W9-AMT-584

JOURNEY TOWARD PROMINENCE

JOURNEY TOWARD PROMINENCE

The Edwin L. Cox School of Business at SMU, 1920–2005

THOMAS E. BARRY

EUGENE T. BYRNE

EDWIN L. COX SCHOOL OF BUSINESS

DALLAS, TEXAS

Published by the Edwin L. Cox School of Business
6212 Bishop Boulevard
Dallas, Texas 75205

Library of Congress Control Number: 2006937843

ISBN-13: 978-0-9790268-0-5

Printed in the United States of America
10 9 8 7 6 5 4 3 2 1

FRONTISPIECE: *Joseph Wylie Fincher Memorial Building, circa 1956*

෴

The authors have made every effort to give credit where credit is due for every photo used in this book. We believe we have been able to identify the appropriate sources in all instances. If we have missed recognizing someone who should have been credited, please inform us at your convenience.

Photos courtesy of: **SMU and Cox School of Business Archives**: frontispiece, 11 (Clogenson-Franz), 15*tr*, 15*bc*, 17, 19, 20, 24, 28, 30, 32, 34, 40, 42*tl*, 43*tc*, 46, 50, 54, 62, 64, 65, 67, 73, 74, 83, 88, 90, 93, 94, 98, 114, 116, 118*tl*, 118*bl*, 119, 121, 125, 130, 131, 132, 135, 136, 139, 148, 149, 152, 156*bl*, 156*br*, 157 (Scott Metcalfe), 161, 165, 166, 168, 172, 174, 183, 186, 189, 192, 195, 199, 200, 203, 204, 205, 206, 208, 216, 219, 226, 228, 230, 231, 236, 239, 248, 251, 268, 274; **Jack Grayson**: 71, 77, 91, 96, 105, 110, 112; **Cchea Nugent**: 234, 237, 240, 242, 243, 258; **Bobby B. Lyle**: 86, 102*tc*, 102*bc*; **Darwin Payne**: 9, 63, 178; **Nora Katherine Bilton**: 42*bl*, 57; **Texas Instruments**: 43*bl*, and *br*; **Hillsman Jackson**: 190; **Helen Jo Potts and Patricia Macsisak**: 37, 95; **Tom Barry**: 85; **David Blake**: 221; **ClubCorp, Inc.**: 137; **Janet and Alan Coleman**: 146; **Dallas Area Rapid Transit (DART)**: 188; **John Daniel**: 155; **Pam and Roy Herberger**: 180; **Junior Achievement of Dallas, Inc.**: 169; **Mick McGill**: 223; **Mike Morgan**: 245; **Maria and Al Niemi**: 261; **Parkland Hospital**: 8; **Dee Powell**: 259; Images From the Collections of **The Dallas Historical Society**: 3, 7, 14, 45; **The Texas/Dallas History and Archives Division, Dallas Public Library**: 2, 4, 10

To the past and current deans,
students, faculty, and staff of the Edwin L. Cox School of Business
in the hope that those present and those to come will carry on the progress
of their predecessors toward the achievement of prominence

CONTENTS

ACKNOWLEDGMENTS

IF EVERYONE who contributed to this book were properly acknowledged, the authors would have to write another chapter. However, there are people who must be singled out as significant contributors to the final product. These contributors include first the five deans in chapters 3 through 7: C. Jackson (Jack) Grayson Jr., Alan B. Coleman, Roy A. Herberger Jr., David H. Blake, and Albert (Al) W. Niemi Jr. Without the contributions of their administrations and willingness to share openly and candidly their decanal lives with the authors, this book would be much less interesting and relevant. Next the authors must acknowledge the acting deans (all also long-time faculty members), including Bobby B. Lyle, Eugene T. Byrne, John W. Slocum, and Michael (Mick) E. McGill. Acting deans are the unsung heroes of academic schools and colleges. They do all the work of permanent deans and get virtually none of the credit for doing so. Without the stabilizing efforts of these temporary and selfless leaders, the Cox School of Business would have been less fortunate than it has been in its growth toward national and international prominence.

The authors thank the entire faculty they have known over the cumulative fifty-plus years of their tenure at the Cox School of Business. Two very important ones, other than those mentioned above, talked with the authors at length about their significant experiences in Cox: Professor Rhonald D. Walker worked under six deans from Aaron Sartain to Al Niemi; Professor Richard W. Hansen worked under five deans from Jack Grayson to Al Niemi. Both also held various administrative positions in the school. Michael van Breda, associate professor of accounting, provided us with information about Aaron Sartain. The authors also thank all the staff of the school—people who work as hard as or harder than our faculty colleagues for significantly lower pay and stature. Betsy Bayer, Nora Katherine Bilton, Dee Powell, and Monica Powell, through interviews, all provided valuable insight into the administrations of the deans under whom they worked. We thank Marci Armstrong, Joan Gosnell, Laura Graham, Lindsay Hogan, Hillsman Jackson, Linda Kao, Kevin Knox, Dick Lytle, Russell Martin, and Jerry White for providing documents, photos, and other archival information. Kathryn Lang and Keith Gregory provided valuable publishing information.

There have been so many important alumni and friends of the Cox School of Business (and SMU) who have contributed significantly to the institution's quest for excellence. The authors interviewed only three, including, of course, Edwin L. Cox, a significant donor and external leader for the school, and the man for whom the school is named. The first chairman of the Cox Executive Board, Cary M. Maguire, has had a long and generous history with the school and SMU as a member of the Board of Trustees. The second chairman of the Cox Executive Board, Carl Sewell, is an alumnus of the school and a member of SMU's Board of Trustees. All three of these gentlemen represented extremely well the thousands of alumni and friends of the school and SMU who continually work to help assertively promote and achieve excellence at the Cox School and SMU.

The authors had the pleasure of interviewing Robert Hyer Thomas, grandson of the founder of SMU. He provided fascinating insights from documents and family stories about his grandfather's founding vision for Southern Methodist University. Our colleagues Mick McGill, Darwin Payne, and Marshall Terry provided very valuable insights into early drafts of the book. Payne and Terry allowed us liberal use of their works on the histories of

Dallas and SMU, respectively. To the three of them we are most grateful. Barry's long-time administrative assistant, Alice Doster worked on the very early phases of the project. His current assistant, Cchea Nugent, provided significant technical help in producing this book, including taking several photographs used in the book. Without their help, the quality of this work would be less.

Gerald Turner was kind in his support of the project, including reading the entire manuscript. We also received some editorial insight from Michelle Byrne, who read early drafts of the manuscript. We appreciate Al Niemi's strong endorsement of the project as well as his funding support.

We also benefited from the guidance of Mark McGarry, who designed and produced the book and served as project manager. Together with copyeditor Melanie McQuere, flap copy writer and proofreader David Allen, and Robert and Cynthia Swanson, who indexed the book, Mark took us from manuscript to finished book. Our former student Win Padgett stepped forward early to underwrite the press work for this book and provide technical support during manufacturing. At Padgett Printing Corporation we thank Chuck Baker, who provided timely estimates and guided the job through the pressroom and bindery. The staff at Padgett—from pressmen to support personnel—treated our project with care and attention to detail.

Finally, a special note of gratitude is reserved for our families and especially our wives, Kathy Barry and Te Byrne. As throughout our careers, they encouraged us and enabled us to bring our initial thinking to a completed project. As always, they have our love and admiration.

The contributions of all of these people, as well as scores of unmentioned ones, have added to the knowledge and fun the authors have had and hope you get from this work. In spite of the contributions of all of these people, any errors in this book are the sole responsibility of the authors.

THOMAS E. BARRY
EUGENE T. BYRNE
Dallas, Texas
December 2006

PREFACE

In April 1971, Willis M. Tate, fifth president of Southern Methodist University, commented,

> Universities have a history worth remembering. As keeper of the memories of society, the university will not protect itself if it is forgetful of its own. Universities are never complete, never finished. They are forever in the process of being made, and the makers are people, you and I and all the other people who put their minds, bodies, and worldly goods to the task.

This is the story of how a department of commerce journeys from a modest beginning in a small wood-frame structure in 1920 to become a business school seeking international prominence early in the twenty-first century. The school grew and prospered as a young university grew and prospered in a growing and prosperous city—Dallas.

Institutional growth results from the complex interaction of forces that change constantly. Among these forces, the deans of the Edwin L. Cox School of Business have always played a central role in the growth and development of the school. In its history, the Edwin L. Cox School of Business has had eight deans. Three of them passed away before this book was started. The other five provide testimony, in these pages, of their and their administrations' roles in this journey of a business school striving toward excellence and prominence among the historically elite schools of business.

The journey starts in chapter 1 with the founding of Dallas in 1841 and the founding of Southern Methodist University in 1911—and their mutual growth. The important, interwoven nature of Dallas and SMU is introduced in chapter 1. The founding of the School of Commerce (Business) then unfolds in chapter 2 through documents and memories from and of the first three leaders—we call them the foundational deans—of the business school in its formative years. The journey continues in chapter 3 with an account of the radical change of the Grayson years.

Chapter 4 presents the stabilizing efforts of the Coleman administration, and chapter 5 highlights the expansion of the physical facilities of the Herberger years. Chapter 6 documents the international thrust and innovation of the Blake administration. Chapter 7 continues the journey toward excellence under the leadership of the current dean, Al Niemi. In chapter 8, the final chapter, the authors discuss the leadership challenges of moving a business school along the path of progress toward the world of top-tier, elite business schools.

History can be written by those who did not live that history in a literal sense, but the story of this historical journey is told principally by those who were at the Cox School of Business as it began a concerted effort to attain national recognition. In the spring 2001 issue of *Legacies,* a history journal for Dallas and North Central Texas, editor Michael Hazel comments:

Personal memories form one of the cornerstones of the historical record. The histories of many cultures were preserved only through oral tradition, passed from one generation to the next. Even in sophisticated societies with a wealth of documentary records, the recollec-

tions of individuals may still provide the only clues to bygone places
and events.

This book is dependent to a large extent upon the personal memories of
the authors, the deans who were interviewed, and other people who were
interviewed and who knew the deans and presidents of SMU since its founding in 1911. While we relied heavily on documents to provide facts about presidential and decanal administrations, including SMU and business school
bulletins, it is the personal recollections that breathe life into the historical
account of the journey of the Cox School of Business toward national and
international prominence. As a caveat to the reader, we make no claim to be
historians in any scholarly sense of the word. We do, however, claim to be two
storytellers, and what follows is our story of the growth of a local business
school that has achieved a national reputation and continues to aspire to become elite.

Thomas E. Barry was working on his PhD at North Texas State University
(now, The University of North Texas) in the spring of 1970 when his dissertation chairman, Paul McWhorter, told him that SMU was looking for a visiting
assistant professor of marketing, and McWhorter recommended Barry for the
position. As Barry considered the possibility of joining SMU, he attended a conference in Dallas that included a panel of several deans. One was C. Jackson
(Jack) Grayson Jr., dean at SMU's business school, and another was George
Kozmetsky, dean of the business school at the University of Texas at Austin.
Both of them expressed radical views of business education, and that piqued
Barry's interest.

As a result of the panel discussion, Barry decided to interview formally at
SMU. Upon his arrival at the School of Business, he learned that Grayson was
out ill and Barry was to to be interviewed by Eugene T. (Gene) Byrne, then
the associate dean. They had a very amiable chat, and Byrne convinced Barry
that it would be good for his career to have this one year of experience under
his belt before returning to the academic marketplace upon completion of his
doctorate the following year. Barry accepted the one-year, non-tenure-track

offer, expecting to be gone after the year was up, but early into the spring semester, Byrne notified him that the school was making him a three-year, standard tenure-track offer.

So what started out as a one-year, temporary appointment has turned into three and a half decades of change and challenge at SMU and the Edwin L. Cox School of Business, as it came to be known in May 1978. Barry received a contract renewal, earned tenure after six years, and achieved full professorship after nine years. In 1981, Byrne was asked to be dean *ad interim*, and cajoled Barry into being associate dean for academic affairs. When Roy A. Herberger came in as dean and asked Barry to continue as associate dean, he turned him down because he missed faculty life. However, five years later he agreed to a stint as associate dean for Herberger.

A year later, Herberger left to become president at Thunderbird, and Barry went back to the faculty, where he felt he belonged. When David H. Blake arrived as dean, he asked Barry to be his associate dean. Initially Barry told him "no," but then accepted the offer eight months later. After five years, the new president of SMU, R. Gerald Turner, asked Barry to consider becoming SMU's first vice president for executive affairs. Barry hardly knew Turner and was shocked at the request since he was once again about to go back to his preferred faculty lifestyle. After much thought, he decided that the position of vice president would be a good career move because it could provide him with a host of potential alternatives down the road. Barry continues to serve as one of the vice presidents of the university as well as professor of marketing in the Cox School of Business. He has spent more than half his life and his entire full-time career at SMU, and he has a passion for the university and the school. Barry has worked with five of the eight deans in the history of the business school, and met two of the three others—one of whom he knew fairly well. He has worked with six of the ten presidents of SMU. This book is, in part, his recollection of those presidents and deans as well as the incredible experiences at an institution that has changed dramatically over the last thirty-five years.

Eugene T. Byrne's tenure at SMU spanned sixteen years, during which time he served as associate dean, department chair, professor of management, director of research, and dean *ad interim*. In addition to his faculty and administrative experience, he had a close, long-term working relationship with Dean Jack Grayson Jr. and an eventful association with Dean Alan B. Coleman. Byrne was at SMU during some of the most innovative and energetic times in the history of the school.

Byrne first met Grayson while a student in the MBA program at Tulane University in New Orleans. In 1963, Grayson accepted an appointment as professor of finance at l'Institut pour l'Étude des Méthodes de Direction de l'Entreprise (IMEDE) in Lausanne, Switzerland, and invited Byrne to accompany him as his research assistant. When Grayson returned to New Orleans, he was appointed dean of the business school at Tulane, and Byrne received an appointment to the Tulane faculty. Two years later, Grayson persuaded him to serve as associate dean of the Tulane business school. In 1968, Grayson accepted the position of dean of the SMU School of Business and asked Byrne to join him as associate dean. Byrne devoted most of the next three years helping to implement major changes to the curriculum, promoting student involvement, hiring new faculty, and establishing guidelines for faculty advancement and development. In the fall of 1971 Grayson was appointed chairman of the Price Commission in Washington, D.C., Bobby B. Lyle was appointed acting dean, and Byrne continued as associate dean until 1973, when he returned to full-time teaching.

When Coleman was appointed executive dean in 1975, Byrne agreed to serve as director of research. He also spent a major part of his time as co-project manager of a three-year federal grant from the Fund for the Improvement of Post-Secondary Education. Coleman became dean in 1976 when Grayson resigned, and in 1979 Byrne accepted an offer to serve another term as associate dean. When Coleman left the deanship to become head of the prestigious Southwest Graduate School of Banking (SWGSB) in 1981, President L. Donald Shields appointed Byrne as dean *ad interim*. He served in this position for fifteen months.

In 1984, Byrne resigned as professor of business policy and left the Cox School of Business. He accepted a position as director of education for the Federal Home Loan Bank System and worked in the bank system for about nine years, after which he entered private consulting. From 1994 to 2004, Byrne taught part-time courses at SMU, including courses on leadership in the school's executive education area.

JOURNEY TOWARD PROMINENCE

CHAPTER ONE

AN INTRODUCTION TO THE
EDWIN L. COX SCHOOL'S PARTNERS:
THE EARLY YEARS OF DALLAS AND SMU

*On inspection, I found that the one hundred acres north of Mockingbird
Lane was most attractive because of a small wooded ravine running
diagonally through it, and also because there was a beautiful knoll
north of this tract which would be an ideal site for the main buildings of
a university. This is the knoll on which Dallas Hall now stands.*

FRANK L. MCNENY

JOHN NEELY BRYAN founded Dallas. He was a pioneer and a builder. Robert Stewart Hyer founded SMU. He was a pioneer and builder. William Hauhart founded the SMU Business School. He, too, was a pioneer and builder. And all the men and women who had and have leadership roles in Dallas subsequent to Bryan and at SMU subsequent to Hyer and Hauhart were and are builders. They exemplify the spirit in the next to last stanza of "The Builders" by Henry Wadsworth Longfellow:

> *Build to-day, then, strong and sure,*
> *With a firm and ample base;*
> *And ascending and secure*
> *Shall to-morrow find its place.*

This book tells the story of the journey of the School of Commerce at SMU from 1920 to the Edwin L. Cox School of Business in 2005. The focus of this journey is on the deans of the business school at SMU. But that journey begins first with the founding of Dallas in 1841 and second with the founding of SMU in 1911.

Because of the long-standing partnership between Dallas and SMU, we set the stage by briefly introducing these two key Cox School partners.

Early Dallas

In 1839, John Neely Bryan, described as a friend of Sam Houston's and one who got along quite well with the Indians, searched for and found an easy crossing of the Trinity River. Bryan was a pioneer who, according to Dallas historian Darwin Payne, used his claim to 640 acres of land not for farming but for developing a trading center. He was indeed a businessman, and though he had customers (the Caddo tribe) in the Dallas area, other trading business took him to Arkansas. When he returned in November of 1841, most of his customers and many of the local Indians were gone. He decided to establish a permanent business center in the then unnamed area and founded the city, later to be called Dallas, on the east bank of the Trinity River at a natural crossing point with a narrow floodplain. No one is sure of the source for the name Dallas. Three likely suspects include George Mifflin Dallas, vice president of the United States; his brother, Alexander J. Dallas, commodore in the U.S. Navy; and Joseph Dallas, who settled in the

John Neely Bryan with wife Margaret Beeman

area two years after Bryan's founding of it. Other accounts suggest that influential locals may have suggested the name Dallas to Bryan. In any event Dallas it was and Dallas it is.

In 1843, Bryan married Margaret Beeman, and that same year the first doctor arrived in town. In 1844 Dallas was surveyed, and J. P. Dumas developed a site map. A year later, Dallas became part of the United States and the first lawyer arrived in the area. In 1846 Dallas became the temporary county seat of Dallas County. During this same year the first hotel, private school, and church

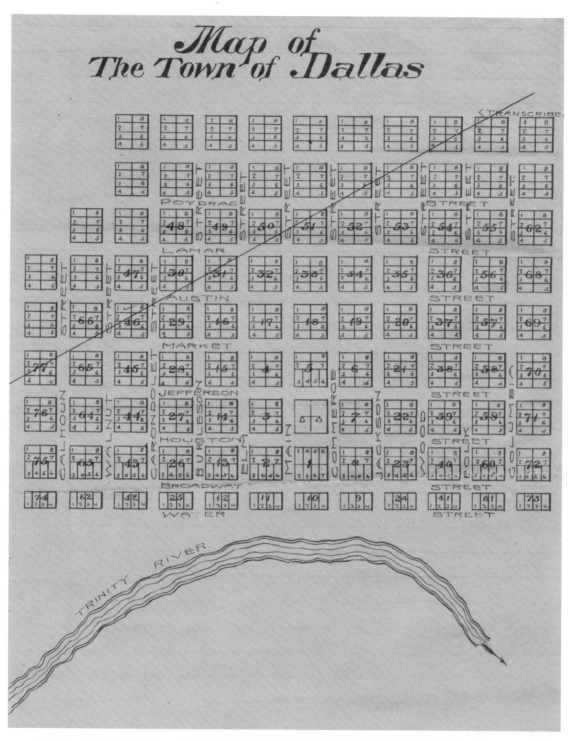

Site map by J. P. Dumas, circa 1844

were organized. Three years later, the *Cedar Snag* (later to be called *The Dallas Herald*) newspaper was founded.

When the first census was conducted in Dallas in 1850 the population had grown from around 100 to 430 people. It was evident already that commerce was thriving and that the leaders of the community would emerge from the ranks of the city's entrepreneurs, just as would be the case for decades to come. In 1852 a French immigrant established a carriage and wagon manufacturing concern, and Alexander and Sarah Horton Cockrell purchased the remainder of Bryan's interest in Dallas for $7,000. They built a brick hotel, a steam sawmill, a general store, and a flour mill. They also built a bridge across the Trinity River that brought in local skilled craftsmen and artists, including brickmakers, cabinetmakers, tailors, milliners, brewers, and musicians from surrounding areas to work and settle in Dallas.

At the start of its third decade, Dallas was a rather diverse city. Its population of close to seven hundred included almost one hundred African Ameri-

Home of John C. McCoy, Dallas lawyer and politician, 1860

cans as well as French, German, Swiss, and Belgian families. But misfortune hit Dallas early in this decade when a fire in July 1860 started in the Peak Brothers Drugstore and destroyed it and most of the other businesses on the square in Dallas. Several slaves and Northern abolitionists were blamed. A vigilante committee formed, and it ordered and oversaw the hanging of three slaves on the banks of the Trinity near the courthouse. Two abolitionist preachers were run out of town. However, by the end of the 1860s, many Southerners moved to Dallas in search of rebuilding their fortunes lost in the Civil War.

In 1871, Dallas's town charter was replaced with a new city charter, and the first volunteer fire company—Dallas Hook and Ladder Company #1—was formed. A year later the Houston and Texas Central Railway arrived at last in Dallas. Then, in 1873, the Texas and Pacific Railway reached the city, making Dallas the first crossroads in the state. Dallas was no longer a "one-horse town." Neither railroad had come by chance. Committees of businessmen had determined that they were desperately needed if the town was to reach its potential, and they had taken the necessary steps to bring both railroads to Dallas. Their impact marked a major turning point in the city's history. Merchants opened their flagship stores along the railroad route as it moved north through Dallas.

Luring the railroads to Dallas foreshadowed the role of business in the community. A partnership in spirit and in action had been formed. It would lead to the founding and development of the university and the Cox School of Business.

Dallas's bawdy side showed in the 1870s. Belle Starr, born Myra Maybelle Shirley in southwestern Missouri, supposedly sang and danced in dance halls, sold stolen horses, and provided safe havens to local outlaws.

The famous Doc Holliday attempted to restore his poor health (from tuberculosis) in Dallas and opened a dentist's office in 1873. But he soon turned to gambling and drinking in the saloons not far from his office. He left Dallas after shooting a man in 1875 and fought in the famous gunfight at the OK Corral with Wyatt Earp and his brothers in 1881.

Belle Starr

Doc Holliday

The *Dallas Morning News* was founded in 1885 and the *Dallas Times Herald* in 1888 with the merger of the *Times* and *Herald*. Under the leadership of men like William Gaston and William Cabell, banking and insurance emerged as major industries in Dallas. Aggressive business leadership led to the organization of a state fair in Dallas, a board of trade, and a merchant's exchange. In his book, *Dallas: An Illustrated History,* Darwin Payne provides an interesting account of the history of the annual State Fair of Texas in Dallas. Prior to 1887, there were two fairs held in Dallas: one on the property of J. H. Cole and the other on the property of W. H. Gaston. These competing fairs lasted one and two weeks, respectively, and remained separate until the *Dallas Morning News* convinced the principals through repeated stories that the fairs should be combined. The agreement came in February 1887. It was clear that the business climate of Dallas, Texas, was alive, vibrant, and prosperous.

In the early 1890s, Dallas ranked as the most populous city in the state of Texas. Its population growth was aided by its annexation of the town of East Dallas, which was geographically larger than Dallas. In 1894, Parkland Hospital opened, and was to become a significant medical facility in the North Texas area. It currently ranks high among *U.S. News & World Report*'s best hospitals in a variety of categories. The hospital was given its name because it was built on land that the city had purchased for the purposes of building a park.

The boom of the 1880s stalled in 1893 when a national financial panic impeded the growth of banks, and the prices of cotton, lumber, and flour dropped drastically. Only two new manufacturing firms opened in Dallas during the 1890s, and in 1899 the American Federation of Labor granted a

Brochure from 1890 State Fair of Texas

Parkland Hospital, circa 1894

charter to the Trades Assembly of Dallas. Residents began to leave Dallas for better fortunes, but soon recovery and growth entered into Dallas's progressive picture once again.

In the early 1900s, Dallas citizens saw the establishment of the Dallas Public Library, the operation of interurban electric lines, the annexation of Oak Cliff, and the purchase of Fair Park from its owners. Dallas had become a leading book, drug, jewelry, and liquor wholesale market in the Southwest. Dallas leaders set a goal to have a population of 150,000 by 1910, but the population reached only about 60 percent of that goal. In 1907, Dallas's first "skyscraper"—the fifteen-story Praetorian Building—was built. Dallas bought White Rock Park in 1909 with the intent of forming a lake. Dallas doubled its geographic size to about eighteen square miles in 1910. In 1911, White Rock Lake was created by damming White Rock Creek and was declared full three

FACING PAGE *Main Street in Dallas, 1889*

years later. In 1912, the Houston Street Viaduct was opened and billed as the "longest concrete bridge in the world."

One of the key events in 1914 that inspired and seemed to ensure the economic growth of Dallas was spawned among the business leaders of the city. Detecting the prospect that Saint Louis, not Dallas, would be awarded one of the twelve Federal Reserve Banks under the new banking law of 1914, Dallas business leaders mounted a concerted effort to turn the tide. They were successful, and on April 2 Dallas got a Federal Reserve Bank, the smallest city in the nation to become headquarters for a regional Federal Reserve Bank. Dallas was beginning to make its mark as a financial center. The decision would be another milestone in establishing the central role of the business community.

Establishment of Love Field in 1917 marked the beginning of Dallas as an aviation center, a key event. Pilots were trained here for combat, and the facility was kept after the war through efforts of the Dallas Chamber of Commerce. By 1930 Dallas would be a leader in scheduled air transport. Air transportation continues to be a significant business asset for Dallas, even today. But for our purposes, the most significant event of this time period was the founding of Southern Methodist University in 1911.

Houston Street Viaduct, 1920

Early SMU

With the enthusiastic support of the Dallas business community, Southern Methodist University was founded in 1911 by the United Methodist Church with generous help from Dallas citizens. More than six hundred acres of land and $300,000 were provided to fund the university. Frank McNeny was a junior real estate salesman when he heard about the plans for a new university in Dallas. His employer told him to devote all his time to the project, which he did. McNeny met with influential Dallas leaders in attempting to find land that would be suitable for the university. The Methodist Church, in the meantime, appointed a Texas Educational Commission to which representatives of Fort Worth and Dallas were invited to submit proposals to build a Methodist university in their respective cities. McNeny extended the invitation for Dallas. (See the sidebar on pages 12–13 for a fuller, firsthand account by Frank McNeny of SMU's founding.)

The first charter for the university was filed on April 17, 1911. Before settling on its name as Southern Methodist University, founders and supporters considered other possibilities, including Southland University, Trans-Mississippi University, and Central University. The combined growth and

Dallas Citizens Committee gives $300,000 toward SMU's founding

THE STORY OF SMU'S FOUNDING

by Frank L. McNeny

I N THE FALL OF 1909 there was a movement on
foot to move Southwestern University from
Georgetown to Dallas. This sentiment had crystal-
lized to such extent by the spring of 1910 that the
Dallas Chamber of Commerce raised $300,000 in
pledges to induce the trustees to move Southwestern to Dallas. But while the Chamber of
Commerce was raising pledges, the alumni were
raising Cain—to put it mildly—and when the trustees met in the early summer of 1910 there was such
a storm of protest that the trustees voted that inso-
far as they had the authority the school should for-
ever remain in Georgetown.

The leaders of the Methodist Church then
began to lay plans for building a great university for
Methodism west of the Mississippi River.

I was employed at that time as a junior salesman
in the office of Hann and Kendall, a large real estate
organization. I told my employer about the plan to
build a new university and suggested that we try to
get it for Dallas. He authorized me to devote my
entire time to it and advised me that Mrs. Alice T.
Armstrong, owner of Highland Park, had offered to
give one hundred acres to Trinity University if they
would move from Waxahachie to Dallas. He suggested that I see if Mrs. Armstrong would not do
the same thing for this new proposed university and
if she would undertake to get the Chamber of
Commerce to give the $300,000 in pledges to this
new university, also.

I discussed the matter with Mr. Hugh E.
Prather, Mrs. Armstrong's son-in-law, and Mrs.
Armstrong agreed to give either one hundred acres
where Highland Park West is now located or the
one hundred acres which she owned north of
Mockingbird Lane. On inspection, I found that the
one hundred acres north of Mockingbird Lane was

most attractive because of a small wooded ravine
running diagonally through it, and also because
there was a beautiful knoll north of this tract which
would be an ideal site for the main buildings of a
university. This is the knoll on which Dallas Hall
now stands.

I found that the tract north of Mrs. Armstrong's
one hundred acres was a 106 acre tract extending
from [A]irline Road west to Turtle Creek and
belonging to heirs scattered throughout Texas. It
was also under a ten-year lease for grazing purposes. I located one of the owners at Cedar Hill in
Dallas County, and found that her son had been
handling the property for his aunts and uncles. I
began negotiations with him and he went to visit all
of his kinspeople and got them all to agree to sell
with the exception of one aunt who owned a one-
fourth interest. But I could not get this nephew to
sign a contract even for the three-fourths undivided
interest.

Meantime, the annual conferences of the
Methodist Church had met during the fall of 1910
and appointed a Texas Educational Commission
composed of two ministers and two laymen from
each of the five conferences. Bishop James C. Atkins
called a meeting of this commission in Austin
January 18, 1911. I went down as the unauthorized
representative of the city of Dallas and invited them
to locate the school here. Judge William Capps, one
of the leading attorneys of Fort Worth, was there
representing that city. They asked me to leave the
meeting while he extended an invitation to the commission to locate the University in Fort Worth, and
asked him to leave while I extended the invitation
for Dallas. The commission agreed to come to
Dallas on February 1st and to Fort Worth on
February 2nd, coming back to Dallas on the morn-

ing of February 3rd meeting at the Methodist Publishing House to make a decision as to where the University should be located.

When the commission came to Dallas various real estate promoters and various sections of the city vied for the location of the University. On February 2nd the commission visited Fort Worth. They went by interurban from Dallas and returned late that evening. The *Dallas News* on the morning

who were older men and knew him better, to discuss the matter with Mr. Caruth. He immediately agreed to give an undivided interest in 672 acres lying between Lovers Lane, Northwest Highway, Preston Road, and Airline Road.

Just at this time I was called on the telephone by my office and advised that Mr. L. M. Finley, who represented his kinspeople who owned the 106 acres we wanted so badly, was in my office. I went imme-

The leaders of the Methodist Church then began to lay plans for building a great university for Methodism west of the Mississippi River.

of February 3 gave prominence to the story from Fort Worth which stated that the schools had turned out, the school children lined the street waving flags as the interurban approached, sirens blew a hearty welcome, and the committee, after an elaborate luncheon, escorted the commission out to what is now Camp Bowie Boulevard to a high point near the Rivercrest Country Club and offered one thousand acres as a site.

So, I went immediately to the Methodist Publishing House and there found Mr. H. H. Adams, who was Chairman of the Chamber of Commerce committee which raised the $300,000 in pledges and who also, on behalf of himself and his brother, had donated a strip of land from Turtle Creek west to Preston Road. Also with him was Dr. John O. McReynolds, who had been helpful to Mr. Adams and me in getting Mr. W. W. Caruth to contribute some forty acres of land including a strip from the University campus to the Greenville Road.

I suggested to these men that we simply had to have more land in order to get the University. They asked where we were going to get it. I said from Mr. Caruth. Mr. Adams said, "I haven't the nerve to ask Will to give any more land." I said I had and picked up the phone and phoned his residence. Within ten minutes he was at the publishing house and I had prevailed upon Messrs. Adams and McReynolds,

diately and found that he and his brother were both there and were ready to close and wanted me to go to their attorney's office. I took them both with their attorney to our attorney's office.

Somehow or somehow else I got word to our attorney that these men must not be permitted to leave his office until this matter had been concluded. About one o'clock I heard [the shouts of a newsboy announcing] an extra on the street and quietly slipped out to get one. It was announcing the location of the University on this very tract.

About two o'clock, as I remember, we concluded the negotiations and Mr. Finley signed the contract for three-fourths of the land. About four o'clock that afternoon I left with the firm car and chauffeur for the southeast corner of Rockwall County to see the aunt who had refused to sell. I went by the town of Rockwall and took a Notary Public with me, and we stayed there until nearly eleven o'clock at night before getting the contract signed.

And that's the story of the founding of Southern Methodist University.

Signed: Frank L. McNeny

Note: Frank L. McNeny bought 106 acres of land for SMU, bounded by Daniel Avenue, Airline Road, McFarlin Boulevard, and Turtle Creek, from the heirs of Frances A. Daniel.

Dallas Hall

developing economic wealth of the city of Dallas and the strength of the educational reputation of the Methodist church throughout Texas were key factors in SMU's naming.

Methodists had previously founded six colleges in the state, but only two
remained in operation by the early 1900s, and some felt that those remaining
colleges could not meet the needs of higher education throughout the twentieth century. Because of the growth of Dallas in particular and North Texas in
general, Methodist and Dallas leaders felt that North Texas was the right area
for the new university, which would, they promised, add considerable intellectual capital to the community.

Southern Methodist University opened its doors in 1915 to a surprisingly
large class of 706 anxious and excited students and 35 eager and dedicated faculty. Today, SMU boasts a full-time faculty of about 600 and a student population of 11,000. The original campus consisted of two buildings. The first,
Dallas Hall—then, now, and forevermore the "crown jewel" of SMU's physi-

cal plant—housed the entire university at its beginning. As Marshall Terry notes in his cogent history of SMU, *"From High on the Hilltop . . .": A Brief History of SMU,* Dallas Hall included a bookstore, a soda fountain, a barber chair, science labs, administrative offices, the registrar's office, classrooms, professors' offices, a library, the School of Theology, the Music Department, and a small auditorium where students met for compulsory chapel. Not until 1940 would the compulsory chapel requirement be eliminated. The second building was the Women's Building, a dormitory for women students. Later it was renamed Atkins Hall and then Clements Hall, which it remains today as an office and classroom building. When SMU opened its doors, the two buildings were complete but without furnishings, heat, water, or lights!

SMU Bulletin, June 1916

In terms of land, the SMU campus is considerably smaller today than in the past. Most people do not know that SMU's campus once sprawled from Mockingbird Lane on the south to Northwest Highway on the north and from Preston Road on the west to Greenville Avenue on the east. Much of the

Women's Building/Atkins Hall/Clements Hall

land was provided by W. W. Caruth Sr. Unfortunately, as a result of difficult financial times coupled with the Great Depression, much of this land had to be sold to insure SMU's survival.

Robert Stewart Hyer

Robert Stewart Hyer was the founder and first president of SMU. He was born in 1860 in Oxford, Georgia, and earned his AB and MA degrees at Emory University. He taught physics at SMU and was widely recognized for his research, and especially for inventing the resistograph used for locating oil fields in West Texas. Hyer served as SMU president from 1911 to 1920. He died on May 29, 1929.

In his booklet on Robert Hyer and Dallas Hall, James Early, now deceased professor emeritus of English, suggests that Hyer was a remarkable man who more than any other person was responsible for the founding of SMU. It was Hyer's vision of a strong university being placed in the North Texas region that culminated in the establishment of Southern Methodist University. Hyer began his plans for a new university in partnership with Hiram Boaz, who soon would become Hyer's vice president at SMU and who would succeed Hyer as president.

Hyer began to think about the establishment of a new university while he was president of Southwestern University in Georgetown, Texas, where he had begun his career in 1882 as a professor of natural sciences. Hyer's fascination for scientific laboratory work began at Emory University during his student days and continued as he attended scientific lectures and participated in various laboratory experiments at Harvard in the early 1890s. Many of these experiments dealt with light waves, heat, and electricity. A few years later, Hyer sent wireless messages from the campus of Southwestern to the courthouse in Georgetown. He was a true pioneer in broadcasting experiments. James Early notes that Hyer also created a machine that took a picture of a bullet in a man's neck. That picture became the first x-ray used to serve as evidence in a criminal trial in Texas.

President Robert Stewart Hyer

As Hyer advanced in his career, he became president of Southwestern University. In her book on the founding and early years of SMU, Mary Martha Hosford Thomas notes that Hyer, as early as 1906, hinted that he wanted Southwestern moved to Dallas, but this was not generally known until a few years later. Hyer simply did not believe that Southwestern's location, far from a major metropolitan area, was suitable for a major university. He estimated that about $300,000 would be required to move Southwestern to Dallas.

At the same time that Hyer was considering a move to Dallas, Hiram Boaz, president of Polytechnic College in Fort Worth, proposed that Southwestern be moved to Fort Worth. When the citizens of Fort Worth became interested in providing land and raising money for the move, the business and political leaders of Dallas became interested in having a university located in Dallas. According to Thomas, this was a time in Texas when people were beginning to see the need to develop adequate financial support for public colleges and universities (the University of Texas was founded in 1883), simultaneously creating a favorable climate for the development and expansion of private education. As Early states in his booklet, "These developments were to influence the formation and early years of Southern Methodist University."

In 1910, as president of Southwestern University, Robert Hyer proposed moving the university to Dallas, Texas. The university's board opposed his plan, and he resigned. In April 1911, Hyer was named as president of the new and yet unnamed university to be founded in Dallas. His Fort Worth "partner," Hiram Boaz, who wanted the university in Fort Worth, was named vice president. This partnership forged the beginning of what was to become Southern Methodist University.

Hyer and Boaz began to plan for the building of SMU. They wanted $1 million, a modest goal that paled in comparison to two outstanding and ideal universities in Hyer's mind—Stanford University and the University of Chicago. The former had received $20 million from Leland Stanford and the latter $30 million from John D. Rockefeller. As Hyer began to plan for his new university, he met with the architects from both Stanford and Chicago. His administration and classroom building was to be called Dallas Hall, and, according to

Thomas, it was to be "a magnificent, fireproof structure and of such architec-
tural beauty as to be worthy of the crowning feature of the campus." Thomas
notes further that the contract for Dallas Hall was let at $212,902, and Hyer
asked Dallas citizens for prepayments of their pledges. This likely did not
occur, but she further notes that ultimately Dallas paid slightly over 90 percent
of its $300,000 pledge while the Methodists paid only about one-third of their
"subscriptions." Thus, Hyer began his university with a little over $600,000,
only about 60 percent of his million-dollar goal.

Hyer created a master plan and a vision for his new structures to insure
that they were "stylistically harmonious." This harmony was to be in the form
of Collegiate Georgian architecture using a consistent brick known today as
"SMU brick" with a very specific color scheme—No. 1 hard burned common
brick: 35 percent No. 319, 34 percent No. 318, 21 percent No. 316, and 10 percent
No. 329. Most of Hyer's nine successors have retained his vision of harmonious construction style as a high priority.

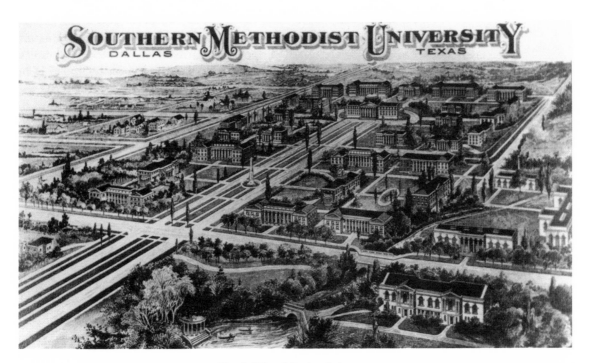

Hyer's "Grand Design," circa 1912

In 1915, Hyer opened the doors of SMU as a small liberal arts college that also included a theological seminary and a music school. Three years later, requirements for the bachelor of arts degree were established. Soon, following trends toward vocational education, SMU began offering courses in business, home economics, and journalism, which eventually led to the offering of a bachelor of science degree as well.

The times were financially trying for SMU's new president. Hyer estimated that the annual cost of educating an SMU student was $274 and the per-student income was $170. The university was accumulating a significant deficit, and Hyer made public his feeling that a private university could not survive on tuition and fee income alone. It must have an endowment to support its programmatic and building activities. According to Thomas, Hyer said, "For a number of years there has been a growing feeling that a college president must be a diplomatist in politics or a promoter in finance; the president of a state institution should be the former, the president of a private institution should be the latter; while the president of a church institution must be both."

In 1920 the SMU Board of Trustees called for Hyer's resignation. Robert Hyer Thomas, Hyer's grandson, told the authors in an interview that his aunt reported that Hyer came home "weary and pale" one day in 1919. He sat in a chair and said, "Oh, they asked me to resign the presidency." Thomas suspects, from family accounts to him, that Hyer was shocked at the request. Hyer felt that the trustees were supposed to raise the money and he was supposed to run the university. In his letter of resignation, Hyer told the board that since he was neither a politician nor a financier, he would have to resign the presidency. His resignation in no way dilutes the important and lasting impact that Robert Stewart Hyer had on the founding and initial growth of SMU. Hyer's dream to have a university of substantial reputation in Dallas had begun in good form in spite of the financial difficulties facing SMU and the unexpected departure of its founding president. Without Robert Stewart Hyer's dream of a great university in Dallas, Texas, a history of SMU and the Edwin L. Cox School of Business might not be necessary.

Building University Boulevard west of Dallas Hall

Hyer's impact upon SMU was well expressed by Bishop Edwin D. Mouzon, former trustee of SMU during Hyer's early years. In 1933, Bishop Mouzon wrote a letter to the Reverend Shettles regarding some historical questions about SMU. In the letter Bishop Mouzon stated:

> It should never be forgotten that but for Dr. Hyer we would not have had Southern Methodist University. Other men have come on later who have raised money for the university, but Dr. Hyer was the father of Southern Methodist University. . . . [I]t should go down in any history of the university that but for R. S. Hyer Southern Methodist University would not now be in the city of Dallas.

Shortly after Hyer left SMU, the business school at SMU was founded. It is to this topic—the focus of this book—that we now turn.

CHAPTER TWO

THE FOUNDING AND EARLY GROWTH
OF THE SMU BUSINESS SCHOOL, 1920–1968

*The foundation for a future business career is best laid by learning
methods for analyzing business data, by training the mind to deal
with human relationships, and by developing a sense of moral
responsibility.*

LAURENCE H. FLECK, CIRCA 1952

T HE SIX EARLIEST business schools founded in the United States still in
operation include five of the most prestigious business schools in the
world. The first, founded in 1881 at the University of Pennsylvania, is the
Wharton School. Second is the Haas School of Business at the University of
California, Berkeley. The Haas School was founded in 1898, just seven years
after Wharton. The University of Chicago's Graduate School of Business was
also founded in 1898. The Amos Tuck School of Business, founded at Dartmouth College, joined the business school ranks in 1900. In 1908, the Harvard
Business School was founded at Harvard University.

Wharton was almost forty years old when SMU's business school, called
the Department of Commerce, Finance, and Accounts, began in 1920 and was
housed in rather humble facilities. The classroom and office building of the
newly formed Department of Commerce was one of three wood-frame structures. The other two structures housed engineering and chemistry.

The SMU Department of Commerce, Finance, and Accounts (subsequently often called the School of Commerce in official university publications) was part of the College of Arts and Sciences as a result of the Board of

Trustees' authorization in February 1920. An important initial catalyst for
starting a business school at SMU was provided by the Dallas Chamber of
Commerce in 1919. At that time, the Chamber "urged" that a business school
be started in Dallas and recommended SMU as the best place for the school.
This is further evidence of the importance of the Dallas/SMU partnership
noted in chapter 1. In a document entitled, "The Courses in Business" (circa
1922), likely composed by the first dean, the following comments were made
about the department's founding:

> Special attention is called to the Department of Commerce, Finance,
> and Accounts. For obvious reasons the Executive Committee of the
> Board of Trustees has designated that this department shall be called
> the Dallas School of Commerce. This school has the active support of
> the various business organizations of the City, especially of the Dallas
> Chamber of Commerce. In fact the Chamber of Commerce thinks so
> much of the school, and is behind it to such an extent, that it gives
> down town class room quarters to the school without charge.

Engineering, Chemistry, and Department of Commerce buildings, 1925

In chapter 1, we suggested that SMU and Dallas have been in partnership since the former's founding. A strong aspect of that partnership was and continues to be the business school at SMU. Further, Dallas provides a marvelous business laboratory for business school students. This has been the case for most of its history. Testimony to the importance of the partnership of the business school and Dallas as a laboratory is found in the document mentioned above and as it states further:

> [T]oday more than ever before big business is calling for men who have already been trained in the theory and principles of business, and our colleges, recognizing this need, have included in their curricula courses which have largely been suggested and recommended by the various lines of business. . . . To the young men of Texas who contemplate business as a career, no better advantages for laying the foundation of this career can be had than those offered by the Department of Commerce, Finance and Accounts, with the City of Dallas as our great laboratory, especially since we have absolute cooperation not only of the business men individually, but of their various organizations, such as the Dallas Chamber of Commerce, the Wholesale and Retail Merchants Association, Insurance Exchanges, the Real Estate Board, the Advertising Club, and similar organizations.

In the next chapter on Jack Grayson, we will talk about "experiential learning" as one of the hallmarks of Grayson's tenure as dean. The philosophical groundwork for Grayson's experiential learning was laid at the very beginning of the SMU business school's founding. Again, in the document noted above, the writer states:

> The old adage that "Experience is the best teacher" doubtless holds true to this date, but how much better can this experience be won if at the beginning of it the person who is entering upon a business life can equip himself with theories and principles which have been obtained

from the experience of others. This school proposes that all the theories and principles advanced in the class rooms shall be tested by actual experience of business concerns.

So, the Department of Commerce was formed offering courses in a Dallas laboratory setting with a curriculum that included "Business Administration and Organization, Personnel and Office Management, Advertising, Salesmanship, Accounting, Insurance . . . Real Estate Methods, Business Law, and the various financial subjects." Before focusing on the first dean of the SMU business school, let's look at the environments within which he worked.

Dallas during the First Administration of the Business School
Throughout the 1920s, Dallas established the first municipal radio broadcasting station in the country (WRR) as well as WFAA radio station, and purchased Love Field as a municipal airport. Dallas women had been active in reforming child-welfare practices as well as legislation for pure food and drink. Throughout this decade, women increasingly entered the workforce. In 1927 the local chapter of the National Association of Business and Professional Women estimated that some 15,000 Dallas women were in the workforce in 125 occupations, trades, and professions. As Dallas was becoming a major center for textiles, it employed many women as dressmakers in the garment industry.

Between 1920 and 1930, Dallas added over 100,000 citizens to its population. In 1930, the Cotton Bowl was built, but the next year the Great Depression put 31,000 people out of work and 15,000 on relief roles. C. A. "Dad" Joiner's discovery of oil, one hundred miles east of Dallas, attracted a flood of oil-related businesses to Dallas. The city's leading banks became pioneers in boldly making loans based on unproven oil reserves, and Dallas became a banking center for the oil industry in Texas and Oklahoma. One of the nation's earliest grand shopping centers—Highland Park Village—was opened in 1931 in the Dallas suburb of Highland Park. Perhaps most significant to Dallas's growth and governance was the establishment in 1930 of the city manager–city council form of government. The city manager would become the CEO of Dallas. Not surprisingly, the new form of government based on a business model was promoted by a dedicated group of business and civic leaders demanding change. The group formed the Citizens Charter Association, which would be prominent into the 1970s, maintaining their role as a force in business and city political affairs.

In 1943, the University of Texas Southwestern Medical School was founded. Throughout the 1940s there was a trend for corporations to move and grow in Dallas. Chance Vought (later, LTV) moved its headquarters to Dallas, and smaller, local companies began to grow and add to the number of corporate and regional headquarters that would call Dallas home thirty years later. Prior to World War II, Dallas could boast of manufacturing industries only in food processing, apparel manufacturing, and printing and publishing. However, by 1944, Dallas's industrial labor force grew to 75,000, energized by the war effort. Toward the end of the 1940s, five new businesses opened each day, and thirteen new manufacturing plants opened each month. Dallas continued to grow as a thriving business center.

SMU during the First Administration of the Business School

During the early years of the SMU business school, the deans worked under three presidents. They were Hiram Boaz, Charles Selecman, and Umphrey Lee. Each contributed to building the foundation of the business school.

Hiram A. Boaz

In 1920, the year of the founding of the School of Commerce, vice president for SMU, Hiram A. Boaz, became president. Boaz was born in Murray, Kentucky, on December 18, 1866, and later educated at Sam Houston Normal Institute and Southwestern University. An ordained Methodist minister, he became Bishop of the Methodist Episcopal Church, South. Boaz was a trustee before he became president of SMU. He died in 1962.

Boaz wrote in his autobiography, *Eighty-Four Glorious Years,* that he had been a student at Southwestern University and that his favorite teacher was Robert Hyer. When Boaz was the vice president at SMU, he received a letter from Hyer that said, "Dr. Boaz, your job is to raise money, and my job is to spend it."

The board wanted Boaz to serve as president in anticipation of his ability to raise money to help the struggling new university. One of the conditions under which Boaz was offered the position was to design a campaign that would raise $1 million. The General Education Board of New York promised to contribute one-third of the campaign target if Boaz could raise two-thirds of it. According to Terry, Boaz worked alongside the chairman of the Board of Trustees, Bishop John M. Moore, in raising money for SMU.

President Hiram A. Boaz

During the two years that Boaz was president of SMU (1920–1922), times in Texas were prosperous. According to Mary Martha Thomas, the oil discovery in Beaumont in 1901 and the discovery of oil in Ranger, Texas, in 1917 helped create the foundation for that statewide prosperity. Among those creating extensive wealth were Texas Methodists. Through the efforts of Boaz, Moore, and others, SMU was to be a direct beneficiary of that Methodist wealth creation. By 1924 SMU had an endowment of $1.5 million and was out of debt for the first time in its young history.

As SMU became more stable financially, Boaz thought that it would be possible to begin to emphasize the development of a winning football team. It is likely that Dallas businessmen, who tended to have significant influence through the Board of Trustees, promoted this notion. As noted in Terry's history of SMU, Boaz commented later, "Since the University was on sound financial basis and the spiritual atmosphere on the campus had been greatly improved, and since the faculty was doing most excellent work in the classroom, it seemed to me that we ought to lay some emphasis on securing a winning football team."

At the end of two years as SMU's president, Boaz left SMU to return to Polytechnic College in Fort Worth. Shortly after that, he moved to New York and studied at Columbia University and at Union Seminary and was selected a Methodist bishop. About Boaz, Terry notes, "His idea of generating School spirit was to have a revival." Boaz served SMU well, especially through his partnership efforts with Hyer in founding SMU. His partnership with Bishop Moore created financial stability for the university on the hilltop.

Charles Claude Selecman

SMU would be without a president for a year after Hiram Boaz left. Finally, on March 31, 1923, the SMU Board of Trustees appointed Charles Claude Selecman as SMU's third president. Selecman was born on a farm near Savannah, Missouri, in 1874. He attended Savannah High School and then entered Central Methodist College in Fayette, Missouri, in 1892. However, he

President Charles C. Selecman

did not finish his degree. He was considered by some to be one of the best athletes in Missouri and played on Central's varsity football team. He was also quite a track star. While pastor of the Trinity Auditorium in Los Angeles, Selecman received a call to come to the First Methodist Church of Dallas as its pastor. In later years he received an honorary doctorate from the University of Southern California.

Selecman came to SMU with the vigorous backing of the Methodist Church. He was known as a very dynamic minister and had served Methodist congregations in Saint Louis, New Orleans, and Los Angeles. However, the faculty greeted Selecman with suspicion and concern. Although the new president had attended college in Fayette, Missouri, he never earned his degree. His time was spent on his theological calling. This was not unusual, however, as the noted Princeton University mathematician Oswald Veblen described conditions at American universities in 1924.

By 1924, one year after Selecman arrived, SMU's student population had grown from its initial size of 706 to over 2,500 students. This put strains on the faculty and the physical facilities of the university. Fifteen-hour teaching loads were common, and research was nearly nonexistent at this time. Selecman's reputation as a practical man extended to his tight rein on expenses. As an example, he discouraged faculty from using their offices at night (ostensibly for research activities) in order to curb the costs of electricity. However, one area that faculty were likely in agreement with their new president was Selecman's perspective that Dallas businessmen should not have too large a say in the affairs of the university. While the university wanted good relationships with the business community, it did not want those business leaders managing the university. That was the business of the university's administrators.

In addition to concern over Selecman's lack of academic credentials, another area that may have caused a rift between Selecman and the faculty was his rather conservative approach to the interpretation of the Bible. This approach led the president to fire Mims T. Workman, a faculty member who told his students that parts of the Bible were myth. As a result of Selecman's actions, another faculty member—Harvie Branscombe, a member of the theology faculty—wrote a rebuttal that was published in the *Morning News*. Selecman called Branscombe and fired him over the phone. Branscombe later became chancellor of Vanderbilt University.

During Selecman's tenure as president, the campus of SMU continued to expand. He was responsible for the erection of Florence Hall, Perkins Administration Building, McFarlin Auditorium, Ownby Stadium, Hyer Hall, Virginia Hall, Patterson Hall, Snider Hall, and the Blanton Student Observatory. These buildings came to a total cost of about $1.5 million. Selecman continued to add to the dream of Presidents Hyer and Boaz. Like his immediate predecessor, President Charles Claude Selecman left SMU when he was elected bishop at the General Conference of the Methodist Episcopal Church in May 1938.

Umphrey Lee

Umphrey Lee was selected to follow Selecman as president of SMU in 1939. Lee was born on March 23, 1893, in Oakland City, Indiana. He earned degrees at Trinity College, SMU, and Columbia University. Lee served as dean of Vanderbilt University School of Religion before coming to SMU. He died on June 23, 1958.

With the appointment of Lee as the fourth president of SMU, the university gained a true scholar. Lee did his undergraduate work at Trinity College and earned a master of arts degree at SMU. He was a scholar in church history and was the first SMU president to hold the doctor of philosophy degree, which he earned at Columbia University. The author of several books, he was considered to have a broad and liberal mind. He was well respected by faculty,

President Umphrey Lee

students, alumni, and the citizens of Dallas and the surrounding areas. Lee added academic credibility to SMU. In the words of Terry, "He [Lee] truly turned SMU around, from prairie college to a real University."

In a way, SMU was home to Lee. He had been one of the first students to enroll at SMU when he matriculated to the graduate program in 1915. He was much more attuned to the faculty (at least in their eyes) than his immediate predecessor. The faculty could identify with his academic credentials and supported his liberal arts view of SMU's core educational experience. Lee was the first to succinctly articulate the importance of the liberal arts being at the center of all educational experiences at SMU. As noted in Terry's history, Lee said, "Southern Methodist University should emphasize its college of liberal arts. . . . [A]n institution . . . that . . . is committed to a unified philosophy of the nature of the world and of man may well have a significant place." Umphrey Lee practiced that belief, and his successors did as well.

William F. Hauhart: The First Business School Dean

In September of 1921, the SMU business school got its first leader, William F. Hauhart. Hauhart became the director of the School of Commerce and was to stay at the helm of the department/school for twenty-five years. According to the historical account of the history of the Cox School of Business by Helen Jo Potts and Patricia Macsisak, Hauhart was the son of German immigrants. He was a scholarly man and had earned his PhD in German at Columbia University in 1909 after studying and earning two degrees at the University of Missouri in 1901 and 1902. Immediately prior to being named as director of SMU's School of Commerce, Hauhart served as a professor of economics at the University of Michigan. When called to serve SMU, Hauhart convinced one of his young colleagues, Laurence H. Fleck, to forgo his summer plans for "fishing and loafing" and join him at SMU. Fleck would succeed Hauhart as dean of the SMU business school.

Both Hauhart and Fleck likely were surprised at the SMU campus upon their arrival. The facilities at the University of Michigan were probably much

Dean William F. Hauhart

plusher than the temporary School of Commerce office that was to be Hauhart's home from 1922 until 1941.

Work in the School of Commerce required students to take three courses in each of the following subjects: mathematics, history, business English, general economics, accounting, general business administration, and business law. (SMU had three terms to its academic year, each lasting twelve weeks.) Additionally, students pursuing the business degree had to take eighteen hours (six courses) in advanced work in the department. The School of Commerce awarded its first degrees—two of them—in 1922.

Both Hauhart and Fleck taught in the department, initially with three other professors. Courses were offered in accounting, money and banking, commerce, and marketing. There were also co-operatives offered by Dallas businessmen at the School of Commerce. Classes included Real Estate Methods,

Insurance, and Life Insurance. Several School of Commerce courses were cross-listed with the Department of Economics. It is interesting to note that there were four professors in the Department of Economics, three of whom were also in the School of Commerce. Two of those were Hauhart and Fleck. What makes that situation even more interesting is the rift described next.

Often, when departments/schools of economics and business are housed together, tension arises. The tension apparently has existed from the earliest of times at SMU's business school. The row will be noted again in chapter 3 as the conflict between business and economics surfaced early in Grayson's adminis-tration. In any event, recall that the School of Commerce was housed in the College of Arts and Sciences. The college was composed of several depart-ments, including Liberal Arts, Education, Journalism, Economics, Chemistry, and the newly formed School of Commerce. Things came to a head in the col-lege in March of 1923 when a serious issue was presented to the SMU Board of Trustees. The secretary of the board read to the trustees a letter dated March 5, 1923, written by the dean of the college, E. D. Jennings, to James Kilgore, act-ing president.

In essence, Jennings told the board that the Department of Economics was focused on a BA degree and that the School of Commerce was focused on a BS degree. The business degree was more "vocational" and applied in nature, and the two areas should be separated with separate curricula. He indicated that "the men are all well qualified in their respective fields," but course and departmental separation was important and the right thing to do. (The full text of the letter appears in the sidebar on page 36.)

As a result of the disagreements between the Department of Economics and the School of Commerce, the faculty of the School of Commerce offered their resignations *en masse* to Jennings. As noted above, the faculty of the School of Commerce was, in essence, the faculty of the Department of Economics. However, since the suggestions in the letter to the dean were approved by Kilgore, the Executive Committee of the Board "decline[d] to accept the resignation of the Professors in the School of Commerce." In 1923, the School of Commerce listed six faculty members; the Department of

EARLY BUSINESS-ECONOMICS CONFLICT

Dear Doctor Kilgore:—

In regard to the differences between the heads of the School of Commerce and the Department of Economics, I desire, to make the following statements and recommendations, as the Dean of the College concerned:

1: I have interviewed various people who might know of the conditions involved and have come to the final conclusion, that stripped of all personal feelings that have since developed, the original source of friction has been a difference of viewpoints, one having developed the social science idea as contribution to culture,—the other the economic idea as a contribution to vocational and cultural pursuits with emphasis on the former. They are both more affected in their attitude now by the seeming demands of their Departments than by their training: one Department aiming at a direct contribution toward the B.A. degree, and the other toward the B.S. degree and vocational work.

2: Both aims are needed in our school, and the men are all well qualified in their respective fields.

3: Under the present circumstances, the Departments should be completely separated by September 1923, according to their chief aims. Courses that are traditionally given under Economics should be given in the Department of Economics in so far as they are Academic,—(historical, general, social or political)—in nature. Courses of the applied nature, (bearing directly on vocational pursuits,) should be given in the School of Commerce. Academic courses in Economics should also be given in the School of Commerce only to the extent that they are necessary pre-requisites to applied courses of the same nature. The future expansion of all courses should be made along lines laid down above and should be determined by the College Council from time to time.

4: The separation of courses would then be as follows:

(a)—Department of Economics would give similar courses to those laid down in last catalog except that Money and Banking should be given only as an expansion of the topic in Economics 11, 12, 13, and should be of a general nature under the name of Theory of Money or Financial Organization of Society. Business and Public Finance and Transportation should be given as a study of the development of trade routes, etc., with only a summary of railway transportation.

(b)—The School of Commerce would give similar courses as laid down in last catalog except that Railway Transportation and Business and Public Finance should be brought over from Economics. A course in Business Economics as a pre-requisite to other courses and numbered 14, 15, 16, named Principles of Economics and courses in Money and Banking should be added to meet the needs as pre-requisites to applied subjects of the same fields.

5: No student should receive credit toward a degree for both General Economics and Principles of Business Economics. Either course should count toward a degree but not to be a pre-requisite to courses in the other Department. All other courses should be counted as other electives in Majoring in the other Department.

6: Teaching forces should be employed as needed to properly carry out the program but in keeping with the general policy of the administration with other Departments.

7: The School of Commerce should have charge of its own work down town. The Economics Department should have charge of any of its work down town that might be demanded by the Extension Department for Academic purposes only.

Yours sincerely,

E. D. Jennings

Economics listed only one. In 1924, commerce had nine faculty or student assistants and economics had five. It is interesting to speculate on what eventually may have happened to SMU's business school had the board accepted those disgruntled business faculty resignations in 1923.

The SMU *Bulletin* for 1924–1925 included a separate *Bulletin* for the College of Arts and Sciences that published "announcements" for the School of Commerce, Day and Evening Courses. Early in the announcements, several paragraphs highlighted the value of training in business at the university level. (Because of the importance of this document as an early guide for the philosophy of what was to become the School of Business Administration, and later the Edwin L. Cox School of Business, the statement appears in full in the sidebar on pages 38–39.)

Dudley Curry, professor of accounting, 1937

In 1925, the American Association of Collegiate Schools of Business (AACSB) accredited the School of Commerce. Today the AACSB is named AACSB International (The Association to Advance Collegiate Schools of Business). This was important to the neophyte School of Commerce at SMU because, according to Potts and Macsisak, only thirty other business schools had received the AACSB's blessing by 1925.

Over the next two decades, Hauhart and his colleagues worked diligently to improve the quality and reputation of the School of Commerce, and to increase the size of its student body and full-time teaching faculty. Not all of the hard work paid handsome dividends. On June 4, 1940, just fifteen years after receipt of accreditation by the AACSB, the minutes of the annual meeting of the SMU Board of Trustees recorded the following comments:

> Dr. [President Umphrey] Lee is in receipt of a communication from the Secretary of the American Association of Collegiate Schools of Business stating that The Dallas School of Commerce does not meet the minimum standards of the Association and several particulars: separate status, training of the members of the staff, salaries and perhaps

in teaching load. In view of these facts, the Dallas School of Commerce has been put on probation for two years.

While we can find no evidence of our opinion, we believe that the probationary action resulted from the differences in loads, salaries, and so forth between faculty teaching at the SMU campus during the day and the faculty teaching at the downtown campus in the evening. The disparity between the faculties likely existed because the evening faculty consisted of adjuncts. Adjunct faculty are not on tenure track and typically do not have terminal

THE VALUE OF UNIVERSITY TRAINING IN BUSINESS*

THE RAPID EXPANSION of business has placed on Universities and Colleges the duty of giving students systematic preparation for a business career. The call for business instruction at Southern Methodist University has been pressing, both from students and from the public. This demand became so imperative that the Dallas Chamber of Commerce formally suggested that the University establish a Department of Business Training. The Chamber of Commerce pledged support of the proposed business department and agreed to assist in obtaining full cooperation of all the business interests of Dallas. The Board of Trustees of Southern Methodist University, February 20, 1920, established a Department of Commerce, Finance, and Accounts.

Many of the business institutions of Dallas are furnishing lecturers who are assisting in instructing students in the practice of their business. These lecturers are associated with members of the Faculty who devote their full time to teaching. Wherever possible, students will supplement their class work with business experience gained as part time employees.

University instruction in business has long since passed the experimental stage. It has been amply proven that young men and women who take such a course, master the details of business more quickly than they otherwise could. Everywhere businessmen are themselves seeking a more fundamental knowledge of their problems and are demanding a higher standard of training for the young men they employ. American economic life is continually becoming more complex and highly organized. It is a field for experts. Universities are giving more attention to this type of practical achievement.

The Dallas School of Commerce recognizes business as a profession. It aims to give prospective businessmen a thorough training for their future work. Education in fundamental principles rather than drill work in technical details is the object of instruction. The foundation for a future business career is best laid by learning methods for analyzing business data, by training the mind to deal with human relationships, and by developing a sense of moral responsibility.

It is believed that this end will be best attained by laying a broad general foundation in the study of cultural subjects before proceeding to the more technical work of the actual business courses. The degrees. They were likely recruited from downtown businesses by the dean or department chairs. In any event, as a result of the probationary status, an Instruction Committee of three trustees (M. K. Graham, Frank L. McNeny, and Eugene McElvaney) was appointed by the Board of Trustees to study the situation and make a report to the Executive Committee of the board regarding the necessary action to be taken.

The school and the AACSB resolved this issue amicably. However, as we will discuss, philosophical differences created a major schism in the early 1970s when the school would face the possibility of losing accreditation.

---

first two years, known as the Pre-Commerce Course, will therefore be devoted largely to the basic subjects of the regular college course. The last two years will then be given over to the study of technical business courses.

At present there are offered courses in Accounting, Banking and Finance, Marketing, Secretarial Training, and a General Course in Business. As the school grows other courses of specialization will be offered.

1. Course in Accounting.

The work is designed to meet the needs of those persons who are preparing for public accounting, the teaching of accounting, or for positions as accountants in financial or business establishments.

2. Course in Banking and Finance.

These courses are recommended to those who are looking forward to positions in banks and bond houses. Dallas offers many advantages to the student of Banking and Finance. It is the seat of the Federal Reserve Bank of the eleventh district. The surrounding territory with its predominating cotton and cattle industry offers some of the most interesting and important credit problems of the entire country.

3. Course in Marketing, Advertising and Salesmanship.

The courses in marketing include those subjects directly bearing on problems of selling. The courses are in charge of an instructor from the University, and in most cases the work is augmented by lectures given by business men, who are specialists in the particular subject in which they lecture.

4. Course in Secretarial Training.

This is planned for those contemplating positions as private secretaries, or assistants to executives, or general stenographic work. The training is directed toward proficiency in general business supplemented by the ability to transcribe dictation accurately and rapidly.

5. General Course in Business.

This course is recommended to those persons who desire a well-balanced training in the important fields of business education or for those who are not yet able to decide upon a specialized field of study.

*From SMU *Bulletin* for 1924–1925, Announcements for the Dallas School of Commerce, Day and Evening Courses.

On February 3, 1941, President Lee stated to the board that the Instruction Committee would report its recommendations to the board later in the meeting. In its report, the committee recommended that SMU establish a new school to be called the School of Business Administration, which would replace the old School of Commerce in the College of Arts and Sciences effective September 1, 1941. Committee members recommended that the new school be allowed to confer the bachelor of business administration (BBA) degree. They further recommended, assuming available financing, that a Department of Marketing and a Department of Secretarial Training be formed. As stated specifically in the minutes of the board meeting:

The
SOUTHERN METHODIST
UNIVERSITY
BULLETIN

The School of
Business Administration

Announcements for 1941-1942

DALLAS, TEXAS
September 1, 1941

Bulletin *for the School of Business Administration, September 1941*

It is understood by the present School of Commerce and those involved in the establishing of the new School of Business Administration, that no expansion requiring additional financial outlay will be recommended or attempted unless proper financial support can be provided in the budget of the University.

At the board's annual meeting on June 3, 1941, Lee presented the income budget for 1941–1942. Included in the budget report was the initial financing for the new School of Business Administration, a healthy $28,000. At that same meeting, the board recommended that William F. Hauhart be named dean of the new School of Business Administration, and be paid a salary of $4,300, a sum likely equivalent to a contemporary dean's coffee allowance! Thus, in two decades, the School of Commerce became the School of Business Administration. The SMU *Bulletin* incorporated a new separate section that included announcements for 1941–1942 in the School of Business Administration. (The sidebar on page 44 provides a revision of the document that appears on pages 38–39.)

Hauhart would continue as the dean of the school until his announced retirement in 1945. He would be succeeded, as mentioned earlier, by his friend and close working partner, Laurence Hobart Fleck, in 1946. In the interim between Hauhart's retirement and Fleck's selection as dean, a committee would run the affairs of SMU's School of Business Administration. A summary of enrollment for 1945–1946 showed that the school had 519 students, 420 men and 99 women. The student body was composed of juniors, seniors, certificate candidates, and special students. So, in a quarter of a century, Hauhart took the business school from 2 students and a handful of faculty to over 500 students and almost 30 faculty, including professors, lecturers, special lecturers, and evening division lecturers. The foundation for the Cox School of Business had been laid.

Laurence H. Fleck: The Second Foundational Dean

As did his predecessor and friend, Fleck would serve in the dean's office of the business school at SMU for almost two decades. He had already contributed twenty-five years of service as a professor and administrator in the school, and he was poised to move the School of Business Administration forward after having helped Hauhart lay the groundwork. Fleck had studied at the University of Michigan in 1919 and 1920 and received his CPA in Texas in 1926. He was a professor of accounting at SMU. Fleck's early years would be filled with issues precipitated by World War II. Fleck inherited the professors, lecturers, and student assistants from Hauhart's tenure as dean, and was faced with an influx of veterans. The cover of the SMU *Bulletin* for the School of Business Administration in 1947–1948 included the following subhead: "Containing the Program for Veterans."

Fleck had to add some staff and faculty to teach the influx of veterans to SMU and the School of Business Administration. One of his key staff additions was a young graduate of the business school in 1944. She was only twenty years old and would go on to serve the school as secretary of the school, secretary to the dean, administrative assistant to the dean, assistant to the dean, and director of Support Services. Her name was Nora Katherine Bilton, and she would serve the business school through the end of Roy Herberger's tenure as dean in 1989. In 1948, the business school had 1,093 students, including 104 women and

Dean Laurence H. Fleck

Nora Katherine Bilton, 1940 SMU freshman

989 men. The faculty size increased to include 15 professors along with 29 day lecturers, 13 lecturers in the evening division, and 55 student assistants. Two new student organizations, the Delta Commerce Club and the Sales Association, were added in 1947. They joined Alpha Kappa Psi, the professional business fraternity, which started on campus in 1923, and Phi Chi Theta, the professional sorority, begun in 1944. In the summer session of 1947, the school had 786 students. During the 1947–1948 academic year, there were 1,265 men and 106 women students for a total of 1,371 students, almost triple the number of students inherited by Fleck a mere two years before. Fleck had to set up "Trailorsville," temporary housing for all of the veterans that flowed to SMU after the war.

Dallas during the Fleck Administration

Early in the 1960s, Dallas began a process of racial integration through the work of a biracial committee appointed by the Dallas Chamber of Commerce and the Negro Chamber of Commerce. But soon after, a very dark day descended on Dallas with the assassination of President John F. Kennedy on November 22, 1963. The tragic event occurred at Dealey Plaza, which was (and remains) only yards away from the location where Dallas founder John Neely Bryan had settled 119 years earlier.

The SMU Environment

Umphrey Lee was still SMU's President when Fleck became dean. According to Terry, Lee was a strong

"Trailorsville" housed World War II veteran students, circa 1946

"town and gown" president for SMU. He very much enjoyed interacting with the general citizenry, and he apparently was very effective in those interactions. During Lee's tenure as president, he oversaw the construction of twenty buildings. They included DeGolyer Library, Perkins Natatorium, Engineering Lab Building 2, Lettermen Hall, Caruth Hall, Fondren Science Building, Peyton Hall, Storey Hall, Carr Collins Hall (Lawyer's Inn), Smith Hall, Perkins Hall, Bridwell Library (Phases 1 and 2), Martin Hall, Kirby Hall, Hawk Hall, Perkins Chapel, Engineering Lab

Jack Kilby, inventor of the integrated circuit, 1958

Kilby's circuit

Building 1, Selecman Hall, and the Fincher Memorial Building. These projects cost almost $15 million. Also during Lee's presidency, SMU gained national attention for its football program with athletic stars like Doak Walker and Kyle Rote.

Lee served as president of SMU longer than any president before him. He was, in a sense, a man for all seasons, and, in the eyes of the faculty, he brought academic respectability to the presidency. At the same time, he created enthusiastic support from the local and regional population for SMU's continuing

SCHOOL OF BUSINESS ADMINISTRATION

History

COLLEGIATE TRAINING for business was introduced into the colleges and universities of the
United States during the first two decades of the
present [twentieth] century. The Dallas Chamber of
Commerce in 1919 urged the necessity of a School
of Business for Dallas, and suggested that it be
established by Southern Methodist University. The
trustees of the University responded by adopting a
resolution on February 20, 1920, which provided for
the founding of the School of Commerce.

The preliminary work of organization was done
jointly by the late Professor John Wynne Barton and
Mr. C. J. Crampton, who at that time was Executive
Secretary of the Dallas Chamber of Commerce.
Messrs. Hauhart and Fleck, from the University of
Michigan, joined the staff in 1921. The school was
organized on a two-year basis, with a preliminary
requirement of two years of general college work.
The degree of Bachelor of Science in Commerce was
conferred after the successful completion of these
four years of study. The first graduating class in 1922
was composed of two men. At the present time,
approximately seventy-five students are graduated
each year. Both men and women are admitted to the
privileges of the school. During the last few years the
number of women students has been increasing per-
ceptibly, and at present, about 20 percent of the
annual enrollment are women. The school has developed its offering of courses as rapidly as possible, and
since 1925 it has been a member of the American
Association of Collegiate Schools of Business.

As its February (1941) meeting, the Board of
Trustees of Southern Methodist University established the School of Commerce as a separate unit,
this action to become effective as of September 1,
1941. Upon recommendation of the staff of the
school and the President of the University, the name
"School of Business Administration" and the new
degree of Bachelor of Business Administration
(B.B.A.) were approved by the Board.

The school enjoys the hearty support of the business men of Dallas. It has an ideal location for a collegiate school of business; for Dallas is the financial,
insurance, and distributing center of the Southwest,
and business in its larger aspects may be observed at
first-hand by students in the school. Furthermore,
this favorable location gives the school an opportunity to draw upon outstanding business men for assistance in the instructional work.

Purpose and Aims

It is recognized that under modern conditions the
apprenticeship system alone no longer offers adequate training for a business career. On account of
the complexity of the present-day economic production and distribution of goods, it is no longer
feasible to learn to do merely by doing. The School
of Business Administration of Southern Methodist
University recognizes business as a profession. It
aims to give prospective business men a thorough
training for their future work. Education in fundamental principles rather than drill work in technical
details is the object of instruction. The foundation
for a future business career is best laid by learning
methods for analyzing business data, by training the
mind to deal with human relationships, and by
developing a sense of moral responsibility. If a student has thus equipped himself, he may rest assured
that business life later will offer him abundant
opportunity for doing creative work for his own satisfaction, as well as for the promotion of human
welfare.

It is believed that it is best for a student of business to lay a broad general foundation by the study of
cultural subjects before proceeding to the more technical work of the actual business curriculum. The
first two years, known as the pre-business administration course, are therefore devoted largely to the basic
subjects of the regular college course in arts and sciences. The last two years are then given over to the
study of the more technical business courses.

vision to become a notable academic institution. He
continued the dreams of his predecessors through significant building of the campus, and SMU began to
gain national recognition, albeit through its football
prowess. His health declining, Lee resigned in 1954.
Lee continued at SMU and spent his time researching
and writing. According to Terry, he completed his
book, *Our Fathers and Us,* on the day he died while he
was at work in his office in Fondren Library in 1958.
The book dealt with the heritage of Methodism.

Dealey Plaza under construction

Willis M. Tate

Following Lee's resignation, SMU called on one of its most charismatic leaders to head the university—Willis M. Tate. Tate was born on May 18, 1911, in
Denver and was educated at SMU, where he earned BA and MA degrees in
1932 and 1935, respectively. He also studied at the University of Texas and the
University of Chicago. Tate died on October 1, 1989.

In 1954, Willis M. Tate became SMU's fifth president and would serve
admirably for almost two decades. Of all SMU presidents to date, he served
the longest term—eighteen years. Willis Tate was no stranger to SMU. He
held undergraduate and graduate degrees in sociology from SMU and was an
all-conference tackle on the 1931 Southwest Conference championship football
team. In 1945 he was lured back to campus by Umphrey Lee to serve in the
capacity of assistant dean of students. He moved through the ranks of administration by becoming dean of students, vice president, and, ultimately, president of SMU.

In *Willis M. Tate: Views and Interviews,* edited by Johnnie Marie Grimes,
Terry says,

And I must also write from the perspective of one who has steadily
cherished, no matter what disagreement there may have been on spe-

cific issues along the way, the personal and professional association
with Willis Tate, whose qualities of loyalty to institution and to
human beings, whose integrity, hard and endless work for the good
cause, and social and educational statesmanship I much admire.

Academic freedom was an essential ingredient in the educational philosophy of Willis Tate. This was recognized by his faculty colleagues, who nominated him for the prestigious AAUP Alexander Meiklejohn Award (1966) for
his "significant support" of academic freedom. Besides academic freedom,
the fundamental dimensions of education in Tate's mind also included quality and substance. Substance, according to Tate, began with the curriculum
and was developed, maintained, and enhanced in the classroom experience
through interactions with those who did the teaching and those who did the
learning.

Tate believed strongly in the liberal education essence of SMU. In a
speech to the Southwestern Social Science Association in March of 1959, he
commented,

A statement of the purpose of a
university which I learned many
years ago was simply that it was
for education of the whole man
to live in a free society. In a college or university, liberal learning,
of which the social sciences are a
part, is not placed at the heart of
the education experience to teach
businessmen business or to teach
grammarians grammar. Rather,
liberal learning should help each
person bring to his total life the
greatest possible assets of intelli-

President Willis M. Tate

gence, resourcefulness, judgment, and character. Liberal education must include an intellectual approach not only to what is fact, but also to what is lasting, what is beautiful, what is true, and how this must relate to life as it is lived.

Tate's educational criteria of quality, substance, and freedom were in place. The substance was centered in the liberal arts arena, and the fifth president of SMU was about to venture into a major planning phase.

Growth under Fleck

In the 1947–1948 academic year, Aaron Q. Sartain appeared on the faculty list of the School of Business Administration. Sartain was professor and chairman of psychology at SMU, and he joined the business school, at Fleck's urging, to begin a Department of Personnel Administration that would be the precursor to the Organizational Behavior and Administration Department in the early 1970s. The SMU *Bulletin* for 1949–1950 included a catalog for the School of Business Administration. In 1949–1950 and for the first time in a couple of years, the cover of the school's supplement did not mention veterans, likely because many of them had graduated. Enrollment in the school included 1,132 students, virtually all undergraduates. Graduate students in certain programs on campus could take selected upper-level business school courses toward a minor in business administration. The downtown school by this time had been renamed Dallas College and was still staffed by special evening division lecturers.

The very next year, the business school had a total of 777 students in business, a significant shortfall from the previous academic year. Enrollment would continue to worsen. In 1951–1952, the school's enrollment showed only 635 total students. However, now some of them were graduate students. In June 1950, the first master of business administration (MBA) graduated from SMU. He was Isham Lee Wilson, who specialized in accounting and wrote a master's thesis entitled "Installment Basis of Reporting Income for Federal Tax

Purposes." Thirty more MBAs would graduate between June 3, 1950, and June 4, 1951. The school now had three institutes: the Institute of Insurance Marketing, the Institute of Building Materials Distribution, and the Institute of Management.

Fleck was a strong advocate of business students receiving broad educational experiences. However, a business education should focus on free enterprise. In an undated booklet (circa 1952), "Careers in Business Administration," Fleck notes:

> The foundation for a future business career is best laid by learning methods for analyzing business data, by training the mind to deal with human relationships, and by developing a sense of moral responsibility. The first two years, known as the pre-business administration course, are devoted largely to the basic subjects of the regular college course in arts and sciences; the last two years are then taken up by the study of professional business courses.
>
> The School of Business Administration of Southern Methodist University is frankly and definitely committed to the principle of free enterprise as the best system for employees, employers, and the public.

In that same booklet, Umphrey Lee continues the language of the strong partnership between SMU, particularly the business school, and Dallas:

> The location of Southern Methodist University in a metropolitan area . . . offers unusual opportunities for a School of Business Administration. The combination of theory and practice . . . is found only in a city. . . . The School . . . has had the cooperation of business and industry in this region since its beginning.

By the early 1950s, the business school was offering majors in accounting, banking and finance, business education, business law, business statistics, insurance, management, marketing, personnel administration, real estate, retail merchandising, and general business. The Hoblitzelle Foundation contributed $50,000 to establish a chair of real estate to be known as the Frank L. McNeny Chair. Had this chair come to fruition, it would have been the first endowed chair in the School of Business Administration. However, in the early 1970s, Willis Tate requested that the Hoblitzelle Foundation transfer the funding from an endowed chair position to a scholarship in the "same name and field." Tate made his request because the original funding and its accumulation were insufficient to support an endowed chair position.

The School of Business Administration continued to grow and prosper under the leadership of Fleck, and he was about to be handed a significant gift for his efforts. In the account by Potts and Macsisak, Tate, then vice president of development for SMU, and Bishop Hiram Boaz, second president of SMU, convinced Mary Nored Fincher to provide SMU with a gift to build a new facility for the School of Business Administration. Evidently Mrs. Fincher, widow of one of the four original stockholders of Humble Oil, Joseph Fincher, left $1.5 million of Humble stock to SMU the night before she passed away. Her generosity and the persuasiveness of Boaz and Tate led to the design, construction, and dedication of the Joseph Wylie Fincher Memorial Building. The story is often told that Fincher Parlor, a room in the new building, was furnished with items from Mrs. Fincher's home in memory of her wish to have a place where faculty could meet in tasteful and comfortable surroundings. The Fincher Building was dedicated on November 4, 1954. The beautiful Collegiate Georgian structure offered outstanding classrooms, as well as offices for the faculty, staff, and administration, and would be the foundation structure of today's Cox School of Business.

The 1955–1956 *Bulletin* was the first that mentioned the new Fincher Memorial Building. A glossy black-and-white photograph was placed in the middle of the business school supplement and included the floor plan for the first floor of the building. The configuration of this floor plan has changed dramatically over the last fifty years. The dean's office was located then where

Joseph Wylie Fincher Memorial Building, circa 1956

Barry served two of his three terms as associate dean for academic affairs and Byrne served his two terms as associate dean.

Surprisingly, enrollment had fallen to 425 students, still mostly undergraduates. The majority continued to be men. While no records indicate why enrollment decreased, one could surmise that World War II veterans had completed their education by 1955, thus causing the enrollment sheets that had swelled immediately after the war to be depleted. The next year enrollment for the academic year inched up to 472 and then to 520 the following year. The Building Material Distribution Institute fell by the wayside, and the Southwest Graduate School of Banking (SWGSB), which continues today, was founded by Richard Johnson, an economist who eventually taught in the business school.

In a memo dated January 9, 1961, Fleck responded to an invitation from Dallas-area business leaders suggesting that the School of Business Administration begin a joint work-study cooperative program. In the memo he stated that the faculty had long realized the need for sharing the responsibility of educating young men and women to prepare them for careers in business. More specifically he said:

> Realizing the need for the establishment of a joint cooperative work-study program and acknowledging that education for business responsibility is a joint effort of higher education and business and industry, the Faculty of the SMU School of Business Administration is happy to accept the recommendation of a group of business leaders in the community to establish a joint work-study cooperative program.

Just prior to his retirement, Fleck received the report from the Task Force on the School of Business Administration. The cover letter was dated December 15, 1962, and was signed by Walter Boles, Theodore Eck, and Syd Reagan, who chaired the Task Force. The letter stated that the Task Force had "sought the counsel of our colleagues in the School of Business Administration, including the Department of Economics." The signers admitted their recommendations would necessitate additional funding for the school before all could be implemented. The second and third paragraphs and the first sentence of the fourth paragraph provide a clear picture of what the faculty in the school thought about business education at the start of the 1960s:

> The School of Business Administration should strive to produce a graduate who has developed the values, knowledge, skills, habits and motivation to make constructive contributions to society both as a citizen and as a businessman in a future that will contain many developments not yet known. As a citizen and a businessman, he should be equipped to recognize and define a problem, to determine alternative solutions, to evaluate the consequences of alternative solutions, to decide on a solution, to take action, and to analyze the results of the decision. He should be equipped to understand the consequences of a course of action to himself, to his business, to his employees, and to society. He should have a concern for these consequences both as a citizen and as a businessman. He should be equipped to think and to think responsibly. He should understand and appreciate his cultural heritage. He should be prepared and motivated to continue his education as a citizen and as a businessman throughout life and should understand that education does not end upon graduation.
>
> This goal can be achieved through more rigorous professional training within the context of a liberal education.
>
> The gulf between liberal arts and education for business should not and need not exist.

The Task Force made a recommendation that the school have six priority goals in the following order: full-time undergraduate education, cooperative internship program, part-time (evening) undergraduate education, graduate education, Southwest Business Research Institute, and program of continuing business education (non-degree programs).

Fleck retired in June 1963. During his last academic year, enrollment dropped slightly to 500 students. Thirty MBAs graduated during Fleck's last year and his successor's first year as dean. When Fleck left, the School of Business Administration had 42 professors and instructors, 4 daytime lecturers, 39 nighttime lecturers for Dallas College, and 19 student assistants. Fleck came to SMU when called by Hauhart. In an article dated May 5, 1963, a month before Fleck's retirement, he said his greatest challenge as dean of the school was the creation of mutual respect between businessmen and business educators. He did not believe schools of business could "unlock the door to creative ability" or teach business students how to be leaders. Fleck was supposed to come to SMU and teach economics for one summer in 1921. He said, "It turned out to be a long summer." His "summer" lasted forty-two years, during which time he was an admirable and tireless contributor to both SMU and the School of Business Administration. He had built up the foundation started by Hauhart by increasing the quality and quantity of the faculty and opening the Fincher Building. He built bridges with the business community. He set the tone for Aaron Sartain to take the helm in July 1963.

Aaron Q. Sartain: The Third Foundational Dean

Aaron Q. Sartain was trained as a psychologist and was brought to the business school by Fleck to initiate a Department of Personnel Administration that would one day become the Organizational Behavior Area. To the best of our knowledge, Sartain was the first and, to date, the only person to hold chairmanships in two different schools at SMU (psychology in the liberal arts and personnel administration in the business school). Sartain earned bachelor and master's degrees in psychology from SMU in 1923 and 1928, respectively. He went on to earn his PhD in psychology at the University of Chicago in 1939. He began teaching at SMU in the Psychology Department in 1932, prior to beginning his graduate work at the University of Chicago. He was the first president of the Faculty Senate, and was coach of the debate team from 1933 to 1942. Sartain began his shift from psychology to business through his consulting work at North American Aviation during World War II.

Dallas and SMU during the Sartain Administration

Early in Sartain's administration, several campuses of the Dallas Community College system were established. It was also the year that NorthPark Center opened as one of the early indoor malls in the nation. In 1966 Joseph Lockridge became the first African American elected to the Texas legislature from Dallas, and SMU's Jerry Levias became the first black scholarship football player in the Southwest Conference. The following year, Dr. Emmett Conrad became the first African American elected to the Dallas school board. In 1969 Anita N. Martinez was the first Hispanic elected to the Dallas city council.

Dean Aaron Q. Sartain

Sartain's administration saw the genesis of the University of Texas at Dallas (UTD). Officially located in the city of Richardson, UTD was the result of the foresight and daring of Eugene McDermott, Cecil Green, and J. Erik Jonsson, the founders of Geophysical Sciences, Inc., later to become Texas Instruments. To foster the growth of scientific talent in the area, McDermott, Green, and Jonsson established the Graduate Research Center of the Southwest in 1961. They decided to donate the center and its land to the University of Texas System, and in June 1969 the Texas legislature formally created the University of Texas at Dallas. UTD initially offered only graduate programs but has since provided undergraduate education as well.

When Sartain took responsibility for the School of Business Administration, he inherited President Tate's master plan. According to Terry, the 1962–1963 master plan would be central to understanding SMU and its educational philosophy. The master plan reaffirmed the centrality of the liberal arts core to the educational model of SMU. SMU students were to be educated as citizens of the world first, and members of their professions second. In designing the master plan, Tate insisted that SMU should not be a copycat of other universities in spite of how outstanding their reputations might be. Instead, SMU should develop its own "character and style." In his opening remarks at the first of two separate conferences on SMU's shared governance program that was being instituted by the master plan, Tate noted,

We have tried to define, to understand, and to establish ways of orderly self-renewal and change here at SMU. Our "image" becomes what our various publics see. While we are certainly concerned with what they see, as our very life depends upon our publics believing we are worthy, we are most concerned to be what we say we are. We must be flexible, progressive, and subject to improvement. Even so, no single segment of the university (president, faculty, students, alumni, or trustees) has the right to change unilaterally this university's purpose and goals.

A key question of the master plan, according to Terry, was whether a church-based school such as SMU could achieve academic excellence and be a "truly first-rate institution." Faculty and administrators involved in the master plan planning process believed that the answer was "yes" but only through "commitment, dedication, and support." One of those key planners was Sartain.

School of Business Progress under Sartain

Everyone who knew Sartain considered him very bright and uncommonly congenial. As Nora Katherine Bilton told us in her interview, Sartain was very calm, and, while slow moving and slow talking, he had more energy and stamina than most people she knew. Because of his love of students and psychology, Sartain continued to teach a course in psychology while he was dean of the business school. He also started a course in business for first-year undergraduates. Sartain was a rather informal dean, in terms of personal style, and continued to maintain his ties with his colleagues throughout the university while he led the business school faculty through the middle 1960s.

Sartain was well known nationally as an excellent arbitrator, a skill that likely came in handy during his administrative stints in psychology and business. He was well liked by the business community in Dallas. He often contributed his time and efforts to local business organizations and seldom turned down a request to give a speech or provide service for a Dallas organization. An open and tolerant person, he was well respected among his business and academic colleagues. Sartain was a strong motivator who helped people gain confidence in themselves.

In 1963, Sartain inherited forty professors, two instructors, four day lecturers, thirty-nine night lecturers, and nineteen student assistants. Student organizations that were operating in the School of Business Administration at the time included Alpha Kappa Psi, Phi Chi Theta (a women's business fraternity), Delta Sigma Pi (to foster the study of business), Student Marketing Club, Society for the Advancement of Management (SAM), Alpha Delta Sigma and Gamma Alpha Chi (advertising fraternities for men and women, respectively),

Aaron Sartain and Nora Katherine Bilton at her retirement party, 1989

the Personnel Management Association, Beta Alpha Psi (accounting fraternity), Sigma Iota Epsilon (professional management fraternity), the Students' Association, and several social fraternities and sororities to which business school students belonged.

As Sartain began his administration, tuition and fees at SMU were up to $450 a semester, board was $250 each semester, and rooms varied between $150 and $200 per semester. There was also a student service fee of $50 each semester. So students were paying between $1,800 and $1,900 annually, excluding personal costs and books. At the time, freshmen interested in studying business were entered into the university as "pre-business administration" majors. Regular students admitted into the business school had to meet the pre-business requirements and have completed sixty hours of acceptable college credit. The business school also allowed "conditional admits" and granted select correspondence credit. Special students were admitted but were not candidates for a degree. An MBA student could focus on accounting, finance, management, marketing, real estate, or statistics.

Enrollment in the School of Business Administration totaled 500 students. Only 71 were women. Most were seniors, followed by juniors, and then "others," including MBA students. During ceremonies in August 1961, January 1962, and May 1962, 30 MBA candidates received their degrees. One of Sartain's first tasks was to expand the role of graduate education in the business school. In 1964, 161 MBA students were enrolled in the school. Only 6 were women, possibly indicating that graduate business education was not yet interesting to many women. In 1965, there were 228 MBAs, 13 of whom were women.

According to the account presented by Potts and Macsisak, and an interview with Nora Katherine Bilton, Sartain was dean when the SMU Foundation for Business Administration (SMUFBA) was formed in January 1965. The impetus for the foundation was the organization of a committee by President Tate to encourage influential businessmen to get engaged with the School of Business Administration and SMU. The focus of the committee was, generally, financial support of the business school and, specifically, faculty expansion, scholarships, and building of better facilities. Twenty-five influential businessmen in Dallas were nominated by the SMU Board of Governors, a nineteen-person group of trustees that made week-to-week decisions in an effort to streamline Board of Trustee decisions. The appointees included William P. Clements Jr., Robert H. Stewart III, Charles Pistor, and the first chair of the foundation, Edwin L. Cox. Clements and Cox were successful in the oil business while Stewart and Pistor were prominent Dallas bankers.

As reported by Potts and Macsisak, the first priority of the SMUFBA was to analyze the strengths and weaknesses of the school. A visiting committee of high-ranking officials from premier schools and industry was brought to the SMU campus to study the school of business. The committee included Ernie Arbuckle from Stanford University, Ross Trump from Washington University in Saint Louis, Willis Winn from the University of Pennsylvania, and O. V. Cecil and Arthur Smith from industries in Dallas. In its report submitted to Tate on March 1, 1966, the committee concluded that the undergraduate program lacked an analytical curriculum and was not very challenging; the graduate program was not at all distinctive.

According to the committee's recommendations, both the undergraduate and graduate programs should undergo significant revisions. Entrance requirements for both programs should be raised, and courses that were narrow, skill-focused, and descriptive should be replaced with more analytical and challenging courses. Committee members told Tate that the School of Business Administration's budget was not adequate to make the reforms necessary to improve, significantly, the quality and reputation of the school. As one example of the inadequate budget, the maximum salaries of full professors at the SMU School of Business Administration were less than the minimum salaries of professors at Stanford University and at the Wharton School of the University of Pennsylvania. If the SMU School of Business Administration was to become an elite school, it had to pay its faculty more appropriately. The committee also noted that the evening program courses were seriously lacking in quality.

As a result of the Master Plan Task Force of 1962 and the visiting committee's report in 1966, there came a clarion call for bold, new leadership of the business school. The call came as a signal that both SMU and the business school wanted to see greater national prominence established in the school. To respond to this call, in the fall of 1966 Tate formed another committee that included himself, Sartain, Clements, Cox, and Smith. In addition, Provost Neill McFarland; Syd Reagan, a real estate professor; and Cliff Wendler, a statistics professor, joined the committee.

In fall 1967, Reagan interviewed the young dean of Tulane, C. Jackson Grayson Jr., who indicated no interest in SMU. The writing, however, was on the wall, and Sartain submitted his resignation as dean of the School of Business Administration on November 10, 1967, to be effective on September 1, 1968. During Sartain's last academic year, there were 23 professors, 4 instructors, 6 daytime lecturers, 43 nighttime lecturers, and 19 student assistants. Tuition, room, board, and fees had increased to slightly over $2,200 annually. The MBA program had 368 students, 11 of whom were women.

The goal to increase the prominence of the School of Business Administration became part of the mindset of university and school administrators. What Hauhart had begun in 1921 was maintained and nurtured by Fleck for almost two decades. Sartain, as the third dean setting the foundation of the school, would increase, significantly, the enrollment in and focus upon graduate education in the school. It would be some twenty-five years later that the MBA program would gain significant national prominence and become the flagship program of the School of Business Administration. And it would be the next dean, C. Jackson Grayson Jr., who first would put the school on the national map.

CHAPTER THREE

GRAYSON AND RADICAL INNOVATION, 1968–1975

We have the opportunity to transform business education in the U.S.

JACK GRAYSON

C. JACKSON GRAYSON JR. was born on a prosperous cotton farm in north-west Louisiana. He graduated from the Wharton School of Finance and Economy at the University of Pennsylvania. A highly regarded researcher in decision sciences, Grayson studied under Howard Raiffa at Harvard University, where he earned his doctorate. His dissertation explored decision-making risk and uncertainty. He arrived at Tulane University in 1959 having spent time as an FBI field agent and a staff writer for a New Orleans daily newspaper. At Tulane, Grayson quickly earned a reputation as an outstanding classroom teacher to go along with his research and writing prowess. He would dabble in the racehorse business and become a licensed pilot. From 1963 to 1964 he served a stint as a professor of finance at IMEDE (Institut pour l'Étude des Méthodes de Direction de l'Entreprise), now IMD (International Institute for Management Development), a management development institute in Lausanne, Switzerland. This was an interesting background, but it did not hint at the innovative and aggressive manner in which he would go about implementing his vision of significantly transforming business education.

Dean C. Jackson Grayson Jr.

The Dallas Environment

In 1970, Dallas erected and dedicated the Kennedy Memorial. Throughout the 1970s, Dallas continued its population surge toward a million citizens. A key infrastructure variable to Dallas's growth was the opening in 1974 of the Dallas–Fort Worth Regional Airport (later to become Dallas/Fort Worth International Airport) located between the two cities. Four years later, Dallas opened its new city hall designed by I. M. Pei. Regional and corporate head-quarters continued to move to Dallas, further stimulating its growth. Grayson came to Dallas during a time of significant change. He would try to capitalize on that atmosphere of change.

The SMU Environment on Grayson's Arrival

Grayson would serve as dean under two presidents: Willis Tate and Paul Hardin. These two presidents operated within very different environments.

Willis Tate

Grayson would work under Willis Tate for only a short time before Tate's retirement in 1971. Just prior to his retirement as president, Tate, in a speech to SMU alumni, stated twelve important things that happened during his watch as president. These included the master plan of 1962–1963; the growth and develop-ment of professional schools on campus; the creation of University College with its liberal learning core curriculum; the creation of the School of Arts; the founding of the Master of Liberal Learning Program, which offers the

Kennedy Memorial

MLA degree; and SMU's increasing ability to attract faculty from first-class universities. Further, Tate noted more selective admissions, recognition that

President Willis M. Tate

SMU could face controversies without having disruptions, recognition that openness is more valuable than dogma, the completion of one of the most impressive physical plants in the United States, the recruitment of great friends and supporters of SMU, and a sense of community involvement and trust in all major SMU affairs.

Willis M. Tate, as the fifth president of SMU, had continued to plant the seeds of excellence in the beds prepared by his four predecessors. He had focused on academic freedom, substance, and quality. Tate was a tremendous stabilizing force in the history of SMU, and the original two-building university had spread its wings and was ready to fly higher and higher in the last three decades of the twentieth century.

Paul Hardin

Paul Hardin served as SMU's president for only a brief period of time, 1972–1974. He was born in Charlotte, North Carolina, and educated at Duke University and Clemson University. Hardin was a young, energetic man—just forty years old—when he took the SMU helm. He came to SMU from Wofford

College, where he was serving as Wofford's president. Prior to that, Hardin had taught law at the Duke law school. Hardin was a strong believer in developing plans and setting goals. With the help of James E. Brooks, his provost and academic vice president, Hardin set out a planning process for the next several years in SMU's advancement toward academic excellence.

In addition to his penchant for planning, Hardin was an ambitious and inquisitive man. According to Terry, Hardin asked about the wisdom of football at SMU at his interview dinner. Evidently the subject was quickly changed when one of the members of the Board of Governors insisted that football at SMU was not a topic for debate. But Hardin, as president, asked the Board of Governors difficult and pointed questions regarding issues he believed important to the future of SMU. He even went "so far" as to report SMU football infractions to the NCAA, an action not commonplace in the early to mid-1970s.

Hardin did not have a lot of time to implement his planning procedures at SMU. A short two years after his appearance as the sixth president, he left to be president of Drew University. Why Hardin left so suddenly is not known.

President Paul Hardin

Some hypothesize that he was fired. Others suggest that because of his constant probing about the value of football at SMU he was placed on probation by select members of the Board of Governors. Unable to tolerate the situation, he resigned. In any event, SMU lost a potentially good leader who had proven himself at Duke and Wofford College and would subsequently do the same as the president of Drew University and then the University of North Carolina. While Willis Tate was enjoying life without the presidential duties, he did respond to the call from SMU to return as interim president until Hardin's replacement could be found.

Change Agent Grayson

Grayson was dean of the school of business at Tulane University when he was invited by officials of SMU to consider moving to Dallas as dean of the SMU School of Business Administration. Upon meeting with Tate and other university staff and faculty, Grayson was impressed with the strength of their intention to improve the school of business. No less important to Grayson's decision was the effort of two important members of the SMU Board of Trustees, Edwin L. Cox and William P. Clements. Both were successful Dallas businessmen. They were able to assure Grayson of widespread business support and their personal commitment to help him move the business school into national prominence.

Grayson made two appointments at the beginning of his term as dean of the SMU business school. Eugene T. Byrne was appointed associate dean for academic affairs. Byrne was associate dean at the Tulane school of business and had been Grayson's research associate at IMEDE. John M. Dutton, Grayson's classmate at Harvard, was appointed professor of business administration, a position he held at the prestigious Herman Krannert School of Management at Purdue University. Byrne and Dutton were the two key figures who worked with Grayson to plan the future direction of the school of business in his first year at SMU.

The Foundation for Transformation

As Grayson began the task of creating a plan to develop the school, there was no specific planning process in place. Rather, planning was a continuous stream of meetings, with Grayson, Byrne, and Dutton wrestling with issues of what to change, how to produce change, the timing of specific changes, and how to raise funds to support program revamping and innovation. Although Grayson met periodically with Cox, there was virtually no contact with the business community to seek their input.

During late fall 1968, some of Grayson's guiding principles became clear. The first was that the learning environment should focus on actual business problems. Grayson was attracted to the power and utility of learning through experience, and the phrase became a mantra in the business school. Working on real business problems would motivate students to learn, faculty to guide learning, and men and women in business to solve problems and gain access to untapped faculty and student resources. The environment envisioned by Grayson and his colleagues was not simply a senior elective seminar but the foundation for an entire curriculum. Periodically, students, faculty, and business people would jointly assess the amount and quality of the student's learning and assign a "grade" as a measure of completion of a learning activity. Different business problems and situations would provide many different learning opportunities, and students, guided by faculty, would make choices that determined their business educa-

Students studying a business issue

tion. After successfully completing the equivalent of the normally required undergraduate credit hours, the student would be granted a degree.

While Grayson's pedagogical approach engendered enormous opportunities, it also presented a quagmire of problems for everyone involved. This form of education at the undergraduate level previously had not been attempted in any business school. The idea of learning in real-life or clinical environments had been successful in other disciplines, such as medicine, engineering, and fine arts, among others. Indeed internships and cooperative models of education were common in American education. What Grayson envisioned, however, was a far cry from minor excursions into the real world. He wanted to adopt the real world as the engine for education and research. Freedom to choose was another guiding principle that shaped Grayson's emerging educational philosophy. In the late 1960s the educational format for students was rather rigidly prescribed. The business school accrediting association, the American Assembly of Collegiate Schools of Business (AACSB), now called the Association to Advance Collegiate Schools of Business (AACSB International), prescribed courses of study and degree requirements that offered little choice except that a student might select a major field of study and have elective choices within that field. Grayson believed that prescriptions might be valid in some cases but that the student would gain little or no self-knowledge or learning by following prescribed routes. To the contrary, he strongly believed that students should have the freedom to make their own choices regarding how to develop competence in a field of study. Interestingly, freedom of choice was not restricted to graduate students and, in fact, would find initial expression with undergraduates when a curriculum was adopted that had only one required course!

SMU business school students were not at all unanimous in support of freedom to choose. Many felt as if they were being abandoned and that faculty members were abdicating their responsibility for educating students.

Although it was difficult to oppose freedom of choice for students, the idea of an unrestricted curriculum did not gain universal acceptance among the business faculty. Part of the reason was the strong possibility that the

AACSB might withdraw accreditation from the undergraduate program. Accreditation was considered a hallmark of any quality business school. Thus freedom of choice could jeopardize the school's hard-earned status as a respected business school. In fact, the issue of accreditation eventually became a major challenge for the school.

Shared governance was another principle Grayson used to develop his concept of a business school capable of transforming business education. Just as he was willing to allow students to tackle the most complex business problems, Grayson was confident that students could contribute to the fundamental processes of managing and directing the educational enterprise. He believed that students had the intellectual capacity, motivation, and experience necessary to struggle with such central issues as the nature and scope of the curriculum, questions of faculty evaluation, and the structure and operation of the school's governing mechanism. Working in concert with the faculty, who would continue to have the primary decision role in virtually all matters affecting the school, students would participate in decisions directly affecting them.

This was a highly controversial philosophy in the late 1960s. Few, if any, educational enterprises provided students with an opportunity to participate in decisions affecting the central mission and purpose of the educational organization. The idea of direct participation by students was not only foreign to the thinking of most faculty members, but students themselves did not readily adopt it. The students throughout the country were becoming politically and socially active in the 1970s, involving themselves in everything from protesting the Vietnam War and the invasion of Cambodia to the civil and social rights of minorities and women. In most instances students demanded a say on any and all issues of human rights. However, in discussions or decisions in areas traditionally reserved for faculty and key administrators, students demanded to be heard and to influence decisions but generally did not ask for a direct role in decisions such as curriculum development. Grayson was confident that student participation would help transform the SMU school of business into an exciting and vibrant learning environment that would attract outstanding faculty and students as well as the support of the business community. Student participation would be one of the significant forces producing change in the school.

The Vision for the School of Business

In Grayson's vision, innovation was also one of the guiding elements necessary to transform business education. Grayson stated the bold goal of becoming the best business school in the Southwest region and one of the five leading business schools in the world by 1980. He said, "The main strategy we will follow to achieve our goal will be that of innovations—innovation in management education and in research on management practice."

The reason that this strategy would succeed, in Grayson's mind, was the stagnant condition of business education in the United States. In contrast to existing practices at most business schools, Grayson wanted to individualize instruction and learning through curriculum reform and educational technology; integrate teaching, research, and management practice; and require clearly defined goals, responsibilities, and performance measures to instill accountability in the educational enterprise.

Grayson's vision of a world-class business school would have faculty, students, staff, and business people acting cooperatively in a learning environment that emphasized and served individual differences, focused on developing leaders and entrepreneurial ability, and discovered and distributed relevant knowledge about business. This interactive mix of the three dimensions of teaching, research, and business involvement quickly became labeled the 3-D approach and was often used to represent the school's approach to practical, individualized action learning. The logo became ubiquitous, appearing on reports, letterhead, business cards, envelopes, and so forth. In a few years, however, the university would insist that the business school return to its more traditional logo, similar to that of all other schools on campus.

In the SMU business school of the future, students would have the responsibility for designing their individual educational programs. For most students, the programs they designed would be stimulated by their involvement in teams, with faculty and other students working on actual business problems. They would be guided and assisted by faculty as they sought knowledge and skills to satisfy their need to solve real problems. They were free to choose from many resources for learning, including traditional class-room courses, independent modularized study and research, and the use of technology-based resources such as audio-visual or computer-assisted learn-ing. Periodically, students would document their learning and receive credit for their progress. They were encouraged to be creative in designing their learning through the opportunity to have their accomplishments evaluated on a pass/fail basis. When a student amassed a certain amount of certified learning credits, he or she was granted a certificate of completion. In some cases students could elect to receive certification for a partially completed course of study; e.g., they might choose an 80 percent completion certificate. Most undergraduate students would elect to earn sufficient credits to be awarded their bachelor's degree. Similar options would be available for grad-uate students.

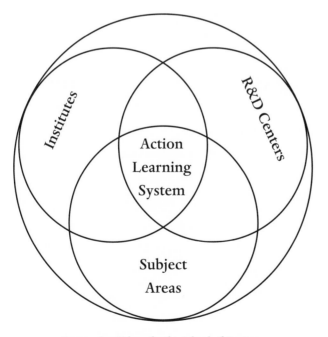

Grayson's 3-D logo for the School of Business

Thus, Grayson's vision for students was to have a business bring a problem to the school, e.g., conduct a performance audit of the company's personnel policies. One or more teams of two to five students would work under the guidance of a faculty member and conduct the audit. Much like a consultancy, the business received a final report from the students. The students would document their learning and be awarded credit. Students might work on three to four teams on different business projects for an entire semester. In following semesters, they may do more or less of this type of learning, perhaps devoting themselves entirely to traditional classroom work in some semesters. Students could move in and out of team settings, independent study, and traditional educational venues, all the while relating to and basing their learning on actual business problems.

The changes for faculty would be no less dramatic than those offered to students in the SMU School of Business Administration as it was envisioned by Grayson. Faculty would be expected to retain their role as important information and knowledge resources for students and business people. They would provide traditional courses and seminars but would spend a significant portion of their time working in teams with students, business people, and other faculty on actual business problems. Their role would be expanded beyond mere knowledge provider. Instead they would become coaches, mentors, and motivators for student learning. This form of involvement by faculty would direct their research focus toward practical knowledge to solve business problems. It would also increase cross-disciplinary research and integrate multi-disciplinary curriculum development since actual business problems cannot be solved by reference to a single academic discipline, which is the usual manner in which knowledge is organized in business schools.

The school would also serve the business community by providing office space over extended periods of time to significant numbers of people from a large variety of business organizations. These resident businessmen and businesswomen would interact with faculty, students, and each other to form learning communities that might further enhance learning and research opportunities for faculty and students.

Students and faculty interacting

Technology had to be a central feature for all members of the business school community. Multi-media and computer services would be available to allow learners access to information on an as-needed basis. Connections would be provided to information resources around the globe, including the ability to access and interact with human resources on a real-time basis. The physical facility would be designed and structured to permit rapid deployment of space to accommodate changing needs as projects were completed and others were begun.

The school would generally accommodate both undergraduate and master's level programs. Despite the fact that most leading schools of business had doctoral programs, such programs were not included in the vision of the school of business in part because of their high costs. Doctoral programs are traditionally devoted to developing expertise in single disciplines and frequently focus on theoretical research. With both the undergraduate and

Fincher Building with gold-leaf cupola, circa 1970

master's programs emphasizing practical business problem solving, essential scarce resources might be diverted by the introduction of a discipline-oriented doctoral program.

It is interesting to note at this point that few people inside or outside the school fully understood the depth of Grayson's concern about the state of business education. He continually and enthusiastically espoused his business education philosophy. For example, he once said, "It seems inevitable that within the management careers of BBA and MBA students that there will be more fundamentally important changes than in all the history of mankind."

Implementing the Vision

"Since you will be in Dallas before me, I want you to visit with Provost Neill McFarland and ask him to gold leaf the dome on the Fincher Building as soon as possible. We are the only school at SMU whose dome is not gold leafed." With these instructions to Byrne, Grayson left on a previously scheduled trip that would delay his arrival to the SMU campus. McFarland was not sure of the purpose of the request but agreed to it, and the gold leaf was added to the dome by the end of the summer of 1968. Gilding the dome was intended as a symbolic message to everyone on campus, and especially to the faculty of the business school, that things were going to be very different! The gold dome on Fincher attracted everyone's attention, but the symbolism may have been lost on most people.

Also symbolic, but even more confusing to the campus community, was Grayson's decision to move the Department of Economics out of the business school. The department had an excellent reputation. It seemed strange not to embrace a department perceived to engender the quality of teaching and research that would be a potential spearhead for improving programs throughout the school. Grayson's view was that the economics department's success as an academic discipline would work against the practical, experiential, entrepreneurial, leadership environment he envisioned. While this decision was accepted as a *fait accompli,* most faculty were surprised and disappointed. (See the sidebar on pages 78–79 for excerpts from a recollection of the Department of Economics by Professor J. Carter Murphy.)

To balance symbolism with substance, Scientific Methods, Inc., was hired to help create a long-range, comprehensive strategic plan for the school. This firm's special expertise involved using a planning and organizational development technique known as the Managerial Grid. An interesting feature of the grid process was to involve the primary stakeholders of the school. The first phase of the project was held during the Christmas break of the 1968–1969 academic year. Students, business school and university faculty, administrators, and staff attended, as did several prominent members of the Dallas business community. The process sought to promote change and garner increased involvement, participation, and commitment to common goals from all the school's constituents. Despite some lively and productive discussions regarding the future of the school and how to implement change, the Managerial Grid process was halted when it was deemed impractical, due, in large part, to the expense of the grid. The process would require years and would drain time from other activities that were critical to create change quickly. It should be noted that the grid process required frank and open discussion among all parties. This dynamic was very new to most participants and, in more than a few cases, provoked anger, confusion, and some disenchantment. This disenchantment, in addition to financial concerns, may have stymied plans for the grid process.

Organizational Innovation

Shortly after the aborted Managerial Grid program, a committee of twelve to fifteen faculty and students, appointed by Grayson, was formed to review and recommend changes to the school's graduate and undergraduate curricula. The Task Force on Curriculum was given carte blanche and encouraged to be bold and innovative in reflecting Grayson's philosophy. The task force members were devoted to their task and met regularly over the course of the next year. Their work would produce some of the most provocative and controver-

SOUTHERN METHODIST UNIVERSITY
SCHOOL OF BUSINESS ADMINISTRATION
POLICIES FOR FACULTY APPOINTMENT
AND ADVANCEMENT

July 1, 1969

The primary goal of the school is to be among the top five (5) professional schools of business. To achieve this position the School must have a faculty and a student body which seeks and provides <u>excellence in every program and product of the school</u>.

sial curriculum changes (discussed in the following section) seen in any business school in the country at the time.

In concert with forming the curriculum committee, Grayson announced two dramatic changes in the conduct of the affairs of the school. The first, in July 1969, was presented in a document entitled "Policies for Faculty Appointment and Advancement." The goal of the school was to have faculty who qualified for compensation levels associated with internationally rated institutions. Productivity and quality were addressed for teaching, research, and applications. One standard, for example, was the production of fourteen refereed articles by a full professor holding a full-time research appointment; an individual professor with a full-time teaching appointment might handle four classes of one hundred or more students per academic year. Quality was also considered, and it was noted that teaching was more than an emphasis on day-to-day classroom activities. The expectation was for faculty to demonstrate superior performance in at least two of the three major functions of the school—teaching, research, and applications. The applications area, later to be called institutes, would consist of faculty, staff, and students devoting part of their time to solving actual business problems. This activity was similar in nature to consulting for business, with the expectation that institute faculty would enrich their teaching and produce findings of general interest that could be reported as academic research or published in the popular business literature. The institutes would bring the school closer to the business community and provide venues for faculty to make major contributions to the school's goal of a practical, problem-solving education in business.

In addition to providing a working point of contact with business, the institutes were expected to attract excellent teachers who may not be inter-

---

THE SCHOOL OF BUSINESS ADMINISTRATION
AND THE ECONOMICS DEPARTMENT

[The following excerpts are from "Recollections: SMU's Department of Economics 1960–1971" by J. Carter Murphy. These recollections were written in September 2002 and sent to Tom Barry by Murphy on April 25, 2005.]

ABOUT 1963, the School of Business was threatened with loss of its accreditation by the American Collegiate Schools of Business because the number of faculty with PhDs fell short of standards. To resolve this problem, the undergraduate budget of the Economics Department was shifted administratively from Arts and Sciences to the School of Business, and the department's offices were moved from Atkins Hall into the Fincher Building—then the only building in use by Business. The department's graduate budget remained in the Graduate School of Arts and Sciences, and the department offered an AB degree through the College of Arts and Sciences as well as the BBA in business.

⋆　⋆　⋆

The department remained in the School of Business and was housed in Fincher until Jack Grayson became dean there in 1969 [*sic*] and wanted both the

space occupied by economics and, I think, freedom from the influence of the economics faculty.

⋆　⋆　⋆

Relations with the School of Business were generally agreeable and without issues until the arrival of Jack Grayson in 1969 [*sic*]. At the time of inauguration of the Economics doctoral program, at the end of the 1950s, Larry Fleck was the Business School Dean. On his retirement, the post went to Aaron Sartain, a kindly and judicious psychologist and personnel manager who was, however, unable to arouse the Dallas business community to provide major financial support for the school. I believe it was at the time of Sartain's retirement, that a dean's search committee found Jack Grayson, then at LSU [*sic*], and a man who had terminated the undergraduate business program there and made innovative changes in the MBA program. With Grayson came changes in the School of Business at SMU and in the relationships between that school and the department of economics. I shall detail some of these changes below, but his deanship brought to an end economics' position as part of the business school and its housing in Fincher Hall, the business School building. It also all but terminated the participation ested in traditional academic research. Their participation in the institutes and teaching would qualify them for membership in the ranks of valued faculty. As one might expect, traditional faculty were skeptical if a colleague was not producing articles for academia while faculty who devoted their time to teaching and institutes worried about being cast as second-class citizens. Such fears were not unreasonable and would require time and action to eliminate.

About a year after his appointment, Grayson set productivity and quality goals similar to those at top-rated schools of business. This caused significant

---

of business school students in economics classes for four or five years. Grayson left SMU in the winter of 1971–1972 for a Washington assignment, and then, after a brief return in 1973, left the university for good, probably in 1975.

Fortunately for economics, and I think for Business as well, Grayson was followed at Business by Bobby Lyle, who served as interim dean while Grayson was in Washington and briefly after his return. His tenure, however, was short, and he was never given full rein by the university administration. He was followed by perhaps the best dean of that school that I think I knew, Alan Coleman. Coleman came to SMU as the holder of the Caruth Chair in Finance but then accepted the deanship a year after coming. He completed the unraveling of the administrative innovations of the Grayson era and, by good appointments and the cultivation of the Dallas business community, started the school on a path to genuine quality. During his deanship, good relations were restored with economics, and business school undergraduates and MBA students came again to the department of economics in large numbers.

I [Murphy] succeeded Dick [Johnson] as chair of the department at the end of the spring term, 1968. At about that time, too, Jack Grayson came to the School of Business as Dean. I remember well a phone call from Jack, one day in July or August of that summer, suggesting we have breakfast when he

was in town the following weekend. Jack was not one to be indirect, and at that meeting he bluntly said he wanted the Department of Economics out of the Business School. He wanted us administratively in Humanities and Sciences, and he wanted the space we were occupying in the Fincher Building. I told him I would give that idea my prompt attention and get back to him. And during the following days, I canvassed my department colleagues and sought the advice of the deans of Humanities and Sciences and the Graduate School and that of the Provost. I am certain that, in my own mind, from the beginning, my own preference was to accept Jack's mandate and take the department without a fight to H and S. The Provost, Neill McFarland, pointed out that Jack had arrived with strong support from the central administration and the trustees and was probably in a position to win any showdown in any case. He was being given a free hand in remaking the School of Business. I found other members of the department, like myself, more in tune with our colleagues in the other social sciences than with our colleagues in business at that time, and so, within a week or two I got back to Grayson and told him it was agreed that economics would become part of the College and the Graduate School for administration, and that when suitable space could be provided on campus, we would move our office from the Fincher Building.

frustration and anger among most of the faculty. SMU business school salary levels were nowhere near the lofty levels announced in the Standards Document, and, for many faculty, the productivity and quality standards were deemed unreasonable, if not punitive.

On September 1, 1969, Grayson announced a Plan of Organization for the school. Academic departments were to become subject areas "to indicate new relationships, responsibilities, and membership." Specific subject areas would be specified in the spring of 1970. The Plan of Organization also included three internal policy councils responsible for making recommendations to the school faculty or administration for final decision: the Educational Policy Council, the School Policy Council, and the Research and Development (R&D) and Institute Policy Council. An External Policy Advisory Council was also established. Councils could develop recommendations regarding the scope of the curriculum, content of courses, requirements for degrees, and continuation or addition of new subject areas, and research and development centers, or institutes. Indeed, any individual in the school could make a policy or strategy recommendation that, in turn, would be considered by the appropriate policy council. Each policy council included faculty, administrators, and students appointed by the dean. All members were granted full voting rights within each council. The External Advisory Council served to advise and consult with the dean.

By September 1973 the organization plan was revised. Grayson wanted to broaden direct participation of all constituents to help govern the school. The revised plan created the Business School Assembly as the school's primary policy authority. The assembly consisted of full-time faculty, two part-time faculty, five administrators, and students equal to 30 percent of assembly membership. All members, including students, had full voting rights. The assembly had concurrent jurisdiction with an executive committee, and there were three standing committees: Faculty Personnel, Student Personnel, and Educational Affairs. Students were also voting members of the executive committee and of each of the standing committees.

Grayson's Plan of Organization thrust students into the middle of the governance structure of the school. The students' presence on each of the policy councils provided them access and input into areas that had always been the sole province of faculty and administrators. These students could ask for information on any topic and request that their ideas be discussed in open forums where students voted on the content and disposition of proposals.

Change came upon the business school in a rush, and much more was on the way!

Curriculum Innovation

According to Grayson, "an undying principle can make one an intellectual pauper." He was convinced that conventional business school curricula were rigid structures primarily oriented toward dispensing knowledge and inadequate to meet the demands of the exploding information age. Critical skills for a graduate included finding and applying knowledge to solve real problems and not simply building a store of knowledge. Perhaps even more important was a student's opportunity to be an active, autonomous learner fully versed in making the critical decisions that determine his or her academic experience. Success in a student's future career would require possessing the skill and ability to maintain life-long learning.

The Task Force on Curriculum struggled for about a year to design an undergraduate curriculum that would meet the challenges faced by graduates entering a world dominated by dramatic change. In the end, task force members wanted students to begin the process of taking full responsibility for their own learning and in March 1970 recommended abolishing all but a single required course. The required course, known as Administrative Seminar 1— more popularly AS1—introduced students to an academic environment virtually unlike any other they may have experienced or expected. Students would craft their own course of study limited only by university requirements for graduation and the business school's requirement that not less than 40 percent nor more than 60 percent of all work could be taken within the School of Business Administration. The environment would be rich with alternative forms of learning, including teams working on actual business projects, as well as simulations, self-study, and traditional classroom activities. There were options for pass/fail grading and contract learning. Contract learning was a formal, structured approach to independent learning. There were no designated major programs of study, and students were free to design any course of study they deemed most beneficial to their development.

More than any other action, this curriculum expressed the philosophy of Jack Grayson and those colleagues who shared his philosophy and values. For some faculty and students, the curriculum created unlimited opportunity for self-expression and self-understanding. For others it was a blatant abdication of faculty responsibility. No matter what view was held, the school of business promised to provide some of the most interesting and challenging experiences in one's academic and professional career.

Shortly after the undergraduate program revision was approved, the faculty reviewed the recommendations of the Task Force on Curriculum for the MBA program. The proposal for the graduate program was as sweeping and revolutionary as the undergraduate changes. The philosophy and values that spawned the undergraduate curriculum were embedded in the design of the graduate program. The recommendation was approved by the faculty in July 1970 and was designed for students to complete the program in twelve months of full-time study. This broke with a national norm (with the University of Pittsburgh as an exception) that MBA programs require two academic years to complete. The one-year program at SMU required forty-two credit hours of graduate work compared to the sixty credit hours required under the national norm. Part of the rationale for a one-year program rested with the assumption that the pace of change in the business world coupled with the information explosion negated any attempt to provide students with a knowledge-based program of study. Instead students would be provided a broad introduction to business and allowed wide freedom of choice of elective content and methods for learning. This curriculum would prepare them for the realities of self-responsibility and life-long learning.

Graduate students were required to take twenty-one hours of credit in specified subject areas covering basic business functions, but they were given complete freedom to choose among elective courses for the remaining twenty-one hours of course work. The learning environment was a rich collection of alternative options for students, who could choose among conventional course work, research, independent study, and internships with little restriction on the amount of each. Faculty members were encouraged to provide non-conventional learning options. Students who could demonstrate proficiency in a basic subject area were allowed to immediately participate in advanced courses in that area.

The grading scale in the new curriculum consisted of honors, satisfactory, and no credit (H, S, NC). While H, S, NC grading was not unusual in colleges and universities, the use of the scheme in required courses was innovative, a privilege usually reserved for honors students in advanced study. It was also an effort to recognize the priority of learning over the quest for grades. As it turned out, there were faculty, students, and some corporate recruiters who did not agree with the underlying concept for the H, S, NC grading scheme, so it was modified to a more conventional system over the next two years.

Graduate students registering for courses

The one-year program was fast-paced compared to the traditional MBA program, which included a summer break between the first and second years. The pace and intensity of a graduate program accomplished in twelve consecutive months were new for everyone in the school and the university. The one-year program provided distinct marketing advantages for the school by attracting some outstanding students, many of whom saw the significant economic advantage of obtaining an MBA in one calendar year. Nevertheless, some faculty found the change to a full-time, year-round program a disruption to the standard rhythm of teaching and research. This was one factor that eventually led to changes in the MBA program.

In September 1972, the Life Planning Center was established to support the curriculum changes. The center assisted students in self-assessment, exploration of jobs and careers, and preparation of action plans to achieve career and job objectives. The staff had a counseling psychologist, and the counseling efforts were coordinated with the school's advising system. Byron E. Williamson, a successful businessman who decided on a career change, was hired to direct the center. Williamson wanted young students to begin thinking about their passions and not simply negotiating the academic terrain. In keeping with Williamson's goals, the center staff was creative and motivated to use many psychological tools to help students "find themselves and their road." However, most students considered the center remote from the things they needed to do in school and afterwards. Coupled with the inability to generate funding from outside sources and total reliance on funds from the general budget, the center was abandoned after two years.

Gathering an Innovative Faculty

In Grayson's view, the existing faculty of the school of business would not be up to the task of implementing his vision. This view was based not on an evaluation of individual faculty but rather on Grayson's sense that faculty committed to and successful within a set of traditional performance norms would sustain those norms at every opportunity. He believed that bringing his vision to life would require a passion for that vision that would not come from traditional academic thinkers. His experience further suggested that it is more difficult to change people's basic values than it is to attract people with compatible values. Grayson hoped that some existing faculty would prove to be compatible, and, indeed, some existing faculty became major contributors to the implementation process. Rather than wait to see who might step forward, Grayson began a vigorous national recruiting effort. Not surprisingly he concentrated his efforts on younger faculty, including those just about to complete their advanced degrees.

With important but modest success in 1968 and 1969, a breakthrough was recorded in recruiting faculty who would join the school in the fall of 1970. Termed the "Baker's Dozen," the group of thirteen new faculty, including Tom Barry, came from east and west, from prestigious universities and from programs with lesser reputations. Their common denominator was their inter-

Tom Barry, 1970,
one of the Baker's Dozen

est in pursuing the vision outlined by Grayson and being open to new ideas and innovation. Joined in 1971 by another equally inspired group, the school now had a nucleus of faculty devoted to implementing Grayson's vision.

One of the "Baker's Dozen" was a young doctoral student, Patrick Canavan, from the Organizational Administration program at Yale University. Obviously bright and talented, he nevertheless stirred a storm of controversy that was to leave its mark on the school. Canavan was a free spirit with a lifestyle reflective of the late 1960s and early 1970s. He arrived in Dallas for the fall semester of 1970 eager to begin his academic career and excited about the prospects for the school of business. From the beginning he lived a rather unorthodox lifestyle. Rather than renting an apartment, he stayed with various faculty and students in their homes for short periods of time.

Commenting in a *Dallas Morning News* interview, Canavan said, "I wanted to get to know people in Texas and you can't do that by being a visitor or a guest. You have to live with them." His campus office was unconventional as well. He removed his office door, replacing it with his old school neckties, "so that it will be open at all times to everyone." Surplus parachute material served as a second ceiling in his office. To open the fall semester, Canavan proposed

Student "Disorientation," fall 1970

a "student disorientation" for new business school students. He was hoping to spur interest in new ways of doing things, which was his perception of the role of an educator. With the help of some of the new "free-thinking" faculty and some eager students, a huge plastic tent was erected on the front lawn of the Fincher Building. Inside the tent there was a constant barrage of loud, contemporary music. Students, faculty, and curious members of the SMU community wondered aloud about this new approach to the fall semester orientation in the business school!

Coupled with his other lifestyle decisions, Canavan attracted immediate attention from all quarters of the university and business community. While many applauded his independence and saw him as a loud voice for change, he was considered an extremist by others. Indeed, a number of influential business leaders wrote angry letters of indignation to SMU officials. Despite their tone and inferences about withholding future contributions, President Tate informed Grayson that he would support his decision. Grayson advised Canavan to consider resigning. (See the sidebar on page 91 for examples of correspondence between two influential businessmen regarding Canavan. The names of these men and their companies have been omitted to protect their privacy.) After a few weeks of intense discussion and meetings about whether he could contribute to positive change, Canavan decided that his presence could not have the impact he wanted or expected. In an emotional speech to a large gathering of students, faculty, and administrators, he announced his decision to leave SMU and the business school. He applauded the efforts to change the school and urged everyone to continue "to determine how we can make this Business School the best in the country."

The Canavan episode had distinct effects on the school. One nationally prominent faculty prospect, who had accepted an offer to join the faculty, wrote to rescind his acceptance, citing Canavan's resignation as the reason for his change of mind. There was little doubt that the incident raised concerns among members of the business community, and created a dampening effect on funding for the school, at least in the short term. Observers felt that Canavan's style created a gap between the school and many people in business that would take time to close. This slowed the synergy that would eventually be a hallmark of the school. For the most part, students and faculty came together in various ways, including joint meetings, that set a positive tone for implementing and sustaining open communication necessary for change.

All was not smooth sailing, however, and a split developed between existing faculty, who felt disenfranchised, and the new faculty, who were impatient to usher in change and innovation to achieve the goal of transforming business education. Soon to be called the "Old Guard" and the "New Guard," the

Patrick Canavan and Jack Grayson, 1970

separation into factions undoubtedly slowed the rate of change Grayson wanted as well as the establishment of a culture he thought was necessary to sustain and nurture an environment for continuous innovation.

Although external funding was slow to materialize, the school received an important gift in 1970 when the Hillcrest Foundation established the Caruth Chair of Financial Management in honor of Mr. and Mrs. W. W. Caruth Sr. This was the first endowed chair established in the business school, and Alan B. Coleman was appointed to the position in the summer of 1974. Coleman would be named dean of the school of business in 1975. Another major gift came from the Lay family in the summer of 1972 when it endowed the Herman W. Lay Chair in Marketing. Richard H. Buskirk was appointed to the Lay Chair in 1974. The Clara R. and Leo F. Corrigan Endowed Chair in Real Estate was established in 1975 by a gift from the Corrigan Foundation. These endowments played a vitally important role in the development of the school by enabling the hiring of several outstanding faculty members.

Recognition for faculty accomplishments in teaching and research was an important part of the reward system in the school. Teaching had always been emphasized in the School of Business Administration, and it would continue, along with a more significant emphasis on faculty research. The Faculty Standards for Appointment and Advancement provided guidelines for recognizing quality teaching and research. The director of research and development played an important role in allocating resources to faculty research and teaching.

In the fall of 1972, the Nicolas Salgo Distinguished Teacher Award was established under a grant from the Salgo Foundation and carried a $1,500 cash stipend. Over time, this prestigious award was given to numerous faculty members in various subject areas. To add emphasis to the importance of intellectual inquiry, the school created an annual award for outstanding research in 1973 that carried a cash stipend. Perhaps more important was the addition of significant funds for summer research grants. Today, teaching and research awards continue to be an important part of the recognition for outstanding performance in the Cox School of Business.

Involving the Business Community

The business community was expected to play a major role in the development of the school of business. Grayson viewed action or experiential learning as the involvement of faculty, students, and business participants in every phase of education that had previously been largely reserved for the traditional classroom or individual faculty research. The interaction between the school and the business community would be fostered by the creation of organizational units called institutes, noted earlier. These institutes, directed by faculty or staff, would offer seminars, workshops, conferences, and briefings that distributed knowledge to individuals and organizations.

Initially envisioned to focus on specific industries such as transportation, manufacturing, or retailing, the very first institute to be created was the result of the imagination and foresight of W. W. Caruth Jr. One of Dallas's true business legends, Caruth, along with the Caruth Foundation and the W. W. Caruth Jr. Fund of the Dallas Community Chest Fund, provided support to establish

Nicolas Salgo Teaching Award presented to Professor Don Jackson by Dean Jack Grayson

BUSINESSMAN'S LETTER
REGARDING CANAVAN

September 23, 1970

Dear ——:

A few days ago you sent me a letter saying that I [*sic*] would be invited to a meeting of [business] people at the SMU Business School on October 13. Later I received a letter of invitation from Jack Grayson and accepted it.

Last week, I picked up a copy of the DAILY CAMPUS, which I am enclosing. Please read the front-page article about the new Business School professor. The article does not mention that his classroom attire consists of blue jeans, T-shirt, headband, and bare feet. I understand that his office is also his home and that he freely uses four-letter words in his classroom, as he is quoted as using in the DAILY CAMPUS.

You and I, like Professor Canavan, are "interested in change." We have been innovators in our businesses, and I think we are both very tolerant of people who share different views. However, I was appalled that "hard to get" funds are being squandered to pay a salary to a professor to teach our students a life style to which we who contribute and raise money are firmly opposed. Do you agree?

Cordially yours,

FRIEND'S REPLY
TO CRITICISM OF CANAVAN

September 25, 1970

Dear ——:

If one accepts the view that another is entitled to his peculiar attitudes and points of view, even down to certain language types and dress types and extraordinarily unusual judgments of the times and of others, then it is a corollary that I am perhaps entitled to mine and you to yours.

In the case you present to me of this Canavan, as far as I know—and that is your letter and the article in the DAILY CAMPUS—, I should say that my case is exactly the opposite of his. I should also say that mine further includes that I should not do anything to advance his, and that mine includes the belief that he and his type are more often than not phonies, dealing in vague, wayout expressions of generalities that are hard to discuss in terms of specifics, and therefore easier to defend than to attack. Mine further includes the belief that anyone who brings this sort of jerk on the campus is making a big mistake, and doing the wrong thing.

These are my views. Perhaps I am wrong, but I further have the view that I don't owe anybody an effort to get more information that would change my views, since I am willing to let a jerk like this and all those who espouse and support him go their way while I go mine.

Perhaps I have disclosed that I am as extreme in some of my opinions and feelings as is Canavan and people of his ilk.

Yours very truly,

P.S. It would seem to me the only possible reason to have a squirt like this on the campus would be to give impressionable people an opportunity to see two sides of life and issues.

the Caruth Institute in June 1969. The institute, originally entitled the Caruth Institute of Small Business but soon named the Caruth Institute of Owner-Managed Business, would, in Caruth's words, "encourage the venturesome spirit of free enterprise." John A. Welch, an entrepreneur in his own right, was hired as professor and director of the Caruth Institute. The institute focused attention from the outset on developing entrepreneurs, cash-flow management, and venture-capital financing for the small and emerging firm and was very successful under the direction of Welch and his current successor, Jerry F. White.

The Business Clinic was formed in 1971 to enable teams of faculty, students, and business participants to tackle specific problems provided by firms. Numerous companies presented actual problems to the clinic, and students received degree credit for solving those problems. Citing an example, a small retail outlet wanted to convert a cash system of accounting to a system that enabled more effective cost control. The problem was taken on by a team of students with a faculty advisor. The clinic continued for a few semesters but was never able to sustain its original momentum although the basic rationale for action-learning programs would continue producing a variety of experiential learning scenarios for the next thirty years.

Other institute programs that were formed during this time included the Institute of Retail Management and the Women in Business Institute, which received support from the Hoblitzelle Foundation. The Aubrey M. Costa Institute of Real Estate Finance was established by the Aubrey M. Costa Foundation to support student and industry programs in real estate. In 1975, Cary M. Maguire established the Maguire Oil & Gas Institute to study management and public policy problems related to the oil and gas industry. One of the more enduring institutes, the Maguire Oil & Gas Institute continues in the Cox School of Business today.

The most visible institute activities were the SMU Management Briefings. Under the direction of Fred Lee, former vice president of the American Management Association, these programs featured nationally and internationally prominent speakers at major venues in downtown Dallas. The brief-

Cary M. Maguire

ings typically attracted 1,200 participants. The inaugural speaker for this series was C. Jackson Grayson Jr., who at the time was on leave from SMU, serving as Price Commissioner under President Nixon. Other notables included federal cabinet officers, Federal Reserve Bank presidents, the chairman of Citicorp, and Milton Friedman, Nobel Laureate in Economics.

In somewhat similar fashion, the school established the Management Center as part of the institute's educational programs for businessmen and businesswomen. Dan Weston served as director of the Management Center, which provided seminars, management development programs, conferences, and workshops varying in length from one to three days. The Management Center evolved over time into what today is one of the very fine executive education programs in the country.

In 1970 the school created the Entrepreneur of the Year Award "to recog-

Early Management Briefing at the Fairmont Hotel, mid-1970s

nize individuals who best represent a model for the SMU business graduate—
those who have significant business and social accomplishments, and demonstrate a willingness to help others enjoy business success, leadership and
integrity." Recipients of the award included W. W. Caruth Jr., Walter W.
Durham, Sam Wyly, H. Ross Perot, Herman W. Lay, Morris B. Zale, Norman
Brinker, and W. W. Clements.

One of the organizations that helped create and define the relationship
between the school and the business community was the SMU Foundation for
Business Administration. Founded in 1965, it was established for three fundamental purposes. The first was to encourage and support educational development in business administration and related fields of study at SMU. The second
was to support and advance the SMU School of Business Administration in

endowing, equipping, and supplying continued expansion of superior faculty, scholarships, the library, and other facilities as required. And, finally, the third was to support and advance the SMU School of Business in organizing and conducting symposiums, institutes, forums, training clinics, and other activities related to the understanding and solution of business or economic problems for the benefit of business and industry.

Under the leadership of Edwin L. Cox and a board of directors consisting of twenty-five leading business and civic representatives, the foundation would provide substantial financial support to aid the school's growth and development. As noted earlier, the foundation was a major driver in attracting Grayson to SMU as dean of the business school.

Norman Brinker, 1974

There was, however, a need for the business community to be directly engaged in making the action-learning philosophy a reality. In 1970, Bobby B. Lyle, serving as assistant dean, approached Ray Hunt and asked him about the idea of creating a body whose sole purpose would be to facilitate the interaction between Dallas business people and the school. Under their leadership, the Associate Board of the school was organized.

Associate Board members were asked to provide their time and expertise in fostering the goal of action learning through meaningful involvement with the school. Curiously, fund raising was specifically excluded from the goals of the board. Fifty-five men and women formed the initial board and immediately began contributing by mentoring students and providing action-learning business problems and resources for faculty and students. The roles of the mentors have expanded over time and include establishing internships and advising administrators. The Associate Board clearly distinguished the SMU School of Business Administration from its competitors.

A Chance for a Giant Leap Forward

In March 1971, Ross Perot invited Grayson and a few of his staff to a meeting at the headquarters of Electronic Data Systems. Perot informed the SMU group that the Perot Foundation was making grants of $50,000 to four regional universities to enable them to create a plan for developing an outstanding graduate school of business. Each university would submit its plan to the foundation with the prospect for additional support. Grayson saw this as an opportunity to move implementation of his vision into high gear. He was excited about the idea of gaining additional resources, and he put together a team of faculty and administrators and set about crafting a plan that would "create an outstanding graduate business school that provides practical management training for effective business leadership in a free enterprise system."

The plan provided specific detail on the implementation of the school's organizing concept that brought together teaching, research, and business

Grayson as Price Commissioner with Vice President Gerald R. Ford

applications. Action or experiential learning would be at the heart of all activity in the school, and very ambitious goals were established to be achieved over a period of ten years. Faculty size would double from 30 to 60, and the number of full-time MBA students would increase fivefold from 110 to 550. Expectations for quality improvements in faculty and students were also lofty, and the support system would grow in concert. In support of the plan, President Tate and William P. Clements, chairman of the university's Board of Governors, conveyed the pledge of the SMU Board of Trustees to raise $10 million in endowment by 1975. The endowment would be restricted for the business school. Cox, chairman of the SMU Foundation for Business Administration, stated "we plan to provide $600,000 per year for the next four (4) years."

A new business school building, estimated to cost $12 million, had been approved in concept. The plan was submitted to the Perot Foundation in September 1971 requesting a total of $12.1 million additional annual operating support over the ten-year planning horizon. The plan envisioned that the school would "generate more revenues than expenditures in 1981, and achieve fiscal soundness." The dean and many in the school were optimistic that the proposal would receive favorable consideration. Things looked bright!

A Change in Plans

In October 1971, Grayson received a telephone call from George Shultz, director of the Office of Management and Budget under President Richard M. Nixon. Shultz, a former academic at the University of Chicago, asked Grayson to accept the position of chairman of the newly formed United States Price Commission. The Price Commission would regulate all price changes for domestic businesses. Price increases would only be approved if a business could demonstrate improved productivity. Grayson faced a major dilemma. An opportunity to serve the country and administer a price-control program for the most advanced industrialized nation in the world was very appealing. The offer had no time frame, but Grayson would likely be gone for one to two

years. His immediate reaction was to decline the offer, but Grayson called
Shultz back the next day and accepted the post. Grayson later stated in the
Dallas Morning News, "I had felt my work at SMU was too important to leave
but as soon as I'd said no, I began to feel like I had missed out on one of the
great challenges of my lifetime." Shortly thereafter he left SMU for the exciting, hectic, and time-consuming job in Washington, D.C.

Bobby B. Lyle

Never one to follow expectations, Grayson decided to recommend Bobby B.
Lyle to serve as acting dean. Lyle was a young instructor when Grayson
arrived in 1968, but he immediately became an ardent and energetic follower.
Appointed as assistant dean in 1970, he was a major force in putting together
the extensive plan for the Perot Foundation. Grayson was confident that Lyle

Acting Dean Bobby B. Lyle

could sustain the momentum of change and opportunity, and President Tate appointed Lyle acting dean on October 20, 1971.

As a major proponent of the ongoing change in the school of business, Lyle had been appointed as the coordinator of the school-wide effort to develop a long-range plan for the school in response to the challenge grant from the Perot Foundation. Even before the grant opportunity, Lyle had convinced Grayson that permanent change would require the introduction of systems to set goals, create objectives, select strategies, and implement tactical action programs. This approach was an adaptation of the G-O-S-T system (Goals, Objectives, Strategies, Tactics) used so successfully by Texas Instruments in Dallas. Lyle wanted to introduce performance accountability into every dimension of the school. The challenge grant was an opportunity to utilize the G-O-S-T framework and was the systematic approach used to define and describe each element of the plan that was submitted to the Perot Foundation.

Moving Forward with Lyle

Grayson had little time to arrange an orderly transition, and he was unsure how long he would remain in Washington. With characteristic confidence and boldness he encouraged Lyle to continue moving the school forward and not merely to put the school in a holding pattern. With Grayson's support and the extensive experience gained in crafting the long-range plan, Lyle had a detailed blueprint for progress, and he moved to implement the long-range plan. It would be fifteen months before Grayson would return, and in that time the school continued to make significant progress.

Among his first actions, Lyle installed a system for managing personal performance. Every faculty member and administrator in the school would initiate a Personal Performance Plan outlining his or her activities for a specific planning period. The plans included objectives, timetables, fiscal needs, personnel needs, a method of evaluation, and performance review dates. Presenting the plan to the faculty Lyle stated: "In the proposed plan faculty members have a great deal to say about what they do, when they do it, and how they do it, but everyone in this School will be held accountable for performance, will be evaluated on that performance, and will be rewarded on that performance."

Progress on All Fronts

Lyle enthusiastically promoted and supported Grayson's ideas for the development of programs in the school. Innovations in teaching were introduced by Professors Robert Frame and Dudley Curry, respectively in finance and accounting. They created an audio-visual program that enabled students to study basic accounting and finance. Students could learn at their own pace and receive credit without attending traditional classes.

In another departure from traditional classroom learning, MBA students were provided with a computerized management simulation implemented by Professors Doug Wolfe and Gene Byrne assisted by John McDorman, director of the school's Computer Resource Center. Students were organized in teams, and they made hundreds of business decisions that were evaluated by a computer model with the results fed back to the students. Each student team had a board of directors consisting of Dallas businessmen and businesswomen who held regular board meetings to discuss results and evaluate performance. In addition, both graduate and undergraduate students continued to earn degree credits by means of the Business Clinic, independent study, internships, and faculty-directed research projects. For MBA students, as much as half of their degree requirements could be obtained through nontraditional methods.

Three new activities involved the school in areas that rarely received attention. Project Concern, a program for development of entrepreneurial activity among Mexican-American and black businessmen, was funded in June 1973 by a grant of $100,000 authorized by the Office of Minority Business Enterprise (OMBE). Co-investigated by Lyle and Professor Bobby Spradlin, Project Concern provided intensive workshop training and direct consulting assistance over a period of a year to thirty-nine minority participants. Another project investigated effective promotional mix strategies for minority entrepreneurs in the Dallas metropolitan area. Professors Thomas E. Barry, Michael E. McGill, and Michael G. Harvey directed the research, funded by a $40,000 grant from OMBE. Finally, the Institute for Women in Business was funded under a grant from the Hoblitzelle Foundation to recruit and support women interested in business careers. In the class of 1972–1973, only 9 women were among the 134 students enrolled. However, only four years later women constituted 39 percent of the full-time MBA class enrollment.

A notable achievement in this period was the reduction of the deficit the school owed the university. Beginning with Grayson's arrival, the university advanced funds to support the long-range growth plan of the business school. Payment of the advance, which reached $601,699 by the end of 1969–1970, was guaranteed by the SMU Foundation for Business Administration. The next year the deficit was reduced, and it was completely paid two years later, in May 1973. During these years the school generated a positive cash flow from operations and in 1972–1973 provided almost $1 million in direct support of the university's budget.

Grayson Returns to SMU

In March 1973, Grayson resigned as chairman of the Price Commission and resumed his position as dean of the School of Business Administration at SMU. While serving as chairman of the Price Commission, Grayson developed a strong interest in the potential of increasing productivity in American business. He noted the success of the Ministry of International Trade and Industry established by the Japanese government. The cooperation between industry and government in Japan was credited with some of the economic advances made in that country in the post–World War II period. Grayson hoped to establish some form of private organization devoted to productivity and felt that SMU might make a good home. He decided to devote his time to fund raising for the school, and productivity would be one of his strategic thrusts.

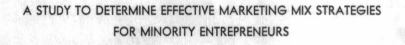

A STUDY TO DETERMINE EFFECTIVE MARKETING MIX STRATEGIES FOR MINORITY ENTREPRENEURS

Prepared for

THE OFFICE OF MINORITY BUSINESS ENTERPRISE
DEPARTMENT OF COMMERCE

by

Thomas E. Barry, Ph.D.
Michael G. Harvey
Michael E. McGill, Ph.D.

School of Business Administration
SOUTHERN METHODIST UNIVERSITY
Dallas, Texas

August 15, 1973

OMBE Report by Professors Barry, Harvey, and McGill

Southern Methodist University School of Business Administration,
A Continuing Report on Business Education, 1973–74

Although the long-range plan submitted to the Perot Foundation was never approved, the underlying ideas became the basis for a fund-raising campaign. In 1973, the university approved a $37-million campaign. Funds amounting to $12 million were designated for a new building while a significant portion would be used to create an endowment. Grayson believed that the school could not make great strides by relying on the growth in tuition and an annual sustentation program. An endowment would allow the school to become self-sustaining.

In a somewhat unusual move, Lyle was appointed executive dean, assuming responsibility for the operations of the school while Grayson, as dean, concentrated his efforts in the critical area of fund raising. This division of responsibility would continue while both remained at the school.

The change in the organization of the dean's office initiated a review of how the academic programs could be more effectively managed. The decision was made to strengthen the focus on the three degree programs, and directors for the Full-time Graduate Program, Part-time Graduate Program, and Undergraduate Program were appointed. The original three-dimensional form of organization was retained, and the new program directors worked in cooperation with subject area chairmen, institute directors, and the director of research to ensure the effective allocation of resources.

Even as administrators worked to improve the existing degree programs, the school decided to add programs. The emergence of dual-degree and joint-degree programs continued the curricular innovation that was a hallmark of the school. A Master of International Management/Master of Business Administration degree was offered jointly with the American Graduate School of International Management (AGSIM) located in Glendale, Arizona. This program provided entry into the field of international business studies and avoided the significant cost of starting from ground zero. Inside the university, the Doctor of Jurisprudence/Master of Business Administration dual degree was offered in cooperation with the School of Law while the Master of Fine Arts/Master of Business Administration degree was offered with the Meadows School of the Arts. Both the SMU degree programs and the AGSIM program represented recognition of the quality of faculty in the School of Business Administration.

In the fall of 1975 the school received a grant that would create another curriculum innovation. The Fund for the Improvement of Post-Secondary Education awarded a three-year grant of $120,000 to Wolfe and Byrne to design, implement, and evaluate an experimental MBA program. Known as the Action Management Program, it allowed students to earn all the required credits for the MBA degree by working on actual business projects. Students documented their learning for review and validation by faculty. The Action Management Program demonstrated the viability of experiential learning as an alternative to traditional methods of learning. It was quite popular among students who enjoyed working independently in unstructured environments. However, it was not as appealing to faculty because it was significantly more time consuming in comparison to traditional methods and required smaller teaching loads, which made it relatively expensive. The program would last only two years.

A Change of Leadership

Toward the end of summer 1975, Lyle was given a leave of absence to pursue a doctoral degree at the University of Massachusetts under the tutelage of Kenneth Blanchard, one of the most respected names in the field of individual and organizational behavior. Soon thereafter, Alan B. Coleman, professor of finance and holder of the Caruth Chair of Financial Management, was appointed executive dean. One of Coleman's first decisions was to reorganize the administration. Marketing Professor Richard W. Hansen was appointed associate dean of Resident Studies with responsibility for graduate and under-graduate full-time programs. Finance Professor Bob Frame was appointed associate dean for Executive Education, and given responsibility for executive education, part-time graduate studies, the Management Center and institutes.

In November of 1975, Grayson resigned his position as dean of the school of business. He would continue at the school for a few months as professor of

Grayson's Productivity Center in Houston

business until he resigned from the university in early 1976 to found the American Productivity Center in Houston, Texas. Grayson continues to head the American Quality and Productivity Center as its chairman. Lyle decided to enter private business after completing his degree at the University of Massachusetts and eventually founded his own energy company, LYCO Energy.

A Look at the Record

Clearly, the period between 1968 and 1975 was one of the most interesting and innovative chapters in the history of the SMU School of Business Administration. There was significant change in virtually every area of the school. Grayson stated in 1970 that the school would achieve its goal by innovating. The record substantiates that strategy.

Faculty changes were dramatic. The faculty more than doubled in size between 1968 and 1975, increasing from twenty-eight to sixty members. In 1968 the school did not have an endowed faculty chair. By 1975 three chairs had been endowed to enable hiring of nationally known faculty. More importantly, expectations were changed. Quality teaching, which had always been important, continued as a priority. However, the standards for teaching productivity were substantially increased. Faculty members were expected to produce the quality and quantity of research demanded at the best business schools. By themselves, the change in expectations for teaching and research could be viewed as extraordinary, but the faculty had to contend with an ongoing process of innovation that produced significant change.

The movement to a single required course for the undergraduate curriculum and the introduction of the one-calendar-year MBA program were dramatic innovations. However, in a sense they paled in comparison with the innovation in the organization of the school. Allowing students to fully participate in generating, evaluating, and implementing school policy was rare and bold (and foolish to some). Each of these innovations drew national attention, enabling the school to attract aggressive, bright faculty and students that made for an exciting environment for learning and growth. It is clear from Grayson's writing and his actions as dean of the business school that freeing individuals to learn in their own ways and to make their own decisions was paramount in his educational philosophy and what he counts as his most valuable contribution to the SMU business school.

In a number of different educational settings the school was able to demonstrate the efficacy of experiential learning. Internships, role playing, and simulations had long been part of the business education scene in the United States, and the SMU School of Business used these effectively. New forms of experiential learning such as the Business Clinic, the Action Management Program, and contracted independent study provided faculty and students with virtually unlimited opportunities to work and learn using actual business problems. What set SMU apart from other schools was the pervasiveness of opportunity. Participation was simply a matter of student choice, and special qualifications were rarely required. The growth in graduate student numbers, 308 to 588, was notable. Undergraduate enrollment grew at virtually the same pace, from 629 students to 1,110 students. In part because of the one-year MBA program, the number of graduate degrees awarded in the period jumped significantly from 86 to 236. The quality of students in all programs increased, and the school was able to attract students to the MBA program from some of the best undergraduate schools in the country.

The business school's relationship with the business community developed into a productive partnership. Business provided actual problems for teams of students and faculty. Business leaders were extremely valuable in recruiting faculty but even more so in helping to grow institute programs. The Management Briefing Series was one of the best of its kind and attracted internationally respected business leaders to speak. SMU's reputation for outstanding executive education owes much to the efforts of the members of the Foundation for Business Administration and the Associate Board. Ed Cox provided leadership during this period to raise funds in order to eliminate the school's debt to the university and generate an endowment of $3 million by 1975. The contributions of Will Caruth to establish the Caruth Institute and the Caruth Chair of Finance go far beyond the simple act of giving. He set an example for others and was an inspiration to everyone with his unflagging support.

Not to suggest that everything worked. It didn't. There were some important setbacks along the way and some dreams that fizzled. There were major disappointments in the personnel area, and some of the highest hopes for institutional reform were not realized for a variety of reasons.

Fund raising must be counted among the major disappointments of Grayson's administration. While some significant progress was made in funding chairs and institutes, the inability to add significant endowments or secure any support for a badly needed state-of-the-art building was critical. The slow progress in securing funding meant that many of the programs had to be delayed and some, such as the Life Planning Center, could not be continued. At the same time, the economy was weak, and some commitments that had been made for substantial funding had to be deferred to the future. Funding problems were among the reasons that Grayson decided to leave SMU.

The accreditation of the undergraduate program was another area where hopes for major change never fully materialized. The school applied for continuing accreditation of the undergraduate program in fall 1971. The hope was to be granted unconditional continuing accreditation on the basis of an AACSB standard that encouraged innovative programs. The requirement for an acceptable innovation was presentation of a satisfactory experimental design that included a plan for evaluating and reporting the results of the experiment. In May 1971, the AACSB granted continuing accreditation of the program but required the school to "submit an annual report, for an experimental period of some five years, that indicates the extent to which the new program is in compliance with the requirement that all students acquire substantial breadth of knowledge." The school submitted a report to the AACSB in October 1974 and May 1975. The association's Continuing Accreditation Committee decided to recommend probation of the undergraduate program "since a satisfactory experimental design to monitor the program's results of the program has not yet been established." In September 1975, the AACSB decided to send another review team to the school. Grayson's resignation delayed the actual visit, and the process would await the appointment of a new dean. Clearly, the school had failed to convince the accreditation authority of the efficacy of the undergraduate program, at least to the extent that the AACSB measured that efficacy.

Another setback in the press for institutional reform was tenure. Tenure has always been among the most fought-for faculty rights. Tenure is awarded after careful peer review of a faculty member's performance over a period of six or more years. It is tantamount to a life-long contract under which dismissal is possible only for egregious behavior. Tenure is seen by some as a deterrent to change. A faculty dominated by tenured individuals opposed to change could significantly slow or even defeat the change process. The American Association of University Professors (AAUP) has staunchly defended the practice of tenure as a way to protect academic freedom.

The business school, under Grayson, decided to test the strength of tenure by awarding five-year rolling contracts in lieu of tenure. The rolling contract indicated the extent to which Grayson was concerned that tenured faculty could slow the change process. He wanted to do everything possible to create an environment that would be open to change. He decided to try the five-year rolling contract and to recruit younger, untenured faculty to foster the change he desired.

A few newly hired faculty who were eligible for tenure agreed to accept the rolling contract. The AAUP immediately announced their opposition and indicated that SMU might be censured. Rather than engage in a protracted battle with the AAUP, Grayson decided that other issues were more important. He was also concerned that the school might lose campus support for change. The faculty members with the rolling contracts were immediately given tenure.

Reflections on Grayson's Administration

What might have been? These words echo in the minds of people who lived the exciting, productive history of the SMU School of Business Administration while under the leadership of C. Jackson Grayson Jr. from 1968 to 1975. Could things have been different? Could the school been moved more rapidly along the path of progress? Suppose Grayson had spurned the chance to serve as Price Commissioner? Lyle did an admirable job as acting dean, but was the school's progress slowed during Grayson's absence for fifteen months? Was the momentum disrupted? If Grayson had devoted more time to developing a broader and more committed support base among business school and key university faculty, some administrators at SMU, the business leadership of Dallas, and the national academic community, would this have made a difference in the development of the school? As noted earlier,

Jack Grayson, Confessions of a Price Controller

the lack of appropriate funding slowed the implementation of numerous programs. Was this due, as some have suggested, to over-reliance on a few key business people for support? Perhaps the lack of funding resulted from Grayson's failure to recognize and address concerns about the direction of the school.

How sensitive was Grayson to the problems that would arise from the rapid growth of faculty? The growth of faculty, while notable, created its own set of problems. In the earliest stages of Grayson's tenure, a few loyal colleagues could promote and drive change. Then, as faculty size grew at a relatively rapid pace and it proved difficult to recruit faculty who fully understood and shared the values required to participate in the innovative, nontraditional environment that was the SMU Business School, was it Grayson's responsibility to ensure compatibility? Perhaps new faculty needed more support to develop their capacity for innovation to go along with their interest in creating new educational forms.

Accreditation was a looming problem. While there were influential deans around the country who were supporters of the innovative curriculum at SMU, they were few in number and not able to persuade the accrediting body to allow the SMU experiment to continue with full accreditation. Should Grayson have spent more time building up this small group of supportive deans in order to be certain of broad-based support for his innovative undergraduate curriculum? Would a similar effort to garner support among a national cadre of faculty and deans have paved the way for the introduction of the five-year rolling contract as an alternative to tenure? Perhaps the concept had been thrust upon the national academic community too quickly and without enough substantive groundwork being laid to create support for the merits of the intended innovations and subsequent change.

The End of a Beginning

Notwithstanding these ideas about what might have been, Grayson placed the SMU Business School squarely on the road toward national prominence. His

Jack Grayson and Carla O'Dell enjoying Antarctica

leadership as an innovator was unparalleled. His 1969 "Towards a New Philosophy in Business Education" is a visionary look into the future of business education. More inspiring was the fact that many of his ideas in that article were implemented in the SMU School of Business Administration, which firmly established Grayson's legacy as an innovator and gave inspiration to others who would be bold.

CHAPTER FOUR

THE STABILIZING AND BUILDING YEARS OF COLEMAN, 1976–1981

You begin to move a school toward excellence by focusing on attracting the best faculty and students at the same time you are building collegiality, strengthening integrity, developing campus relationships, and gaining the confidence of the business community.

ALAN COLEMAN

FORTUNE SMILED UPON the SMU School of Business Administration when Alan B. Coleman was hired as the Caruth Professor of Finance in the summer of 1974. Alan was the first person to hold a chair in the school of business, and his appointment was a coup for the school. He was internationally respected as a teacher, scholar, and administrator and served twelve years on the faculties of the graduate schools of business at Harvard and Stanford. Coleman did his undergraduate work at the University of San Francisco and earned two graduate degrees from Stanford University. He received his MBA in 1956 and his PhD in 1960. While he was in the PhD program he spent one year as a research associate at IMEDE, which was founded as an international school of business in Lausanne, Switzerland. From 1960 to 1963, Coleman taught finance at the Harvard Graduate School of Business.

Shortly after returning to Stanford University in 1963, he was asked to form the first graduate school of business in Latin America. He was appointed the founding dean of Escuela de Administración de Negocios para Graduados (ESAN) in Lima, Peru, and served in that position for three years. At the time

Dean Alan B. Coleman

he undertook the project, sponsored by the U.S. Agency for International Development and Stanford University, Latin America did not have a graduate school of business. Coleman was faced with cultural differences, and there was no blueprint for success. Nonetheless, Coleman built a premier graduate school of business that thrives today. His work at ESAN helped forge his understanding of how to build a quality institution, including the value of relationships with the business community. The government of Peru awarded him one of their highest honors in 1966, and in August 1971 the Alan B. Coleman Library was dedicated at ESAN.

In the four years after ESAN, Coleman continued to serve on the Stanford faculty. He left the academic world in 1970 to become vice president and treasurer of U.S. Natural Resources. This was followed by a two-year stint as chairman, CEO, and president of Yosemite & Curry Co., the largest national park concessionaire in the country. Coleman was serving as president and chief administrative officer of Sun Valley Company, Inc., when he was contacted about the Caruth Chair in Finance at SMU. Anxious to return to academia, he was intrigued by the potential for the SMU school of business. In particular, he believed that the combination of a good university and a dynamic, supportive business community held prospects for the development of an outstanding business school. He arrived in the summer of 1974 with enthusiasm for his new position, but he would be totally unprepared for what would transpire within months of his arrival.

The Dallas Environment

Throughout the late 1970s, Dallas continued its population surge toward a million citizens. Tensions in the oil-producing regions of the Middle East led to a doubling of oil prices and inflation in the latter part of the 1970s. The banking infrastructure was undergoing change that initially stimulated a real estate boom in Dallas but would have dramatic negative aftereffects in the mid-1980s. Dallas continued to move aggressively through the late 1970s and into the decade of the 1980s.

Dallas, 1975

The SMU Environment

About the time Alan Coleman arrived in mid-summer of 1974, President Hardin abruptly resigned. Marshall Terry wrote that the circumstances of Hardin's departure were not clear except that he may have been asked to resign because he challenged the role of SMU football. Nevertheless, the incident created some concern that the university's Board of Governors, a group of the Board of Trustees that made week-to-week decisions in an effort to streamline decisions, could and did exercise too much control. Many years after the incident, Coleman vividly remembers wondering if he had made a huge mistake by accepting SMU's offer. He had made a major change in his personal and professional life, and had not expected the turmoil and tension, especially within the highest levels of the university's leadership. Fortunately for SMU and the School of Business Administration, Coleman made his decision to stay and see what challenges awaited him in the months and years ahead.

James Zumberge

A year after Hardin left SMU, the seventh president, James Zumberge, arrived. Zumberge was a serious academic—a geologist after whom a cape in Antarctica is named. He was also a tough-minded decision maker. He was a highly distinguished man in career and presence and, like Hardin and Tate, was interested in designing his own plans for SMU. He began to tackle some serious budget issues and started his own planning process soon after he arrived on campus in 1975 from the University of Nebraska.

Zumberge was known as a no-nonsense leader and one who relished dealing with crises. Terry suggests that while Zumberge respected the faculty, he did not enjoy a good rapport with them. Zumberge's focus on budget deficits probably made him seem somewhat aloof to the faculty in particular and the SMU business community in general.

As part of his planning process, Zumberge convened a committee of seven faculty members from around the university and asked Marshall Terry to chair it. The committee became known as the Terry Commission and had as its

President James Zumberge

Interim President James E. Brooks

focus the revamping of the undergraduate core curriculum. The Terry Commission would soon emphatically reaffirm SMU's core philosophy that the liberal arts were to be the hub in the educational wheel of undergraduate education at Southern Methodist University. Coleman, the new dean, welcomed this affirmation of the university's philosophy. He saw it as another way to distinguish the School of Business Administration from competitors; it would allow him to develop and enhance programs that were in concert with the liberal arts foundation. However, Zumberge was not especially close to the school of business. Some of the school's faculty felt that a disproportionate share of resources generated by the school were diverted to other parts of the university without full discussion or understanding.

During Zumberge's tenure, in addition to a new undergraduate core curriculum, the SMU Literary Festival was instituted, as was the SMU-in-Spain program that was based in Madrid. The only building erected during Zumberge's term was the Dedman Center for Lifetime Sports.

While things seemed to be moving smoothly for this ambitious problem solver, he surprised everyone when, in 1980, he resigned from SMU to accept the position as president of the University of Southern California, which was experiencing its own crisis. Provost James E. Brooks stepped in and admirably served as interim president until the arrival of Zumberge's successor.

L. Donald Shields

L. Donald Shields arrived at SMU in 1981 as the eighth president of Southern Methodist University. Shields was one of the youngest presidents in the country, having been named president of California State University at Fullerton at the age of thirty-one. Shields arrived with impressive academic credentials—a PhD in chemistry from UCLA; the author of three books, two of which were published in five languages; and an award from the American Institute of Chemists for leadership in science and higher education. His abilities would be severely tested during his time at the university.

President L. Donald Shields

According to Terry, Shields arrived with great energy and ambitions indicating that he was "in the fast lane" with respect to advancing SMU's national and international academic reputation. Shields had a new planning document prepared with the help of his provost, Hans Hillerbrand. Titled "The Decade Ahead," the plan called for the development of financial support to help SMU join the ranks of outstanding universities. The plan indicated that facilities should be improved in order to significantly increase the quality of the faculty, staff, and students. There would be more endowed chairs to attract outstanding faculty and additional financial aid to attract outstanding students. The Decade Ahead Plan called for $24 million to be allocated to the Cox School of Business. Of this total, $14 million would be earmarked for facilities expansion.

The Coleman Years

Having accepted the challenge despite his reservations about the movement within the SMU presidency, the question was how would Coleman proceed? "You begin to move a school toward excellence by focusing on attracting the best faculty and students at the same time you are building collegiality, strengthening integrity, developing campus relationships and gaining the confidence of the business community." These are the strategies that characterized Coleman's term as dean. Coleman made no mention of physical facilities in his broad strategic outline for the school. He repeatedly emphasized that the drive to improve quality is achieved by placing the highest priority on hiring outstanding faculty from the best-known institutions. He also believed in aggressively managing the existing faculty. Not everyone among the existing faculty would be able to contribute to improving quality. Some would have to be moved out of the school and replaced. Upgrading the faculty was the top priority, but improving student quality, especially the MBA student body, was a close second order of business for Coleman. However, his immediate attention was given to the accreditation of the undergraduate program.

The Impact of Accreditation

Accreditation had been a problem for Coleman from the time he became executive dean, something he had inherited from the previous administration. In the spring of 1975, Lyle had convinced the AACSB not to place SMU on probation pending another visit by an accrediting team. When Grayson resigned, the AACSB granted the school a postponement of the scheduled accreditation visit until the latter part of February 1976. On March 17, 1976, Coleman was advised by Ronald R. Slone, associate director of the AACSB, of the school's possible probationary category. Coleman had decided earlier that the loss of accreditation would be a severe blow to the school's efforts to seek excellence. With precious little time to make any significant changes that would stave off probation, Coleman mounted a three-pronged attack.

First, he persuaded SMU's central administration to cede full operational control of the part-time undergraduate business degree program to the business school. Heretofore, that program had been lodged in an organizational unit separate from the school. He also argued successfully to add a number of full-time faculty positions to upgrade the quality of teaching for undergraduates. Second, he worked to mend fences with the AACSB and requested a review of the school's programs and operations. During one visit, the accreditation team, writing about relations with the Grayson administration, noted that "the administration of the School exerted only minimal effort to insure that the School's program fulfilled the accreditation requirements of the

Alan Coleman, Willis Tate, Laurence Fleck, Aaron Sartain, and picture of William Hauhart

AACSB" and that "substantive experimental control and subsequent evalua-tion of results never occurred; no reports that were satisfactory to the Continuing Accreditation Committee were submitted." Coleman promised AACSB officials he would do everything necessary to have the school's pro-grams meet AACSB requirements and hired the former chairman of the AACSB's Continuing Education Committee to serve as a consultant to the school in preparation for the next accreditation visit.

Finally, in the biggest move of all, the Business School Assembly approved a revised undergraduate curriculum a few weeks before the visitation com-mittee arrived on campus. The new curriculum included eight required courses that would effectively meet the standards of the AACSB. The assem-bly's action also included provision for students to meet all the requirements in a fifteen-credit-hour "block." Innovation would be retained to a degree by permitting up to 10 percent of an incoming class of students to pursue their degree through a self-determined degree plan, approved by the faculty. In many ways, the assembly's action seemed to provide the best of all worlds by meeting requirements for accreditation and retaining provisions for some of the provocative philosophies and programs that marked Grayson's efforts.

Buoyed by the positive report of the Visiting Committee and with the strong backing of SMU's central administration, Coleman formally presented the school's request for continuing accreditation at the April meeting of the accrediting association. On May 18, 1976, the school was notified that the undergraduate program was approved for continuing accreditation. A credi-bility crisis had been avoided. Equally important, Coleman was able to gain allies among different faculty factions in the school because a policy of inno-vation was retained. Coleman also began building credibility and support within the rest of the university. He did this with a statesmen-like approach in dealing with other deans. He was their ally in gaining support for their pro-grams and in resolving any other problems where he might be helpful. In another wise strategic move, Coleman took the time to begin reconstructing a positive image with various elements of the Dallas business community.

Next Step: The MBA Program

The MBA program was not part of the accreditation visit to review the undergraduate program. However, the Visiting Committee noted that the MBA program was deficient in three areas. First, there were an insufficient number of hours in the required courses. Second, there was no requirement for students to take a course in the legal environment of business. Third, students were allowed complete freedom in choosing electives, meaning that the breadth-test requirement for all students was not being satisfied.

The solution to the problems outlined by the accrediting team was obvious. Much in the manner in which the undergraduate program was revised, the school set about considering a new MBA program format. On February 11, 1977, less than one year after the revision to the undergraduate program, the Business School Assembly approved changes to the MBA program designed to make it compatible with the accreditation requirements. The assembly approved eight required courses, required students to take elective courses in a minimum of four subject areas, and created a trimester program that required forty-eight credit hours to complete the MBA degree. The previous requirement was only forty-two credit hours. All of this was accomplished against the backdrop of heated and sometimes bitter debates about the viability of a one-year graduate business program. Many faculty voiced the opinion that a two-year MBA was necessary to advance the school's reputation. As a result of these debates, the final vote for a forty-eight-hour MBA program passed, but only by the slimmest of margins.

The school requested the opportunity to submit the MBA program to the AACSB for accreditation. The request was approved, and Coleman presented the school's application at the AACSB meeting in May 1978. A self-study report was to be completed by July 1978. As part of the application, the school was required to include extensive information regarding the undergraduate program as well. The self-study was submitted and reviewed by accreditation officials, who noted only a few minor concerns. The AACSB's Continuing Education Committee conducted its site visit on February 5 and 6, 1979. The master's program was accredited in May 1979, and accreditation for the undergraduate program was renewed. These actions represented major milestones on the road toward achieving Coleman's goal of increasing the quality of all SMU business school programs.

Notwithstanding the positive impact of accreditation, the changes that were wrought had a significant impact on the character of the school. The report of the Visiting Committee provided an illuminating set of comments regarding the school's "block" and "self-determined option" programs that were now available to undergraduate students. It is interesting to note that the availability of these options generally was not known to the undergraduate students, and neither was this availability known to many of the faculty. Further, no students during the year of the visitation or the year of self-study appeared to have elected either of these two options. The committee concluded, therefore, that whereas these options allowed for potential deviations from the standard in the name of experimentation, such deviations were, in fact, not occurring under the school's administration.

Later in the report, the Visiting Committee commented on the school's approach to educational innovation and technology: "Surely, the current capacity for a student to self-design his or her curriculum, the opportunities that are available for internship and hands-on credit, would indicate that the School is capable of educational innovation. It would appear, however, that it will be a number of years before there is a strong desire on the part of current faculty in making major shifts toward curriculum or instructional innovation." This was not the most encouraging outlook, especially from a group of educators not very willing to drive educational innovation. This minimizing of Grayson's efforts to bring change through innovation provided a clear sense of the AACSB's opposition to true innovation.

Another part of the report by the Visiting Committee included Coleman's response to questions that were raised by the officials reviewing the self-study. In his response to a question about whether MBA students would be assured of adequate breadth in their required course work, Coleman wrote: "One basic option was to require fewer credit hours and let the students secure

AACSB

May 18, 1979

Dean Alan B. Coleman
Edwin L. Cox School of Business
Southern Methodist University
Dallas, Texas 75275

Dear Dean Coleman:

It gives me a great deal of pleasure to inform you that the
Continuing Accreditation Committee recommended the continued
undergraduate accreditation of the Edwin L. Cox School of
Business, Southern Methodist University. This recommendation
was concurred in by the Operations Committee of the Accreditation Council and the Accreditation Council membership.

We are pleased to make this report to you and to extend our
congratulations. This action also signfies the belief of the
Accreditation Council that the Edwin L. Cox School of Business
can be expected to continue the fine record of achievement
that has been demonstrated to date.

Sincerely,

V.K. Zimmerman
President

VKZ:jvj

cc: President James H. Zumberge

     Dean Ronald J. Patten, Chairman
     Continuing Accreditation Committee

breadth by self-selecting courses outside their area of specialization. The other option was to require more credit hours, which would, in effect, select for the students the areas in which some of their breadth would be secured. The Educational Affairs Committee, with the support of the faculty and administration, selected the second option."

With these changes to the undergraduate and graduate curricula, the transformation of the business school was virtually complete. Extensive innovation was curtailed, students and faculty assumed more traditional roles, and curricula were reworked by adding a significant number of required courses. Many of the changes that had been introduced during the Grayson years were continued, including the one-year MBA program, a multitude of learning options, a host of joint programs, and continuing involvement with the business community. In general, the Visiting Committee's report of February 1979 was complimentary about the progress and the outlook for the school of business. The committee's members noted no major deficiencies and most often indicated that the school met or exceeded standards for institutions offering master's level programs. Throughout the written report of the Visiting Committee there is a clear sense that the school of business was perceived to be on a path toward improving quality.

The Faculty

Obviously, the issue of maintaining accreditation of the undergraduate program was uppermost in the actions taken at the beginning of Coleman's administration. It was never a consideration to find an alternative to pursuing continuing accreditation, although some faculty thought that the school might lose a competitive advantage by following what they considered to be strict operating and philosophical guidelines of the AACSB. Coleman, and, we might add, most of the business community, did not share this line of the faculty's thinking. Coleman began implementing the model that he had seen effectively employed by the Stanford Graduate School of Business under the leadership of Dean Ernie Arbuckle, the same model Coleman employed during his time as dean of ESAN in Peru.

The school's pursuit of excellence under Coleman made improvement of the quality of the faculty its top priority. This priority was followed closely by upgrading the quality of both graduate and undergraduate students, and building and maintaining strong relationships with the business community. In the 1977–1978 *Annual Report,* Coleman stated that "all school activities are aimed at both enhancing our intellectual climate and expanding and deepening our relationships with the professional business community." Coleman devoted his fundraising efforts to those that would serve these priorities. Soon, the school added five endowed chairs in 1977–1978 and almost $12 million in additional endowment as part of the university's capital campaign. Edwin L. Cox endowed two distinguished professorships. The Corrigan Foundation established the Marilyn and Leo F. Corrigan Jr. Trustee Professorship. The Carr P. Collins Foundation endowed the James M. Collins and Carr P. Collins Jr. Professorship in Finance. Other donors remained anonymous.

Again, in the *Annual Report* Coleman wrote, "Nearly all of the income from the new endowment will be dedicated to people—faculty and students—and most especially to the steady improvement of academic quality."

The size of the faculty remained relatively constant at about sixty during Coleman's deanship. The primary vehicle for improving faculty quality was hiring replacements. His association with Stanford and Harvard undoubtedly influenced the type of individual he thought was necessary to build excellence at the SMU school of business. He wanted people who were skilled teachers and capable researchers, and who had an ability to interact with the business community. Coleman became known as a skillful negotiator who persuaded a number of faculty who did not meet these criteria to leave SMU. His actions provided the faculty with an understanding of the level of performance that would be required for retention and promotion in order to build and maintain a very strong nationally competitive school of business. When the school began hiring senior faculty from the best-known schools, hiring was characterized by the notion of "steeples of excellence."

Coleman's idea of quality in the faculty included a person's level of commitment and is evidenced by a whimsical tale he was fond of conveying to all who would listen. It seems that as a young professor at the Harvard Business

School he was faced with the daunting prospect of getting to his class during a ferocious New England winter storm. He arose early, energetically shoveled his driveway, and cautiously drove to the school. The trip was tedious and dangerous, and he felt quite proud about his determination and commitment. He expected to be one of the few at school. Upon arriving at Harvard, he was stunned to see faculty strolling about the halls. Many had spent the night in anticipation of the storm and acted as if all of this was routine behavior. Coleman's description of this incident was among those he used to describe how he came to appreciate the meaning of quality commitment in a faculty.

In reviewing prospects for appointment to the faculty, emphasis was placed on the quality and prestige of an individual's education and academic experience. Whereas Grayson often sought to add young faculty who were anxious for change and innovation, Coleman mostly chose senior faculty with proven track records. Six new faculty members were appointed for the fall of 1976. Their doctorates or last appointments were at the University of Texas at Austin, the University of Indiana, the University of Chicago, the University of Wisconsin–Madison, and the Massachusetts Institute of Technology.

In a report covering the 1974–1975 and 1975–1976 academic years, Coleman noted that "The SMU Business Program has some distinctive differences . . . differences of which we're proud." He identified practical learning, business involvement, student-centered responsibility, and multiple options for learning as the distinctive differences and called them "the keystone of our educational philosophy." A careful reading of the two-year report reveals the status and focus of faculty efforts as Coleman began his tenure as dean. There are perhaps four or five brief references to research among the faculty. There is not a single reference to research publications, and only one grant is mentioned. The report is devoted primarily to describing different learning options available to students, student statistics, and the various programs that the school offered to the business community. There are pages upon pages of names of students who received awards. There are references to organizational changes, but the director of research is not mentioned once in the report. Even though the school provided some small summer research grants for faculty prior to Coleman's appointment, the research results were minimal. In his early years, one could easily conclude that teaching was the paramount activity under Coleman.

However, judicious use of the Faculty Standards for Appointment and Advancement, along with additional support for research in the form of generous travel funds for faculty presenting papers at national academic conferences and the introduction of a working paper series, encouraged research productivity. From the meager research output beginnings in the early 1970s the school's production of research would increase markedly, as witnessed in a separate report detailing faculty achievements in research in 1980. The faculty of about sixty members produced 122 journal articles, 100 conference papers, 20 working papers, and 17 books between 1978 and 1980. There were an increasing number of grants awarded to faculty, including a $500,000 grant to be shared with the School of Engineering to develop a corporate decision center. Increased research brought recognition to a number of individuals who served as officers in their professional associations or as editors of academic journals. In fact, during this period of growth in research, a number of prominent faculty members were denied tenure because of their lack of research productivity. At the same time, it would be an overstatement to say that teaching had faded into the background as the result of an increased emphasis on research and publication. In fact, the award for outstanding teaching was expanded in 1980 to recognize the outstanding teachers at both the undergraduate and graduate levels.

The strategy of hiring faculty from nationally prominent business schools was accompanied by continuous attention to the needs of an emerging school with lofty ambitions. The increased quality of the student body was another important ingredient used to evaluate the progress of the business school at SMU.

The Students

Although upgrading the faculty clearly was the highest priority for Coleman, he had a keen interest in raising the quality of the student body as well.

Professors Julius Aronofsky, Bob Frame, and Bert Greynolds discussing a research project

Undergraduate students were given a great deal of latitude in designing their own educational degree programs. They received opportunities and responsibility to participate in decision making beyond what most students in U.S. business schools experienced or expected. They occupied important roles on policy, personnel, and curriculum committees, and they were eager and active participants in the change process.

While their official roles were changed little during the period 1976–1981, and the Business School Assembly remained the primary policy-making body in the school, there was less need for change, student activism diminished, and there was continuing pressure to improve the quality of teaching. But the biggest change shaping the character and profile of students was the rise to prominence of the school's MBA programs. The one-year MBA program was seen as a way to distinguish SMU's offerings from almost every other graduate program in the country. The introduction of the executive MBA (EMBA) in the fall of 1976 thrust the school of business to the forefront among local and regional schools of business. The move to a forty-eight-credit-hour MBA program had an important effect on part-time graduate study as well. A part-time student could finish the MBA degree in three years. This was significant to MBA prospects in terms of time and finances devoted to earning their MBA degree. Finally, the growth of full- and part-time graduate programs was a recent phenomenon for the university and allowed the business school administration to negotiate more of a share of the program's revenues.

Professor Marion Sobol and a student discussing a project

It was, and remains, generally understood in the business school environment that the MBA program historically is a flagship business program and an important key to financial and reputational success. Undergraduate programs are important both to schools of business and to universities, but they generally do not have the impact on a school's reputation that is provided by a strong MBA program. Even though MBA programs grew tremendously in the early 1970s, undergraduate programs continued to be valuable sources of workers for American business. Consequently, there was never any serious consideration given to eliminating the undergraduate business program. At the same time, there was never much more than a passing interest in starting a doctoral program at the school. Doctoral programs are very expensive, and, while they can provide some resources for research-oriented faculty members, it is clear that research productivity can be fostered in other important ways.

As a consequence of these conclusions about the three different levels of degree programs, the school undertook to scale back the size of the undergraduate program from 1,000 to 850 and to maintain the size of the full-time and part-time graduate programs. Although somewhat a financial decision, part of the motivation to manage the size of the degree programs was the positive impact that size was expected to engender. The school could maintain relatively small classes taught primarily by full-time faculty in order to enhance the quality of instruction, an important selling point for student recruiting. Furthermore, since scores on the Graduate Management Admissions Test (GMAT) and undergraduate grade-point average (GPA) were used as quality measures for the MBA program, it was easier to improve quality by limiting the number of students admitted each year. Job placement was another measure of performance, prompting the school to analyze who hired MBA graduates at what salary levels. Reading the school's annual reports gives the distinct impression, by virtue of the paucity of data, that placement of graduates improved over time but was an area in need of significant improvement. Despite the importance of placement, the primary measures of quality used by Coleman were the GMAT and GPA. This was also the case for most business schools in the United States.

Despite the restriction on the size of classes in the MBA program, it was not a simple matter to raise the quality of incoming classes. The average GMAT score for the entering full-time MBA class rose from 512 in fall 1975 to 550 in fall 1980, an increase of less than 10 percent, while the undergraduate

MBA students in class

GPA for entering MBAs improved to 3.25. The school began attending MBA recruiting fairs in the late 1970s and hired a director of graduate recruiting in 1981. Even more powerful was the creation of the Dean's Scholars program. The program provided eleven full-tuition scholarships for the class entering in fall 1980, and was a substantial supplement to the funds historically allocated to graduate financial aid. The program was funded by profits obtained from seminars and conferences sponsored by the school's Management Center. Dean's Scholars were required to have a minimum GMAT score in the 90th percentile and an undergraduate GPA of at least 3.5.

During the same period, the undergraduate program hurdles were modified so that admission to the school required a minimum 2.5 GPA. This was a substantial increase from the 2.0 that had been required and was the highest standard for admission to any undergraduate school at the university.

The Business Community

From the outset of Coleman's service as dean, he emphasized the business school's relationship with the business community. He knew that support from the Dallas business community was crucial to the success of his ideas for improving the school. He was well aware of the role that Dallas's business leaders played in the overall economic and political development of Dallas as well as their significant involvement in the establishment and growth of the university. Coleman wanted to capitalize on this fundamentally strong relationship, which had been strained for a while, although Lyle, as executive dean under Grayson, had worked hard and successfully to repair some of the rift.

Coleman's philosophy included the business community as an active partner in the educational process where practical-learning-in-action environments constituted the educational centerpiece of the school. It would not be possible to pursue the school's goals without the direct and extensive participation of business. In addition to working with students and faculty on projects connected with coursework, serving as guest lecturers, providing internships, or acting as a board of directors in a management simulation, the business community contributed to the school through its relationship with the Foundation for Business Administration, founded in 1965 as noted earlier. The foundation was devoted to advancing the interest of the business school through guidance in program, policy, and fund raising. In addition to Ed Cox, its first chairman, the foundation later was headed by Robert H. Stewart III, chairman of the board of First International Bancshares, and then by Charles H. Pistor, president of Republic National Bank. Pistor served through the end of Coleman's deanship.

The Affiliates Program, created in 1975, engaged a select group of local firms dedicated to support timely and pragmatic business education. The affiliates met for half-day sessions to hear experts in all areas of business and government. This group provided an additional supply of resources for SMU faculty and students. The affiliates were important because the Associate Board, created in the early 1970s, became relatively dormant with the departure of Lyle. Coleman was well aware of the potential of the Associate Board concept, and in

1977 he discussed the possibility of reactivating the board. Lyle, now in private business, agreed to serve as chairman of the Associate Board, and it was revitalized. Lyle recruited some of Dallas's finest young businessmen and businesswomen to serve on the board and instituted a program of interaction with full-time MBA students. The mentoring program matched students' and board members' interests. Students would meet with one or more board members during the course of their graduate study. They received invaluable assistance regarding their careers and, in many cases, were provided opportunities for internships and class projects. One frequent form of interaction utilized by the Associate Board members was to invite students to management or board meetings at the mentors' respective companies. Though not specifically part of the mentoring process, employment offers sometimes resulted from student contacts with mentors. The Associate Board provided students with one of the highlights of their educational experience. The revitalization of the Associate Board was an important event in the school's history, and it has continued without interruption today under the watchful leadership of Lyle.

One of the most visible forms of interaction between the school and the business community included the conferences and programs offered through the school's Management Center. As noted earlier, beginning in 1972, the school hosted a number of SMU Business School Management Briefings each year. The format was an address by a prominent national or international business figure. These programs, sometimes offered in cooperation with local business firms or civic agencies, were very popular and attracted sizeable audiences from 800 to 1,800 participants. Prominent speakers included President Gerald R. Ford, Vice President George H. W. Bush, Senator Russell B. Long, and Federal Reserve Board Chairman Paul A. Volcker. Nobel Prize Laureate Milton Friedman addressed a huge gathering at the Fairmont Hotel. Other noted featured speakers included John Swearingen, chairman of the board of Standard Oil of Indiana, and David Rockefeller, chairman of the board, Chase Manhattan Bank. In what seemed almost an annual appearance at the briefings, Editor-in-Chief Lewis Young and a panel of *Business Week* editors provided a review of major economic events and outlooks. In all, there were twenty-five Management Briefings held during the time Coleman was dean.

The Management Center also provided hundreds of one-, two-, and three-day seminars on virtually every business topic and included both specialized programs and general interest programs. Offerings were held in Dallas, Houston, San Antonio, and other Southwest cities. The seminars and workshops continued to be popular throughout the late 1970s and early 1980s, and attendance approached 6,000 participants in the 1979–1980 academic year. As noted earlier, this activity was significant in continuing to foster a strong presence for the school among the local and regional business communities. As significant, though, was the ability to offer the programs at a profit, enabling the discretionary use of funds for such things as the Dean's Scholars program.

In addition to the Management Center programs, the specialized institutes created to serve specialized needs and areas of interest continued their activities. The Caruth Institute of Owner-Managed Business was founded in 1969 by gifts from W. W. Caruth Jr. and the Hillcrest Foundation. The institute focused on entrepreneurs and the formation of owner-managed business. They continued to provide instruction in entrepreneurship for graduate and undergraduate students in courses such as the following: Starting a Business, Cash Flow Management, and the Distinguished Entrepreneur Speaker Series. The Caruth Institute retained its focus on this direction from inception and developed a reputation for a quality program to help individuals who want to start a business.

Bobby B. Lyle, Chairman,
Associate Board

In early 1978, Caruth pledged a gift of $250,000 per year for three years. This generous gift put the Caruth Institute on a sound financial footing and assured its continued operation. In 1981, Neil C. Churchill, distinguished professor of accounting, was appointed director of the Caruth Institute, and John A. Welch was appointed director for entrepreneurship. Jerry F. White was appointed associate director for entrepreneurship. Welsh and White continued to lead teaching and research in entrepreneurship while Churchill added to the institute's activities involving companies in transition to becoming big businesses. New courses were added, and in 1980–1981 a total of 383 persons attended the institute's programs. In 1981 Welch and White authored an article in the *Harvard Business Review* entitled "A Small Business Is Not a Little Big Business," which helped draw attention to the school's work in small business and entrepreneurship.

The Costa Institute of Real Estate Finance, created in 1974 by the Aubrey M. Costa Foundation, was designed for continuing education and research in real estate and mortgage banking. Robert Pease, former president of the Mortgage Bankers Association, served as the initial director and was succeeded by Robert O. Harvey in 1976. Harvey was internationally recognized for his research in real estate and received the Nicolas Salgo Outstanding Teacher Award in 1980. Tragically, he died suddenly on July 11, 1981. Professor William B. Brueggeman was appointed interim director. During 1979–1980, the institute's programs enrolled over 1,200 participants.

Jerry White and John Welch of the Caruth Institute

The Maguire Oil and Gas Institute was founded in 1975 by a gift from Cary M. Maguire, president of Maguire Oil Company. In 1977 the institute named M. Edgar Barrett as director and Daniel R. Weston as administrative director. The institute sponsored an energy panel in November 1977 to discuss national energy policy, and over 2,000 people attended the program, offered in cooperation with the SMU Alumni Association. Speakers included Ambassador Robert Strauss; William P. Clements Jr., former deputy secretary of defense; U.S. Senator Harrison Schmitt; and Edward Vetter, former undersecretary of commerce. Under Barrett's direction, the institute offered courses for undergraduates and MBA students, and in the summer of 1979 it offered the first annual program for senior executives in the oil and gas industry.

In the early 1970s, the Hoblitzelle Foundation assisted in the creation of the Institute for Women in Business. Gerri Hair served as the first director, and the aim of the institute was to enhance the opportunity and potential of women in the business world. The institute's programs were usually a half to a full day in length, and more than six hundred people attended programs in 1978–1979.

Recognizing Entrepreneurs

Under Coleman's announced goal of improving relationships with the business community, he continued the practice of recognizing the careers of some of Dallas's most prominent entrepreneurs at the school's annual awards luncheon. In 1976, the award was given to Robert H. Dedman, founder and CEO of Club Corporation of America, perhaps the most successful business operation of its kind. For the second time since the awards began, the school awarded more than one Entrepreneur of the Year in 1977. Lloyd H. Haldeman was honored for his leadership as president and managing director of the Dallas Symphony Association. John P. Thompson received recognition as the innovative leader of the Southland Corporation, most noted

Robert H. Dedman Sr.

for its 7-Eleven convenience stores. Again, in 1978 there were multiple awards. Three brothers, Lester A., Milton P., and Irvin L. Levy, were recognized for their achievements in leading National Chemsearch Corporation to be one of the fastest growing companies in the nation. Internationally known real estate developer Trammell Crow was presented the award in 1979. David G. Fox, chairman of the board of Fox & Jacobs, Inc., was the recipient of the award in 1980. In 1981 there were multiple awards for Entrepreneur of the Year. Robert Cullum, chairman of the executive committee, and his brother Charles Cullum, chairman of the board and CEO of the Cullum Companies, were recognized for their roles in building the company from a single warehouse grocery operation into a regional supermarket empire under the Tom Thumb name.

A New Name: Edwin L. Cox School of Business

Few events have influenced the business school at SMU as much as the formal naming of the school in honor of one of its most ardent supporters. On May 12, 1978, the Board of Trustees of SMU announced that the School of Business Administration would be named the Edwin L. Cox School of Business honoring Cox's long-standing contributions to the university and the school. His long-time friend and associate, William Clements, was among the many dignitaries who honored Cox at the dedication ceremony. In Clements's words, "Ed Cox has to be the very seed from which the Business School as we know it today has sprouted. The impetus he gave it through the SMU Foundation for Business Administration was the starting point for building the School to the strong position it now occupies. There is no way to evaluate accurately or to express adequately the enormous contribution he has made."

Born in Mesa, Arkansas, on October 20, 1921, Edwin Lockridge Cox would go on to distinguish himself as one of Dallas's most successful businessmen. He attended the SMU School of Business Administration for two years before finishing his undergraduate business studies in 1942 at the University of Texas. He earned his MBA from the Harvard Business School in 1946 after he served

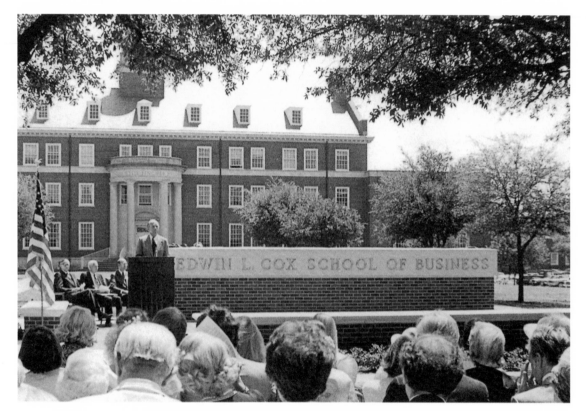

Edwin L. Cox at dedication ceremony for the naming of the Cox School

in the U.S. Navy. He achieved the rank of lieutenant. Cox returned to Dallas and entered his father's oil and gas business. When Cox first founded the SMU Foundation for Business Administration, he worked with a group of twenty-five local business leaders to actively support the development of the School of Business Administration. He was appointed to the SMU Board of Trustees in 1966 and was elected to the Board of Governors in 1968. He served as chairman of the Board of Governors beginning in 1963 and became chairman of the Board of Trustees in 1976.

In the spring of 1978, Cox endowed two distinguished professorships in the school. In a decision that clearly demonstrated his desire to help the school without exerting any personal interests, Cox did not specify where the professorships should be housed within the school. He left that to Coleman's discretion. This degree of commitment and the style of decision making would be a consistent theme of Cox's relationship with the SMU business school.

Financial Support for the Cox School of Business

Lyle, in cooperation with Cox and the SMU Foundation for Business Administration, raised funds to eliminate the deficit of the School of Business Administration by 1975. By 1976 the endowment of the school was about $3 million, composed primarily of the gifts for three chairs, the Stewart scholarship gift, and other restricted gifts. By the time of Coleman's resignation as dean, the endowment had grown to almost $20 million. While about one-half of the increase was due to the addition of eight endowed chairs, there was significant unrestricted giving to build the endowment to this level. In 1977–1978, the university implemented a National Capital Campaign, and the School of Business Administration increased endowment by more than $12 million in one year.

Reflections on Coleman's Deanship

Alan B. Coleman led the Edwin L. Cox School of Business in new directions during his term as dean, and he recorded significant achievements in many areas. He retained some of the interesting and innovative programs of the Grayson administration, but, upon appointment as dean, he immediately established his own agenda. He began to shape and move the school toward a proven model with which he had observed and experienced great success.

Coleman did not hesitate to identify accreditation as essential to the immediate and long-term future of the school. The continuing accreditation of the undergraduate program was in serious jeopardy, and Coleman moved swiftly to assuage the accrediting agency's concerns. He completely revamped the undergraduate curriculum, fashioning one that met all the traditional standards the agency required. Even more impressive was his ability to accomplish this magnitude of change while, at the same time, bringing a sense of purpose to what appeared to be a faculty in disarray and filled with discontent.

Although the MBA program had never been accredited, Coleman knew that obtaining accreditation for it was crucial to his model for building a nationally recognized school of business. Gaining accreditation for all of the school's programs had been an intense, arduous, and frustrating process. But the school had answered a major question and was able to concentrate on the difficult task of improving faculty and student quality while continuing to strengthen relations with the business community.

Notwithstanding the importance of the accomplishments in getting academic programs accredited, Coleman's most notable accomplishments were in faculty development, improving the quality of graduate and undergraduate students, and strengthening the school's relationship with the business community.

By almost every conventional standard that could be used to measure faculty performance and future prospects, the faculty of the Edwin L. Cox School of Business made enormous strides during Coleman's term as dean. Coleman was the first chair holder in the school. Others he hired during his tenure included Richard H. Buskirk, Herman W. Lay Chair of Marketing; William B. Brueggeman, Clara R. and Leo F. Corrigan Sr. Endowed Professorship in Real Estate; John W. Slocum, Corley Chair of Organizational Behavior and Administration; and Neil Churchill, Distinguished Professorship in Accounting.

Thirty-five of the faculty in 1981 were recruited while Coleman served as dean. A review of the appointments clearly shows that academic pedigree and productive histories were important characteristics in those who received faculty appointments. As a prominent scholar-teacher himself, Coleman insisted on hiring people who were above average in teaching and research. It was valuable for an individual to have received a doctorate from one of the highly recognized universities. Standards for tenure and promotion were respected, and there was a general understanding among faculty of the importance of teaching and research. There was support for faculty in the form of student assistants, summer research grants, a working paper series, and travel to professional meetings. Then in 1980 the school, for the first time, provided two awards for outstanding teaching. There was an award for excellence in teaching undergraduates and one for graduate teaching excellence.

The emphasis on teaching permeated much of the school, and the support for research was reflected in the dramatic increase in research productivity during Coleman's years. The school reported 46 articles, 11 books, and 22 speeches and professional proceedings produced by the faculty in 1977–1978. In the fall of 1980 the school published a report on research productivity covering 1978–1980. The faculty published 122 articles, 100 conference papers, 20 working papers, and 17 books. In the following year the school reported 179 faculty publications. The school was also able to obtain grants for research. In 1976–1977 a sum of $68,000 in grants was awarded to faculty for research. The amount reached $165,000 in 1978, and a grant of $500,000 from the Atlantic Richfield Foundation was awarded jointly to the Cox School of Business and the SMU School of Engineering in 1980.

Student quality improved during the period from 1976 to 1981, but, as in the case of the faculty, improvements did not come swiftly. The graduate program showed increases on both important dimensions of quality from 1975–1976 to 1980–1981. The GMAT admission test score rose from 525 to 550, while the undergraduate GPA of the MBA class rose from 3.15 to 3.25. The addition of the Dean's Scholar program in 1980 requiring GMAT scores in the 90th percentile and a minimum undergraduate GPA of 3.5 further strengthened the drive to improve student quality. At the undergraduate level, the school moved to require a 2.5 GPA for students requesting admission. At the time it was the strictest GPA requirement of any upper division school in the university. This, coupled with a reduction in the target level of enrollment to approximately 850 students, ensured the use of small classes and fewer adjunct faculty in classrooms.

Interaction with the business community was an essential element in Coleman's model for making the Cox School of Business a success. It was important to the school's academic programs and critical as a source of financial support. The immensely popular Management Briefings played an important role in keeping the name of the school before the community and helped to build a reputation of competence and business initiative. The Management Center offered hundreds of programs at all levels of management and added to the school's reputation for practical business education. The Entrepreneur of the Year award was well publicized and helped create some special relationships for the school. The Associate Board not only provided an inestimable resource to MBA students but established a cadre of young business leaders who would support the Cox School of Business immediately and ensure growth in the future. The institutes provided another means of business interaction. Coleman aggressively supported both the Caruth Institute of Owner-Managed Business and the Maguire Oil and Gas Institute, enabling them to develop courses for graduate and undergraduate credit as well as programs designed for continuing education. This broadened and deepened the impact of each of the funded institutes.

Heading toward 1981, the Cox School of Business was on a solid financial footing, and overall progress was steady. From an operational standpoint there was little cause for concern. But Coleman made an important statement in his annual report of 1979–1980: "All office and classroom space is very heavily used and is not now fully adequate for the school's needs." Overall, however, he expressed satisfaction with the progress and direction of the school. But he was very concerned that the central university administration continued to experience changes in leadership as noted earlier, including the abrupt departure of Hardin. When Zumberge left after only five years, it was cause for concern to Coleman. He believed that strong, continuing central leadership was essential to success. Each change in administration brought changes in leadership through-out the central administration. Despite the best intentions of qualified people, changes at the highest levels produce "culture shock." Invariably it would take time for the university faculty and administration to regain lost momentum and move forward as a unified whole. His belief in the value of a unified administra-tion led him to work diligently to have the Cox School of Business be recog-nized as a model citizen. Part of the recognition of that effort included his being named to head search committees for deans of three SMU schools, including the Meadows School of the Arts and the Perkins School of Theology.

Amid these concerns about fragmented central leadership was Coleman's recognition that the character of the business school faculty had changed dur-ing the last five years. Understanding the need to rekindle a sense of direction and purpose led Coleman to create a strategic planning committee in 1980. The committee was composed primarily of elected senior faculty and others appointed by the dean. Their task was "to enunciate a strategic plan to guide the decision-making process of the school during the 1980's." The committee's report was issued in the summer following Coleman's resignation as dean.

Lessons Learned

Coleman's success as Dean of the Cox School of Business can be attributed in some significant measure to his strong interpersonal skills coupled with the confidence to implement a vision for the school that was different from those of his predecessors. Coleman steadfastly followed an approach to building excellence that he had learned as a junior faculty member at the Stanford and Harvard business schools and which he implemented as founding dean of ESAN in Peru. The watchword under Coleman was always quality—steeples of excellence. His decisions about the business school rested on whether there would be an improvement in quality.

Coleman's academic and business experience prior to his arrival at SMU gave him the background to recognize and understand the many different stakeholder interests that influence the operation of an institution such as the

Cox School of Business. He was not only at ease with university faculty, deans, and central administrators, but he was comfortable in the business community. These skills, combined with a high standard of ethics, enabled Coleman to encourage the best from the people he valued and gain support for the school from many different quarters.

During Coleman's term as dean, few things were done with drama, but whatever action was taken had a thorough base of support. Programs were not killed or disbanded but rather gradually eased from sight. This included those instances where Coleman felt that a faculty member would not be a long-term asset to the school. Private conversations usually handled the matter in a way that was productive for everyone.

Even though Coleman's five-year term as dean of the Cox School of Business was relatively free of controversy, there were questions raised about his judgment and decisions. Could the endowed chairs have been filled more quickly? The average time to fill a chair seemed to some to be excessive given that quality of faculty was the highest priority in the school. There seemed to be no specific reasons or disagreements within the school that would account for the slowness in recruiting senior faculty. Would the move along the road to excellence have been swifter with recruiting of more senior faculty?

A similar comment can be made about improving student quality. Were adequate resources plowed into the process for attracting top students to the school? The one-year MBA program seemed to provide a huge edge to the school in recruiting students, but no huge influx of talented students ever fully materialized. At the undergraduate level, did the school merely go along with the university's process for recruiting top students? Could the school have been more aggressive and exerted greater influence in recruiting? Perhaps the attitude was too complacent with regard to student quality. Should the lowered enrollment numbers in the undergraduate program have been instituted sooner? Perhaps the target increases in the graduate enrollment should have occurred earlier even as accreditation was being sought.

The question of aggressiveness surrounds some of the institutes as well. The Caruth Institute seemed to have an eager and active constituency among students and in the business community, and, indeed, its credit and non-credit courses were quite popular. Yet the school seemed unable to fully capitalize on that interest, and no connection was ever made between the Entrepreneur of the Year and the activities of the Caruth Institute. The same was true for the Costa Institute in the real estate area. The Maguire Oil and Gas Institute was more integrated into the school, but it too often seemed to go its own way.

These questions aside, Coleman must be credited with executing a sound plan for building excellence in the Cox School of Business.

Coleman Resigns

In early 1981, Coleman resigned as dean of the Cox School of Business. The very surprising announcement had its origins in three features of Coleman's deanship. First he had a very successful five-year tenure. The future would likely be more of the same. However, the need for dramatic additions to the physical facilities was evident. Second, SMU was soon to acquire a new president, whose style and vision were not clear. Finally, the Southwest Graduate

Janet and Alan Coleman, Northern California, 2005

School of Banking was seeking a president to replace Richard B. Johnson, the banking school's founding president. Leading the prestigious banking school was a challenge and opportunity that Coleman could not resist. He accepted appointment as president of the Southwest Foundation and director of the Southwest Graduate School of Banking, one of the prestigious banking schools in the country. He also retained his appointment as Caruth Professor of Finance. After consultation with the faculty of the Cox School of Business, President Shields appointed Eugene T. Byrne as dean *ad interim*. Byrne had been serving as associate dean under Coleman.

The Transition to Herberger

"An interim dean has to preserve the territory to provide the next permanent dean the best opportunity for immediate and on-going success." This is how Byrne approached the job of serving as interim dean. Although it was not realistic to generate new programmatic initiatives, there were existing programs and short-term goals that had to be achieved. Budget negotiations would be important for the school to retain the financial viability that Coleman had achieved, as would securing the approval for any tenure or promotion recommendations of the Cox School faculty. It would also be crucial to faculty spirit and morale to continue to recruit new faculty for approved positions. Byrne appointed Thomas E. Barry as interim associate dean for academic affairs. He knew that Barry had the respect of the faculty.

Faculty recruiting was productive in 1981, and the school added nine new faculty members for the academic year 1981–1982. It was decided not to actively seek candidates for the open endowed professorships. Having these positions available would be a significant recruiting advantage for a new dean of the school.

Maintaining the developing relationship with the business community was essential while the school searched for a new dean, and the school relied heavily on Associate Dean Weston and the directors of the school's institutes to continue their successful programs. The popular and high-profile Management

Interim Dean Eugene T. Byrne

Briefings series continued, and some of the speakers included Governor William P. Clements Jr. and Robert O. Anderson, board chairman and CEO of Atlantic-Richfield.

Student recruiting was an area where the school could continue to be aggressive and create some additional initiatives. To add emphasis to the growing importance of the full-time MBA program, Norman D. Campbell, a graduate of the MBA program of the Cox School of Business, was appointed director of graduate recruiting. The EMBA program was given additional resources with the appointment of Judy Johnson to serve as program director. This use of a full-time staff person to direct the EMBA differed from the previous practice of having a faculty member serve in the position.

Perhaps the most significant contribution came in assuring the unfettered review of the strategic outlook for the school over the next five to ten years. Rather than put the review on hold pending the arrival of a new dean, Byrne moved the process forward with the full participation of all the existing holders of endowed chairs in the school and selected other faculty and administrators. The Strategic Planning Committee delivered its report to the faculty in summer 1981, and it established a base line for the future of the Cox School of Business. It provided a frank assessment of the existing status of the school and laid out requirements and actions that would be necessary to achieve national recognition. The report recommended continuing the school's stated mission of educating and training current and potential managers employing a variety of techniques and a variety of formats. Thus the committee endorsed the basic educational philosophy that had been developed over the last decade. It also noted that the road to national visibility would emphasize a strong degree program at the undergraduate level along with strengthening the MBA program. The school would attain national recognition in the business community by offering high-quality management development seminars, lectures, conferences, and in-residence executive seminars.

The report stated that, "The ELCSB is viewed as a good business school. It is uniquely poised to become a nationally prominent one." No specific criteria for prominence were given, but the report identified several areas of critical need, mostly addressing resource shortages. The committee recommended increasing the number of full-time faculty to seventy-six by 1986 in order to create a critical mass and to improve the quality of faculty that would support excellence in teaching and research. Faculty salaries and teaching loads had to be adjusted in order to achieve parity with competing schools. A similar requirement was proffered for staff support.

The committee recommended that the goal of the MBA program should be to rank among the top twenty graduate business programs in the nation within ten years. To achieve this goal the school must attract a larger number of high-quality students. Enrollment in the MBA program should be 288 full-time

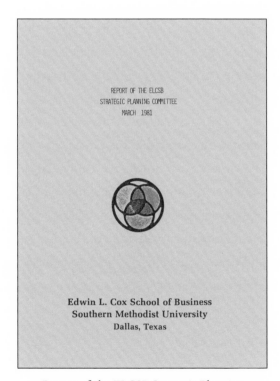

Report of the ELCSB Strategic Planning
Committee, March 1981

and 110 part-time students by 1986, and the EMBA class should be maintained at current enrollment levels. The goal was for the undergraduate program to rank among the top fifteen private undergraduate programs in the nation within ten years. Undergraduate enrollment would be limited to eight hundred students with average SAT scores in the 70th percentile. The strategic planning report dodged the issue of what should be the specific criteria for achieving success in these programs. It does seem likely the school would have benefited by defining measures of success.

The Strategic Planning Committee was critical of the school's lack of programmatic focus for all the degree programs. It endorsed the addition of courses for strengthening core requirements, but importantly its members believed it was imperative to concentrate on educating individuals for the private sector. It would also be important for the faculty to regard core courses as part of a programmatic whole rather than as a collection of department- or subject-area-based courses. The core of any degree program "belongs to the School" while the specialized courses are more properly the domain of each subject area. One possibility would be to appoint educational program managers for each degree program and give them the responsibility to allocate resources among programs.

The committee also laid the foundation that would support and challenge the next permanent dean. It stated that the physical facilities were nothing short of an embarrassment that would prevent the school from further progress. The committee recommended raising funds for an immediate and extensive renovation of the existing Fincher Building followed by the construction of two "wings" extending west from the Fincher Building. The committee provided a timetable calling for one wing to be built "very soon" and the second no later than autumn 1986. The stage was now set for the hiring of a new dean.

CHAPTER FIVE

HERBERGER THE BUILDER, 1982–1989

My vision was that SMU could be in the top category of schools by developing a faculty devoted to teaching and research excellence. We had to fill some gaps in the faculty, and, of course, the physical facilities had to be dramatically improved.

ROY HERBERGER

Roy A. Herberger Jr. earned his BBA and MBA degrees from the University of Texas at Austin. His focus was in communication, advertising, and marketing. He told us that he really wanted to work for a large, prominent consulting firm like Ross Perot's EDS, but his career path turned out to be quite different. One of his professors in the MBA program at the University of Texas persuaded him to enroll in the doctoral program at the University of Colorado. He did, and during his doctoral studies, Herberger spent a good deal of time teaching and doing research, all the while thinking that he would end up in the business world.

Without much conviction, he tested the academic job market as he was approaching graduation at Colorado. He received offers from some excellent schools of business and decided to accept a position as an assistant professor at the University of Southern California. Herberger arrived at USC in 1970, and soon thereafter USC's school of business experienced a change in leadership. The new dean asked him to continue on the faculty and also to serve as assistant dean for student affairs. He accepted the administrative post with some thought that the experience would be useful in the corporate world.

Dean Roy A. Herberger Jr.

About eighteen months later there was another change in deans at USC. Eventually the school named Jack Steele, former dean of the school of business at Texas Tech, as its new dean. It was under Steele that Herberger finally made his choice to pursue an academic career. The school only had a minimal presence in international studies and research, and Steele asked Herberger to direct the program. One of his first responsibilities was to take a group of eighteen students—from the United States as well as several other countries— to Europe. He was very impressed with the domestic students in the four-week course prior to departure to Europe, but he was concerned about the international students, who seemed lost in the complex academic material they were being presented in class.

To Herberger's surprise and delight, the international students made a complete reversal of performance and became the class leaders on the European junket. Their adaptability to numerous complex international situations was outstanding and something he had not previously experienced. He soon realized that the education USC was providing for students who would be managers in the international arena was off target, so he returned to the United States and USC with some ideas for changing the entire area of international studies. Steele was convinced and asked Herberger to develop the area into one of the school's strengths and distinctive competencies. Herberger agreed and tackled the job with fervor. He established the International Bureau of Economic Research (IBER), which attracted capable faculty and students. He created independent sources of funding that placed IBER on a firm financial base. Under his guidance, international activity at USC grew and prospered in significant ways. Subsequently, Steele recognized Herberger's ability as an administrator and gave him primary responsibility as executive dean for running the academic affairs of the school.

Because of his experience and success at USC, Herberger was considered a rising star, and other schools and universities naturally were interested in this young executive dean. SMU showed an interest through its dean search committee, and in an exploratory meeting with Ed Cox and new SMU President Shields, Herberger was impressed by what he deemed were manageable

ambitions. Cox and Shields held high hopes for the school, yet their expectations were consistent with the asset base of the university, the school, and the
Dallas community. Until this meeting, most of the expectations he heard from
other institutions were unrealistic. Herberger was also impressed by the genuine enthusiasm shown by Shields for helping to build a better school of business, and he began to believe that he could have a significant impact on the
development of the business school at SMU. Herberger's conviction that he
could make a difference at SMU, coupled with the fact that he and his wife,
Pam, were both ardent Texans led SMU to announce Herberger's appointment as the dean of the Edwin L. Cox School of Business in early 1982.

The Dallas Environment

Dallas was in the midst of some very unusual economic times during the 1980s
when Herberger arrived. Iraq had invaded Iran in 1980, and hostilities would
last until the latter part of the decade. In the summer of 1990, Iraq would
invade Kuwait, sparking the Gulf War that concluded in early 1991. Throughout the period, oil prices would fluctuate wildly. The energy crisis was coupled
with a significant nationwide real-estate and savings-and-loan scandal that had
roots beginning in the late 1970s. In March 1984, Empire S&L in Mesquite,
Texas, failed, eventually costing taxpayers approximately $300 million. Savings-
and-loan institutions continued to fail nationwide throughout the decade. By
the end of 1987 the Federal Deposit Insurance Corporation noted that losses
at Texas savings and loans comprised more than one-half of all savings and
loans losses nationwide, and, of the twenty largest losses, fourteen were in
Texas. By late 1987, the Texas economy was in recession and commercial real
estate was severely disrupted. Unemployment in the Dallas area was at a low
of 2.9 percent in mid-1984 and jumped to 6.1 percent two years later in the
troubled economy. The unemployment rate remained at these levels until the
late 1980s.

In 1984, Dallas hosted the Republican National Convention at the Dallas
Convention Center. This same year, Dallas voters approved the Dallas Area

Rapid Transit (DART) service plan. The end of the decade was punctuated with the opening of the much-anticipated Morton Meyerson Symphony Hall, and the Sixth Floor Museum was dedicated to the memory of President John F. Kennedy. Toward the end of the 1980s, Annette Strauss became the first woman elected mayor of Dallas.

The SMU Environment

For all of his drive and determination, President Shields was overwhelmed with the issue that had affected several of his predecessors—football. SMU's history had a rather checkered reputation with respect to football infractions. The NCAA had sanctioned the football program several times, and what was to come would be the beginning of the end of successful football seasons at SMU for almost two decades. The glory days of football with names like Kyle Rote and Doak Walker were more than three decades in the past, but football returned to national prominence with new names like Eric Dickerson and Craig James (both seen in the 1983 Cotton Bowl Championship picture at right). SMU just barely missed being named national champions in 1981. SMU was the only undefeated team in the nation, but Penn State was named the champion, and SMU settled, unhappily, for second place.

1983 Cotton Bowl trophy

The story of what was to occur a few years later is both sad and complex. Suffice it to say that SMU was investigated by the NCAA for allegations of illegal payments to athletes, among other things. The NCAA investigative team found SMU guilty of serious infractions, and, because of SMU's history of infractions, it became the first and, at this writing, the only institution ever accorded the "death penalty." SMU was forced to give up football for a year and chose to give it up for an additional year as well. The institution suffered a severe backlash. It was discovered that some members of the Board of

Governors knew about these illegalities, and subsequently the board was abolished for a smaller Board of Trustees that was chaired by Ray L. Hunt. Hunt was instrumental in returning SMU to a focus on achieving academic excellence at SMU. He remains a key figure on the SMU Board of Trustees today.

The faculty backlash at the "death penalty" was significant. Procedures were instituted that made recruiting of student athletes in football very difficult relative to the rest of SMU's competitors in the Southwest Conference. President Shields's health deteriorated, and he resigned in 1986. He was replaced by William B. Stallcup, who served under very trying times as the interim president of SMU. Stallcup, a true scholar and incredible gentleman, held the ship afloat until the arrival of Shields's successor in 1987. SMU was under the microscope; things were looking bad; SMU needed a crisis manager of the highest order. Once again fortune would smile broadly on this university.

Ray L. Hunt

Interim President William B. Stallcup

Kenneth Pye

A. Kenneth Pye came from Duke University to become the ninth president of SMU and inherited what he called "a mess." The football scandal was broadcast throughout the country, and the academic progress that SMU had made was lost in the noise. Pye was an extremely intelligent man and had an incredible storehouse of energy. His accomplishments were recognized internationally as he asserted his leadership in his chosen profession of law and higher education. He had held an endowed chair at Duke's Law School and twice had been chancellor of Duke as well as dean of the law school.

President Pye's focus from the moment he stepped on campus was to restore academic integrity to SMU. However, he inherited a very difficult financial situation and found himself spending much of his time dealing with serious budget issues. He once intimated to one of the authors that he did not have a grasp of the full financial picture of SMU upon his arrival. At one point during his tenure, he called for a 9 percent cut in budgets across the entire campus. As a result, people had to be either relocated around campus or let go altogether. It was a difficult time for all, including Pye.

Pye had to make very difficult decisions, which he did not hesitate to do. He totally overhauled the governance structure of SMU with the help of some key trustees, including Hunt. Some of Pye's detractors as well as supporters felt that he "shot from the hip" and was a "micro-manager." Others, however, felt he was a savior and put SMU back on the right track in attempting to restore its academic integrity. Many faculty lobbied to get SMU to leave Division I athletics, but Pye and key members of the Board of Trustees were steadfast against that move. However, he did put constraints on athletic recruiting to make that process more compatible with the general academic thrust of the institution. SMU would remain a competitor in Division I athletics.

President A. Kenneth Pye

As part of his emphasis on academic integrity, Pye insisted that SMU continue to focus on Willis Tate's fundamental philosophy that liberal arts were the core of the educational experience for undergraduate students at SMU. Pye also created more focus on international curricula and intercultural issues. In order to make SMU more renowned nationally and internationally, he made it clear that additional PhD programs and more faculty research were critical to SMU's future.

Pye's "shoot from the hip" reputation was gained early in his administration when he indicated that he would likely drop engineering and undergraduate business programs. This did not set well with a large group of faculty and external constituents, and, while some programs in engineering were dropped, the undergraduate business program remained intact. Pye soon learned that the financial viability of the university was inextricably linked to the undergraduate business tuition base. Because of Pye's reputation as a tough, even grating, decision maker, faculty and key external supporters continually criticized his decisions. But, there is little question among those who lived through the "scandal," and Pye's subsequent administration, that he was absolutely essential in restoring SMU's focus on its core purpose of education—an education that was, in Tate's terms, one of quality and substance.

Herberger's Philosophy and Managerial Style

As noted earlier, Herberger came to SMU with a very successful record as the associate dean for academic affairs at USC's school of business. The IBER program was both popular and profitable, due in large measure to Herberger's opportunism and business acumen. He also continued his research productivity and was awarded tenure.

During an interview with Herberger about his experience as the dean of the Cox School of Business, Jack Steele's influence on Herberger was evident. Steele arrived at USC's business school following a period when turnover in the office of the dean left the school without a clear sense of direction. Herberger had been serving as associate dean, and Steele asked him to stay in that position and help him develop the school. Herberger agreed. There were a number of traits that were developed at USC that characterize Herberger's style and approach as dean of the Cox School. For one, he used a business-like approach when managing the school. Herberger noted that his mentor, Steele, had come from business and used business logic to make decisions during his time at Texas Tech's business school.

Herberger's academic background and interests had always lured him in the direction of business, and the introduction of business management techniques to the academic process seemed to satisfy his need for a business-like approach in the deanship. It may also have been the source of some discontent toward the latter part of his term as dean. He had some of the same experiences that beset previous deans in the business school at SMU. By virtue of its innate appeal to many business segments and a popular undergraduate program, the school had usually been able to generate significant cash flow. While deans made arguments to use more of the cash flow to improve the business school, the central administration considered the total university in making financial decisions. This typical tension becomes a burden when the decisions seem to frequently go "against deans." Under this budget scenario, deans at the Cox School were unable to institute a salary structure consistent with their internal needs and external market forces. Deans were required to make personnel decisions that were uniform across all schools in the university.

Herberger's attitude toward faculty productivity differed somewhat from what might be considered traditional. He felt that faculty research ought to solve practical business or social problems while contributing to the announced direction and goals of the school. Simply publishing in "A" journals or writing an acclaimed esoteric tome was not enough. If the Cox School aimed to grow executive education for example, then publications directed to this area would be valuable. In their Faculty Activity Report (FAR), faculty would outline their portfolio of activities and ideas for the coming year and would discuss the plan with administrators to decide if the activities and outcomes were valuable. The discussion provided administrators with the opportunity to influence faculty activity. This became an invaluable tool for Herberger, because it enabled him to foster a team environment among faculty. From his perspective, the most important faculty members were those who understood the intent and use of faculty activity planning. Herberger tended to value these team players.

Valuable team players were also defined by their willingness to take on important organizational roles. Herberger's model of the quintessential colleague was someone who questioned his ideas and decisions, not so much probing for weak spots but searching for opportunities to participate and support. One of Herberger's observations was that the Cox School of Business, in his estimation, was underperforming relative to the talent base and the opportunity presented by the Dallas business environment. *Nesting* was blamed for this lack of performance given the perceived capabilities of many faculty. Nesting is when a faculty member establishes a firm position inside a group, such as a department, and then makes all further contributions of teaching and research in ways that strengthen that person's stature inside the group. It is a way to "feather one's nest" and provide some protection against an unknown outside environment. Nesting faculty in protected areas avoid venturing outside the area, as in pursuing new options and directions envisioned by the dean, because innovation is perceived to be both unnecessary and not approved by colleagues. The strong team player is one who recognizes this phenomenon and takes independent action to minimize the impact of nesting and enable the school to move into new areas.

There was a perception among many faculty that Herberger was uncaring and aloof. This perception may have come from his devotion to high quality and the desire to move the Cox School forward rapidly. In addition to possessing a confrontational, problem-solving style, he was also willing to take risks. His desire and efforts to eliminate the academic departmental structure and make all faculty professors of business rather than professors of narrow disciplines (e.g., marketing, finance, accounting, etc.) opposed the organizational status quo. In many ways, this was similar to, and reminded faculty of, some of the organizational changes attempted by Grayson. Herberger engaged a high-risk strategy with a faculty that had come to enjoy stability under Coleman. Herberger's no-nonsense manner was evident in his dealings throughout the

university. Though not generally known, he had productive relationships with the other SMU deans. In his
interview with the authors, Herberger recalled that
they were an outstanding group and that he spent
more time socially with the deans then he did with any
other group at SMU.

Not the least of Herberger's traits was his un-
bounded confidence. He had been successful at every
stage of his career and forged an enviable track record
at USC. Though confident, he was excited to see that
the ambitions at the Cox School of Business were realistic, or, in his words, "manageable." Prior to arriving
at SMU, he surveyed the internal and external environments and thought that moving the school to a higher
level of performance and recognition was reasonable.
When senior university officials shared his assessment
of the school's assets and opportunities, it was the

Lee Iacocca briefing

ideal situation for a new dean. He had unbridled confidence in his ability to
improve performance and appeared to have all the support he needed to get
the job done.

Herberger's Vision, Goals, and Objectives

Once he arrived on the SMU campus and spent some time in the Cox School
of Business, Herberger was less than impressed. "There was no spark—no
fire." At his first faculty meeting, he was surprised and dismayed at the reception to his initial thoughts. He was sure he detected reluctance if not skepti-
cism to the idea that he could lead the school. "My vision was that SMU could
be in the top category of schools by developing a faculty devoted to teaching
and research excellence. We had to fill some gaps in the faculty, and, of course,
the physical facilities had to be dramatically improved." Although not initially
a major area of interest, the idea of developing executive education became

another part of Herberger's vision for the school. Executive education was not a well-defined part of his early thoughts for the Cox School, but the potential for making a significant impact soon became apparent and captured much of his attention. Notwithstanding his initial impressions, Herberger did not see his vision as anything especially difficult to achieve. He believed that moving Cox into the top echelon of business schools would be a relatively straightforward endeavor centered primarily on excellence in teaching and research with a serious upgrade to the physical facilities.

Although major curriculum changes were not part of Herberger's ideas for the school, he expected to be able to capitalize on his international experience. However, he was astounded to find that the Cox faculty did not pay significant attention to international affairs. Neither, in his opinion, did the city of Dallas. The Dallas/Fort Worth International Airport was devoted primarily to international cargo and had little impact on the fabric of the city. While this scenario might provide fertile ground for someone with significant international experience, it would eventually add to Herberger's frustrations.

He attempted to jump-start the international area among the Cox faculty by providing memberships in the Association of International Business (AIB). Cox faculty generally regarded international studies in business as an emerging discipline at best and one that did not attract top scholars. Herberger reasoned that one or more international institutes could be developed using the research interests of a few faculty members, but that approach was unsuccessful. When he tried to obtain approval for a program to take a group of undergraduate students overseas, he spent an inordinate amount of time justifying the proposal and finally shelved the idea because there was little interest and, perhaps, less understanding of the value of international study.

There were two other areas where there was room for major improvement at the Cox School of Business, and Herberger was eager to develop these areas. By almost any standard the school's information technology base for teaching and research was limited. Professor Paul Gray had received a grant to develop a Decision Center, and it earned some recognition, but beyond that there was little to distinguish the school in this area. Herberger was fascinated with information technology, especially personal computers, and believed they would play a much greater role in the future of business education. He was committed to the university's Decade Ahead program that would provide a new building complex for the school, and he was determined to outfit that complex with a state-of-the-art information technology system.

Executive education was another area where Herberger came to believe that he should channel some of the school's resources. Previously, Cox offered a series of mid-level management development programs that had provided some additional funding for the school, but the primary business interface remained the very successful Management Briefing series. Herberger wanted to broaden the school's efforts and believed executive education held the potential for becoming a hallmark of the Cox School of Business.

Implementation

Herberger's legacy is primarily rooted in the outstanding physical facility that was constructed while he was dean of the Cox School. He admitted, upon his arrival at SMU, that raising money for buildings was, in his view, the responsibility of central administration. His job was developing a superior faculty and student body involved in programs of teaching and research that would bring recognition to the school. His view on this matter of fund raising would change soon after his arrival.

In 1984, SMU's Decade Ahead project earmarked $24 million for the Cox School of Business, and 60 percent of that was to be available for new buildings and renovations. The Fincher Building was the sole facility for the school. Built in 1954, it had served admirably, but by Herberger's arrival it was woefully inadequate. Over the years there were attempts to raise money to renovate the Fincher Building, and some modest projects were completed, but until the Decade Ahead project there were no strong, concerted efforts to provide the school with competitive facilities. Finally in 1985, the Cox School broke ground for two new buildings along with a major renovation of the Fincher Building. The Kresge Foundation provided a $500,000 challenge grant for the renovation of the Fincher Building. During construction Cox faculty were scattered around campus; dormitory rooms served as faculty and staff offices until the completion of the new wings and the renovation of the Fincher Building.

Two Collegiate Georgian style buildings were constructed. One, named in honor of Cary M. Maguire, president of Maguire Oil Company and chairman of the Cox School of Business Executive Board, was devoted primarily to serve undergraduates, and included classrooms, faculty offices, and administrative offices. The second building was named in honor of Trammel Crow, the Dallas real estate developer and member of the SMU Board of Trustees. The Crow Building would have classrooms and administrative offices that would serve primarily the MBA student population. It also had faculty offices. The *Dallas Morning News* reported that Maguire provided a multi-million dollar gift in 1983 to kick off the Decade Ahead project while Crow made a $6 million gift in November of 1985.

According to Herberger, representatives of SMU went around the country—from Stanford to Harvard—in search of the best designs for the new facility. Reflecting the predominance of the case method of instruction and the lecture-discussion style of teaching in the Cox School, twelve of the seventeen new classrooms had a tiered, horseshoe-style design. Classrooms were fully equipped with personal computers, VCRs, telephones, overhead projectors, master control panels, and top-of-the-line acoustics. The faculty, staff, administrators, and students moved into the new facilities in January 1987.

One of the more interesting parts of the entire plan for the new buildings and the Fincher renovation was the creation of shared space in the center of the U-shaped three-building design. The three buildings were linked through a common ground floor that also included the Business Information Center (BIC—the high tech, electronic business library) and Georges Auditorium. The 165-seat auditorium, funded by a generous gift from Bill Georges, included state-of-the-art video and data systems as well as translation capabil-

Ed Cox and Governor Bill Clements at Cox School Complex groundbreaking, 1985

ity. It continues to this day as a centerpiece of the school's facilities. Unfortunately, the auditorium was built close to Ray's Creek and would suffer serious water damage a few years later when the entire auditorium was underwater following a severe storm during David Blake's deanship. The flooding situation was remedied, and Georges was remodeled.

However, it was the BIC that changed the character and quality of education at the school. Prior to the BIC, computer and information-technology facilities for faculty and students were primarily provided through a central university system, including Central University Libraries. Herberger had long been an advocate of the power and utility of the personal computer and found a willing cohort in Dan Costello, the school's associate dean for administration. With the added support and encouragement from information systems experts, the BIC was designed to electronically link faculty, students, and the business community in a network for teaching and research. By providing a donation exceeding $500,000, AT&T assured Herberger that the BIC would begin with first-class equipment. AT&T provided one of their most powerful business computers equipped with business software that provided faculty and students with a dramatic increase in research capability. Thirty AT&T personal computers allowed BBA and MBA students to gain access to the latest business periodicals, up-to-date reference materials, and instantaneous market data and news.

During the same period, the school received seventy-five Telecompaq computers from the Compaq Computer Corporation. Twenty went to faculty, fifteen were located in the BIC, and forty were given to the executive MBAs. Connecting the students to each other and to faculty or Cox staff via e-mail, the Telecompaqs offered students and faculty an unparalleled communication system that greatly enriched the executive MBA experience.

In a relatively short period of time the Cox School had acquired substantial classrooms, offices, and information resources, and Herberger could justifiably assert that his school's facilities were as good as virtually any business school in the country.

Construction on new Cox School Complex begins

Faculty Resources

"Teaching excellence is the primary mission of the Edwin L. Cox School of Business." This statement by Herberger, upon reviewing his first two years as dean, succinctly reflects the core of his approach to improving the Cox School of Business. The physical facilities and infrastructure that he developed during his deanship were significant, but he never saw them as the key to raising quality in the undergraduate or MBA programs. He also believed that the undergraduate and graduate curricula were adequate, and he did not devote much time to revising academic programs.

Arriving in June 1982, Herberger moved into the fall semester of 1982 with a total of sixty-four full-time faculty members. Five of the school's six endowed chairs were filled. Over the next three years, one additional chair would be endowed and one more chair would be filled. After the Decade Ahead campaign was announced, there was a significant increase in the number of endowed chairs. By the end of the 1986 academic year, the number of endowed chairs in the Cox School almost doubled to a total of thirteen, with two more added the following year.

As noted earlier, it was Herberger's judgment that the faculty had some gaps in teaching and research and that filling these gaps would be critical to moving the Cox School into regional prominence and national recognition. Budgetary limitations in the first few years prevented Herberger from making significant changes in the faculty, and new additions were, almost entirely, replacements for turnover. Although the faculty would increase in absolute size to seventy-two by the middle of 1988, the net increase was almost exactly matched by the increase in the number of endowed chairs that were filled.

Cox School Business Information Center (BIC)

With the appointment of Wanda Wallace as the Marilyn R. and Leo F. Corrigan Jr. Trustee Professorship in Accounting and Andrew H. Chen as the first holder of the anonymously endowed Distinguished Professorship of Finance, the Cox School and Herberger embarked on an intense period of filling endowed chairs in the fall of 1983. There would be nine additional chairs filled over the next five years. Three of the nine appointments would be made with internal candidates. George Hempel in finance and Roger A. Kerin in marketing were appointed for five-year terms to the Marilyn and Leo F. Corrigan Professorships in fall 1985. At about the same time, M. Edgar Barrett, professor of business administration and director of the Maguire Oil and Gas Institute, was appointed the Cary M. Maguire Professor of Oil and Gas Management.

Richard O. Mason came to the Cox School from the University of Arizona with a background in strategy and the social and ethical implications of information systems. He was named recipient of the Carr P. Collins Professorship in Management Information Sciences in September 1985. One of the most notable appointments occurred in the spring of 1986 when the recently appointed U.S. postmaster general, Albert V. Casey, agreed to join the SMU faculty as the holder of the Ann Cox Distinguished Professorship in Business Policy. Casey was the retired chairman and chief executive officer of AMR Corporation and American Airlines, as well as former president of Times Mirror Corporation of Los Angeles. As a recognized leader in American business, Casey brought business leadership and experience to the faculty and the school's academic programs.

Albert V. Casey

Ronald W. Masulis joined the school in the fall of 1986 as the James M. Collins Professor of Finance. An effective teacher and excellent researcher, Masulis arrived from the Graduate School of Management at UCLA and was serving as associate editor of four academic journals. In the spring of 1987 the school announced that Wayne S.

DeSarbo was named the first Harold C. Simmons Distinguished Professor in Marketing. He joined SMU from the Wharton School of Business.

Alan B. Coleman completed a distinguished career at SMU and was appointed emeritus professor in the fall of 1988. His successor as Caruth Professor of Finance was Rex W. Thompson, formerly of the Wharton School. Rex brought expertise in capital market theory and corporate finance. The final chair holder to be appointed by Herberger was Blake Ives, who was the first recipient of the Eugene J. and Ruth F. Constantin Distinguished Professor of Management Information Systems. Beginning in fall 1988, Ives brought teaching and research distinction to the school. He previously served as a distinguished fellow of the Oxford Institute for Information Management at Oxford University. Both Thompson and Ives would later play significant leadership roles at the Cox School.

By the time Herberger left the Cox School in early 1989, approximately 50 percent of the seventy faculty members were new hires during his term as dean and about 20 percent were chair holders. The increase in size from sixty-four to seventy faculty was less than the seventy-seven that Herberger projected in his *1985 Progress Report*. Not reaching the projected faculty size raises the question whether the faculty appointments provided Herberger the opportunity to "fill the gaps" that would allow the school to move forward aggressively.

Indeed there are two aspects of the growth and management of the faculty that caused Herberger considerable frustration. According to him, SMU's central administration hampered both recruitment of new faculty and rewarding existing faculty by establishing a range of salaries for each faculty rank. This attempt at campus parity was intended to promote a sense of fairness among university faculty. Unfortunately, the market for faculty does not recognize these equity parameters, and there is little doubt that Herberger was hampered in his effort to recruit the best faculty available.

Another factor associated with faculty recruiting was the desire of a few donors to the Cox School to recruit nationally known "superstars." This attitude of "nothing but the best for the school" was well intentioned but could not be achieved since the school had yet to earn the requisite national status. Nor did it have the infrastructure to support these superstars. The school was able to recruit a significant number of outstanding faculty over the five and one-half years of Herberger's term; however, the goal of adding a significant number of superstars was not realized.

Programs

There were few curriculum revisions for either the undergraduate or graduate programs between the 1982 and 1986 academic years. Although there were four new centers and one additional institute founded during this period, they were primarily vehicles for faculty research or business community interaction, both important and necessary activities.

The most notable curricular changes occurred in the undergraduate program. In 1982–1983, the only opportunity for students to formally specialize their education was through a six-course program leading to the certificate in real estate. By 1988–1989 students could select from among five major courses of study and one dual major. The accounting subject area was the first to introduce a major in 1985–1986 with a twenty-four-credit-hour course of study. Not to be outdone, the finance, management and information sciences, and marketing subject areas created major courses of study. The real estate and urban land economics subject area introduced a twenty-one-credit-hour major in 1987–1988 and co-founded a dual major in finance and real estate in cooperation with the finance subject area. The dual major required twenty-seven credit hours in the two fields.

In 1986–1987, the Cox School announced the offering of "honors" sections of the required undergraduate business courses for academically gifted students. The use of honors offerings for BBA students would eventually become a very significant program within the school and be expanded beyond the required courses. There were no honors programs for graduate students. Various sponsored awards provided undergraduates and MBAs recognition for academic excellence at the time of graduation.

A class session in the new Cox Complex

One of the successful efforts to internationalize the curriculum and enhance students' world perspectives was realized in the spring semester of 1985 when the executive MBA class hosted London Business School EMBAs. In April 1986, the Cox executive MBA class went to London for a one-week tour of the financial markets and meetings with business, political, and educational leaders. The journey was a required part of the EMBA curriculum and was offered for credit under an international finance class and a global enterprising class. Students wrote papers summarizing their experience and what they learned. The trip was highly lauded, and an international trip has been an integral part of the EMBA curriculum ever since.

Despite the success of the EMBA trip abroad, the Cox School was still treading lightly in the international arena. In 1983, there were only five global courses offered in the entire school: three in the undergraduate program and two in the graduate programs. By 1989, that number had increased to nine courses at the undergraduate level and only three in the MBA program. This seemingly slow progress in developing the international curriculum was due, according to Herberger, to the university's indifference to the growing importance of international business and the relatively few international business organizations in Dallas. Further, Herberger found it very difficult to generate interest in the international area among the Cox School faculty. They regarded international business as an emerging and secondary field that had not gained any stature compared to long-standing disciplines. Lacking the luxury of a large number of additional openings in the faculty, it was not possible for Herberger to direct faculty resources to what he envisioned as an important, emerging discipline.

A course in corporate ethics and social responsibility was added to the undergraduate curriculum. Dick Mason began offering the course to seniors

in the fall semester of 1986. By 1988, the course was being taught by an interdisciplinary faculty team including Mason; Bob Rasberry and Jack Stieber
from the Cox School; Benjamin Petty from the philosophy department; Will
Finnin, the university chaplain; and William F. May, the first university professor of ethics. The course was not offered at the graduate level in the Cox
School primarily because of a lack of faculty and financial resources.

As we noted earlier, the football scandal had a huge impact on the university, ranging from a complete overhaul of the governance structure to the resignation of President L. Donald Shields due to poor health. The concern for
the viability of the university was at issue when the Board of Trustees
approved the selection of A. Kenneth Pye as president in June 1987. When Pye
indicated that the university would consider eliminating the undergraduate
program in the Cox School of Business, a lengthy and intense public and private debate between Pye and Herberger ensued. Herberger emerged from this
fray as the winner of sorts—the BBA program would stay—but there were
clear budget ramifications for the school and for the rest of the university. The
budget problem was exacerbated by the fact that the university was holding
millions of dollars in trust for the Cox School, but the dean was unable to tap
into these funds for what he considered both a need and an opportunity to
keep the school moving upward. This frustration with the governance and
financial dealings of the university was among the factors that would eventually lead Herberger to decide to go to Thunderbird.

Centers and Institutes

Centers in the Cox School are organizational units created to conduct research
and offer programs to specific business segments. Centers differ from the
school's institutes, which provide courses for credit in both the graduate and
undergraduate programs. The centers also served a very useful financial role
for the faculty and administration. Beginning with the creation of the Management Center, these organizational units have provided financial support that
would not have been otherwise available. The treatment of budgets for the

Graduation Day

degree-granting divisions of schools is bound in tradition and practice. It was very difficult for a dean to obtain additional funding for faculty or to support faculty research by tapping in to the pool of funds generated by tuition. But if the dean and faculty could develop ideas for research and programs directed toward a specific industry group housed in a "center," it was often possible to obtain funding to support their work. The funds could be viewed as "outside of the usual funding sources," and it was possible for the dean to retain a large percentage as discretionary funds to help grow the school.

Beginning in 1970, with the founding of the Caruth Institute for Entrepreneurship, the Cox School worked hard to foster even stronger relations with the Dallas business community. The Management Center offered a variety of programs for industry in addition to the popular Management Briefing Series. The Costa Institute of Finance and the Maguire Oil and Gas Institute were operational when Herberger arrived, but there would be a significant burst of activity during the first few years of his leadership. The Center for Study of Financial Institutions and Markets was established in 1983, and followed the operational philosophy of providing research and educational programs for a specific segment of the academic and business community.

The Center for Enterprising had been funded since the summer of 1984 with income from a university endowment, and the center received additional funding from ARCO Oil and Gas Company. The Center for Enterprising was successful in bringing attention to the school and providing research opportunities for faculty and students on important economic questions affecting Dallas and Texas. The center served an impressive list of clients, including American Airlines, Inc., the Texas Economic Development Commission, the Joint Economic Committee of the U.S. Congress, Gulf States Utilities, and AT&T.

In 1984 Mr. and Mrs. Robert S. Folsom made an endowment gift of over $1 million to the university. Robert Folsom, a former mayor of the City of Dallas and an SMU football star, was a long-time supporter of the university and the Cox School. The Folsom Institute for Development and Land Use Policy was founded in honor of the Folsoms. The mission of the institute was to conduct a program of research and management education focused on issues in land development and public policy. One of the goals of the institute was to pursue research and educational programs on a joint basis with other educational institutions, firms in the private sector, and non-profit organizations and public agencies.

Later in 1984, the Center for Research in Real Estate and Land Use Economics was established. It was created as a research entity with a focus on major issues in the real estate industry. It engaged in a wide range of research, including the federal income taxation of housing and real estate development and real estate investment performance in pension fund portfolios. In an organizational move that provided leverage to three separate organizations, the Costa Institute of Real Estate Finance and the Folsom Institute were housed in the Center for Real Estate and Land Use Economics. The center then coordinated research and education programs among the three organizations.

The Center for Marketing Management Studies was formed in 1985 to serve as a focal point for interaction among faculty, practitioners, and students who share a common interest in applied marketing management research and education. At the outset, the center engaged in a large-scale study on the effectiveness of trade shows and organized numerous research and educational programs for specific companies. The center sponsored a graduate marketing certificate program and became one of the more successful Cox School outreach programs in the school's history.

The Maguire Oil and Gas Institute continued to serve the business and student communities and relied on an executive board of major oil, gas, and financial community leaders for advice, support, and counsel. The institute helped prepare students for careers in management in the oil and gas industry, conducted course development and research programs related to the industry, and acted as a clearinghouse and reference service for selected information about oil and gas management.

The Management Center continued to offer programs for the community, involving over three thousand participants annually. In 1984 a Management of Managers (MOM) seminar was offered as a two-week program. Directed by John Slocum and taught primarily by Cox School faculty, it was successful from the outset. By 1988 the MOM program was offered twice annually. The Management Center reported that overall enrollment in executive education programs increased by 50 percent in 1988. Part of this expansion included more in-company executive programs geared toward senior level management.

Business Community Involvement

The Cox School's strong relationship with the business community dates back many decades. As noted previously, that relationship was strengthened with the formation of the Business School Foundation formed in 1965. Every dean will attest to the importance of developing close ties to the business community. In the case of the Cox School, significant support from the business community is essential to success. While fund raising is among the most vital outcomes of community and business relationships, the interest and contribution of the community affect the entire fabric of education in a business school such as Cox. Faculty and students are profoundly influenced in their daily activity by the level of interest of community leaders.

Herberger was well aware of this crucial factor, and he was quick to develop and nurture alliances with the influential leaders in the Dallas community who had shown their interest in the school. Chief among Herberger's circle was Ed Cox. Cox worked closely with Coleman, during whose time the university honored Cox by naming the school in his honor. It is possible, however, that his influence on the school became even greater during the time Cox worked with Herberger.

To bolster the involvement of the more senior business executives in the Dallas community, Herberger created the Cox School Executive Board. Cary Maguire was named chairman of the board, and Bobby Lyle became its vice chairman. The Executive Board was independent of the Board of Trustees, and its role was to encourage, guide, and support the development of the Cox School of Business. The Executive Board enabled Cox School deans to develop a support base among a high-powered group of business people that had previously not been tapped for their expertise.

This action created some concern among the university's senior administrators, who thought that it might cause the Cox School to embark on a self-serving path that would disrupt the development of the university as a whole. Herberger persisted and defused any problems of perceived independence by requesting that the provost be appointed to the Executive Board. Coupled with the support of influential board members, the Executive Board thrived and became an important instrument in the development of the Cox School of Business.

The Cox School began honoring entrepreneurs in the early 1970s and continued the practice under Herberger as a natural connection to the business community. The first woman ever to be recognized as the Distinguished

Entrepreneur was legendary Dallas businesswoman Mary Kay Ash in 1983. With her life savings of $5,000 and the help of her twenty-year-old son, Richard Rogers, she launched Mary Kay Cosmetics, which grew from a small direct-sales company to become one of the largest direct sellers of skin care products in the world. Robert S. Folsom and Henry S. Miller, among other entrepreneurs, were honored during Herberger's administration.

Reflections on Herberger's Administration

It is interesting that such a significant building program for the Cox School was initiated and completed by Herberger. He did not arrive at SMU with grandiose building plans. His experience at USC had honed his skills outside the area of capital development and building construction. He was engaged as a consultant by some prominent national and international firms, but converting these relationships into financial support for USC's business school was not his primary goal. His growth as a senior administrator was rooted in developing new academic programs, creatively managing budgets, and working to create a strong and balanced faculty recognized for quality teaching and leading-edge research. These were the accomplishments that originally brought him to the attention of the Cox School search committee.

Mary Kay Ash

To define the outstanding contributions of Herberger as being primarily "bricks and mortar" would be unfair. From the outset, Herberger worked closely with Ed Cox to ensure the success of the Decade Ahead program. In reflecting on his time at SMU, Herberger consistently points to the leadership and support of Cox for SMU and the Cox School. Other businessmen, such as John Eulich, Eckard Pfeiffer, Robert Dedman Sr., Cary Maguire, Trammell Crow, and Bobby Lyle, were important factors in Herberger's success and contributed to the rise of the Cox School to regional prominence and early stages of national recognition.

The Fincher, Crow, and Maguire buildings of the Cox School of Business should be viewed as the beginning of a new era for the Cox School. Their completion is one of the many accomplishments Herberger achieved in aiding the school's progress and ambition to be a world-class business school. The Cox Complex formed the platform on which the work of previous administrations could be sustained and future administrations could build. While the buildings themselves are important, their contents are more so. The BIC provided a state-of-the-art information processing and teaching capability. Herberger had fifteen filled endowed chairs by 1988, nine more than when he arrived at SMU. Herberger created or revitalized industry research centers that provided additional opportunity for students, faculty, and the business community to work together and strengthen the school's relationship with all its constituents. Together the buildings, the BIC, the centers, and the institutes provided a spark of vitality and excitement that Herberger clearly felt was missing as he recalled his early visit to the SMU campus. That spark ignited enthusiasm throughout the entire business school community.

As Herberger reflected on his time at the Cox School, he unflinchingly recalled the stellar contributions by faculty and staff. Associate Dean Dan Costello played a major role in overseeing the construction of the buildings and the BIC. Dan Weston, associate dean for external affairs, was instrumental in so many ways in bringing the school and the business community closer to each other. Betsy Bayer, director of undergraduate studies, provided Herberger the same competent performance she provided for his predecessors for a decade. Ken Ferris and Tom Barry, academic associate deans, ensured quality in teaching and research. Andy Chen, distinguished professor of finance; Bill Brueggeman, the Corrigan Professor of Real Estate; and Mick McGill, the popular chairman of the organizational behavior subject area, provided the kind of faculty leadership and collegiality without which a dean's job is unfulfilling if not unproductive.

Not to say that the Herberger's term as dean was all roses. As is often the case, there were faculty who felt they were excluded from the decision process of the Cox School. There may be some truth to that allegation. Herberger's style was not overly inclusive, and he clearly relied on select close associates. One would not describe his style as "warm and fuzzy" but rather as "businesslike." Accountability and responsibility were important characteristics of his approach to managing and leading people. This style put him at odds with some faculty, not only in the Cox School but throughout the university. There were times when, as dean, Herberger felt that an appropriate reward system for the people who made things happen was dismissed as selfish and not in the

Roy and Pam Herberger, 2005

best interests of the university. He recalls that, more than once, his discussions with senior officials were "vitriolic" and "unproductive."

Also, when the university was immersed in the football scandal, there was an inevitable slowing of momentum. President Pye's arrival at SMU did not eliminate all the uncertainty that had plagued the university for more than a year. Finally, the lure of the presidency of Thunderbird, an international business school in the Phoenix area, was too great for Herberger to ignore. He felt as if Thunderbird would give him an opportunity to be totally in charge of an organization since Thunderbird was not affiliated with any university. It would also be highly congruent with his international orientation. In December 1988 Herberger announced his decision to leave Cox for Thunderbird. John W. Slocum was appointed acting dean.

The Transition to Dean Blake

John W. Slocum joined SMU as the O. Paul Corley Professorship in Organizational Behavior in July of 1979. He earned his BBA at Westminster College, his MBA at Kent State University, and his PhD at the University of Washington. Prior to his arrival at SMU, Slocum taught at Seattle University, the University of Washington, Ohio State University, and Penn State.

Slocum had held a number of positions in professional societies and was elected as a Fellow to the Academy of Management in 1976 and a Fellow to the Decision Sciences Institute in 1984. He received numerous teaching and research awards, including the Nicolas Salgo and Rotunda outstanding teaching awards from SMU. He also has been a recipient of the Carl Sewell Distinguished Service Award, which was instituted under Al Niemi, the subject of chapter 7.

Slocum served as the thirty-ninth president of the 8,500-member Academy of Management. He is the co-author of twenty-four books, including the tenth edition of *Organizational Behavior*. He has served as a consultant to a variety of for-profit and not-for-profit organizations, including OxyChem, Associates First Capital Corporation, Pier 1, Fort Worth Museum of Science and History, and the Winston School of Dallas.

Any notion that the service of Slocum as dean *ad interim* would be a holding period until a new dean arrived was dispelled soon after Pye announced Slocum's appointment. Three issues surfaced that required the new acting dean's full attention. Slocum was aware of Pye's strong interest in developing a two-year MBA program and set out to offer Pye his recommendations. In a detailed memo to Pye, Slocum noted that a one-year MBA was an attractive niche that only a few schools tried to capture. In Slocum's thinking, the SMU program was at least as competitive as the others with SMU having greater long-term potential. A major obstacle in shifting to a two-year program was the cost. Slocum estimated that about $2,000,000 would be needed to effectively make the switch. The cloud that was still darkening the SMU skies from the football storm seemed deterrent enough to Slocum. However, Pye was not persuaded and maintained his idea that the Cox School should implement a two-year MBA program.

Somewhat to his surprise, Slocum learned that the Cox School would soon be reviewed for continuing accreditation of its degree programs. Pye felt, as is obvious, that continuing accreditation was essential. Given the state of the university, Pye was in no mood to permit the loss of accreditation by the Cox School. Little advance work had been done, and the process of getting ready for a visit by the AACSB appeared daunting. Slocum requested a delay in the agency's timetable, noting that a permanent dean would be appointed soon. This dean should have the freedom to create and define the school's strategic goals. When Slocum's appeal was denied, he quickly moved to form an accreditation team and appointed Dan Costello to lead the preparation of documents to send to the AACSB. The process eventually proved successful, and Slocum recalls that the faculty and staff put forth a tremendous effort in a short period of time to meet the accreditation demands of the AACSB.

Along with the issues of the MBA program and accreditation, there were questions about the manner in which the financial records of the Cox School were being maintained. The questions centered on how costs were being charged to various revenue accounts. Provost Ruth Morgan suggested to Slocum that the innovative financial revenue and cost-accounting procedures be modified so that the financial situation of the Cox School would be transparent to central administration.

This issue was not a new one for the Cox School. Every dean since Grayson, and perhaps before, had been of the mind that the business school was providing too much cash to the central university coffers. New programs provided the deans with the opportunity to negotiate what they considered fair and equitable distribution of costs and revenues. Frequently, each new program would be set up in a different way regarding costs and revenues. Over more than two decades, this led to a confusing array of agreements and financial practices. After a long period of review and discussion of the financial practices of the Cox School, an agreement was reached that provided some standardization of reporting of revenues and costs. To alleviate any con-

Interim Dean John W. Slocum

cern that the arrangement might have a serious negative financial impact on the Cox School, an agreement was reached for a one-time budget increase of approximately $200,000.

Slocum had not yet served a year when the university announced the appointment of David H. Blake as the new dean of the Cox School. In reflecting on Slocum's service, the benefit of getting reaccredited was obvious. This was critical for the credibility of the school's academic programs. Revising the school's financial structure was necessary, and contributed to improved management practices. It would also build trust because all the school's finances would be transparent.

Executive education was an area where Slocum had hoped to create and instill a vision for the future. He had extensive experience as an instructor in some of the best programs in the country. He also had significant consulting experience at the senior policy level. He wanted to use that experience to shape the future of the school's executive education programs as part of the school's overall effort to rise to excellence. Heretofore, that effort was aimed at middle management. There remained, however, a gap at the most senior executive level, but due to the time requirements of other pressing activities Slocum was not able to solve that problem. While he regrets that, Slocum was clearly responsible for progress on some key dimensions, and the new dean could build on that progress.

CHAPTER SIX

BLAKE'S DRIVE TOWARD GRADUATE PROGRAM CHANGE, 1990–1996

I don't think I had a grand mosaic or a grand plan, but I had a very clear direction of what I thought we needed to do, what would be fun to do, and a pretty good understanding of . . . things that had to be done.

DAVID BLAKE

DAVID H. BLAKE joined the Cox School of Business in January 1990 as its seventh dean. A tall, lean man, he began his academic career at Dartmouth College, where he graduated *cum laude* in history. At Dartmouth he was named a Rufus Choate Scholar as well as a Daniel Webster Scholar. He received an All-American honorable mention for his soccer prowess at Dartmouth. Blake went on to earn his MBA at the University of Pittsburgh and his PhD in political science at Rutgers.

After receiving his PhD in 1966, Blake joined Wayne State University in Detroit as an assistant professor of political science. He began his administrative career early when he accepted the position of director of the graduate assistant program while at Wayne State. He left Wayne State for the University of Pittsburgh, where he moved through the ranks from an assistant to full professor before he became an associate dean. Blake was at Pittsburgh from 1969 through August 1980 and then moved to the dean's position at Northeastern University in Boston. After a little over two years at Northeastern, Blake moved to Rutgers–The State University of New Jersey, where he served as dean from January 1983 through December 1989. Blake noted that

Dean David H. Blake

he had no early intention of being a dean, but he began his administrative journey "by trying to make my environment and my school better, [and] it just seemed kind of a natural thing."

Blake joined the Edwin L. Cox School of Business in January 1990 as dean and professor. He brought with him an impressive array of academic and administrative experiences. When he joined SMU he had accumulated twenty-four years of knowledge across four different universities. He was ready to apply those experiences to the Cox culture, which he describes as one with a spirit of excitement, energy, and inclusiveness, and the main reason for accepting the position as dean at Cox.

Blake initially turned down the offer to be dean of the Cox School of Business. This is not generally known. In spite of the energetic culture of Cox, he was not sure how willing the faculty would be to change. Also, he was uncertain about the culture of the university at the time. An influential friend of SMU and the Cox School "put the heavy rush on" and convinced Blake that Cox, SMU, and Dallas were the right places for him in his career path. Blake recalled how he had recently gone through a burdensome, bureaucratic process at Rutgers and felt that SMU and Cox would offer much more flexibility for a dean that wished to make some significant changes in the school. Blake admits that, while the Cox School did not enjoy the reputation in 1990 that it enjoys today, the energy level was high in Dallas, and he felt he would get the business support necessary to advance and promote the programs and reputation of SMU's business school. Blake was quoted in *The Daily Campus* as saying, "President Pye and [SMU Provost] Ruth Morgan and I are in full agreement with one firm goal in mind—to make the Cox Business School a true national leader among schools of management."

The Dallas Environment

At Blake's arrival in Dallas, the city had grown to just over one million people, and now counted itself among the "million person cities" of the world. The city government was once again amended to include fourteen single-member district council members and a mayor elected at large. At the same time that Blake arrived at SMU, Paul Quinn College, a black college housed in Waco, Texas, moved to Dallas. During Blake's first year as dean, the *Dallas Times Herald* closed, leaving the *Dallas Morning News* as the only major newspaper in Dallas. In 1993, Dealey Plaza became Dallas's second national historic land-mark, joining Fair Park in that honor. In 1996, during Blake's last year as the Cox dean, DART opened its light-rail system. Business was booming in Dallas during the last decade of the twentieth century, and this would be good news for the growth of SMU and the Cox School of Business.

Dallas Area Rapid Transit (DART)

The SMU Environment

Blake arrived in the middle of the presidency of Kenneth Pye, who would retire in 1994. Pye had inherited a very difficult financial situation. He found himself spending much of his time during his service dealing with serious budget issues, and he called for a 9 percent cut in budgets across the entire campus.

Interim President James E. Kirby

Serious health problems forced Pye to retire in June of 1994. The entire SMU community was shocked at his death one month later. Pye had worked long, hard, and enthusiastically to restore the reputation of SMU and to enhance its academic foundation. It seemed unfair that he did not have time to enjoy his life for very long after his arduous administrative service to SMU. When Pye retired, James E. Kirby, former dean in the Perkins School of Theology, stepped in as interim president and, like so many of his colleagues before him, performed admirably in keeping the SMU ship afloat as well as forging ahead while waiting for the tenth president of SMU to be appointed. Kirby told the campus that he was not interested in being a "caretaker" president and that things would move forward and progress would continue. Kirby initiated a strategic planning process that was well on its way to being drafted prior to the arrival of the tenth president of SMU.

R. Gerald Turner

David Blake served as dean of the business school during the presidential transition and continued to serve under the tenth president of SMU, R. Gerald Turner. Turner was born in Atlanta, Texas, in November of 1945 and arrived in Dallas, Texas, to steer SMU into the twenty-first century in June of 1995. He came from the University of Mississippi, where he had served as chancellor for almost a dozen years. He was one of the youngest administrators leading a major university when he first took the helm at Ole Miss. When he arrived at SMU, he was forty-nine years old and loaded with energy and enthusiasm. Always quick to offer a strong handshake and a wide smile, Gerald Turner hit SMU's campus "running," and he has not stopped since.

The title of Turner's inaugural address spoke volumes about his values and mission for Southern Methodist University—"Leadership and Partnership: Reaffirming the Past, Redirecting the Future." In speaking of SMU's partnership with the Metroplex, Turner talked of globalization, communication, health care, and ethical/social issues, and how these issues had to be shared by and solved with the cooperation of the SMU and external communities. In his

President R. Gerald Turner

concluding remarks, he suggested that it was time for SMU to recommit itself unequivocally to being the very best university it could be. Second, there must be a strengthening of the SMU–Dallas Metroplex partnership to produce leaders who could meet the challenges of the twenty-first century. Third, SMU must assure diverse constituents of SMU's commitment to their participation with SMU in taking advantage of opportunities ahead. Fourth, Dallas and the Metroplex must reaffirm their support to SMU. Fifth, all associated with SMU must renew their commitment to the values embodied within SMU that transcend time and person. And, finally, all of us together should make this era uniquely *the* time for SMU. Robert Stewart Hyer would have been proud of that speech, and David Blake's administration had been moving in many of the directions that Turner wanted to go.

Turner moved forward with the strategic plan for SMU initiated by Kirby during Kirby's interim service. Various deans, including Blake, provided input into the document as it was being compiled by Interim Provost William S. Babcock. Turner was on a tight deadline to deliver the plan to the Board of Trustees, and he delivered the Strategic Plan: 1996–2000 to the board by the deadline promised by Kirby. The plan had six major goals: the enhancement of teaching and learning, strengthening the university's research capability, enhancing the international focus of SMU, developing institutional partnerships, enhancing programs to aid students in their lives after graduation, and enhancing programs for the development of students' personal, spiritual, and civic maturity. The strategic plan did not sit on shelves and gather dust. Each year, key administrators throughout the university, including Blake, reported on the strategies and tactics they implemented the previous year in order to meet the specific objectives of each of the six major goals of the strategic plan.

Blake's Philosophy and Managerial Style

One very important dimension of Blake's educational philosophies and managerial style was inclusion. When he first arrived at Cox, he met in a vacant academic associate dean's office with every faculty member who wanted to meet with him. While he had some idea of what he wanted to accomplish at SMU and the Cox School, he communicated clearly to the faculty that he wanted to hear what they had to say. He realized, like most good leaders do, that without the support of the faculty at large—or at least the "key players" of the faculty—deans tend to be powerless in meeting their goals and objectives. Blake was good at selecting key faculty and convincing them that they should side with him to move Cox forward. Not everyone agreed with him, but most respected and liked him. He had an accommodating style and generally was easy to work with and for.

One very important change that Blake made was empowering his key administrative staff—the staff that did not have power through faculty rank. He felt that the staff members were critical in moving his vision and goals forward, and he gave them both the responsibilities and the power (authority) to make things happen. While there is a limit to the power that administrative staff have "over" faculty, Blake made it clear in the Cox School that the heretofore quiet and relatively powerless program directors would have a voice in his organizational structure. So obvious was the change in the Cox School in Blake's early years that some faculty complained that he gave more time to the staff than he did to the faculty. While that was not the case, some faculty believed that it was easier for staff than it was for faculty to get into Blake's office.

Blake both admitted to and delighted in his empowerment of the administrative staff. Those who worked for him in an administrative capacity thought very highly of him because he respected them. They had not always felt that way about previous deans of the school. In any event, Blake believed that the culture at Cox was a good one even before he arrived. He was convinced that the culture was flexible and accommodating and that

STRATEGIC PLAN 1996-2000
Southern Methodist University

SMU Strategic Plan 1996–2000

Cox faculty would be willing to endure change if change could be justified. That meant he had to convince the faculty that he was steering them in the right direction to improve the brand equity of the Cox School of Business. Blake would focus on the full-time MBA program in order to increase that equity.

As noted earlier, most of the faculty respected Blake fully, as did his colleagues around the university. But there were some faculty in Cox who believed that Blake steered the school down the wrong path, especially with respect to the full-time MBA program. Some also felt that his style was not as accommodating for faculty, especially in the face of bad news. They believed that Blake was a positive-thinking person and that he did not have much tolerance for bad news. Because Blake tried to institute wide-ranging changes, there were a lot of negative barbs sent his way. Many of those barbs were delivered (not necessarily originated) by Tom Barry, who finally acquiesced to being Blake's academic associate dean in late 1990. Barry feels that Blake may not have always liked the bad news that he heard, and sometimes he might not have acted upon it, but he did not openly discourage it.

Part of Blake's management style was to encourage people who got better offers to leave the Cox School to do so. He was not inclined to negotiate with faculty who told him that they were underpaid and likely would be more appreciated elsewhere. It was not that Blake did not want to keep these faculty, or that he necessarily wanted to see them leave Cox and SMU, but he was simply "against deals." He felt that most of the highly productive, quality faculty and staff were underpaid. Many of them did not seek other positions or were not sought after. Blake did not want salary differences to get so far out of line that he might create, unintentionally, a significant morale problem.

Above all, Blake valued excellent scholarship. He was well-trained and understood excellent research and teaching. He encouraged faculty to do top-quality research and publish it in the most respected academic journals. While he was a workaholic, he did not expect his administrative staff to work the long hours that he did, but he did admire and appreciate hard work and smart work. He valued people who cared and tried and did not suffer laggards well.

He looked for product champions and change agents—people like him—to implement his goals and objectives.

Finally, when Blake made up his mind, the discussions were generally over. He was a strong-willed leader and believed in his own convictions. Sometimes that would get him into trouble, but he usually got out of it. Irrespective of Blake's strengths and weaknesses, his philosophy and style, both he and the Cox School were poised for change at his arrival in January 1990.

Blake's Vision, Goals, and Objectives

When he joined SMU and the Cox School, Blake was under no specific demands, either from Ken Pye or influential external friends of the university and school, regarding a grand vision or mission for the Cox School. He knew that expectations were high given Cox's recent ascent in perceived quality, and that he would be expected to contribute to moving Cox to a new level, especially via the *Business Week* rankings. Blake knew that SMU and Cox were relatively small in size compared to the perennially top-ranked business schools and universities. He was not convinced in his own mind that Cox was ready to be a top-ten or top-twenty school, but he felt that its small size and energetic faculty, along with a newly energized staff, could move Cox in the right direction. Its small size would allow for more flexibility in the face of change, and it was change that was Blake's main mission.

For no less than twenty years prior to Blake's arrival at Cox, the business school faculty had continually assigned faculty groups to ponder the question of whether Cox should move from its highly successful one-year full-time MBA program to the more classical two-year full-time MBA program. When Barry met with Blake for the one-on-one session, one of the questions Blake posed was "What recommendations do you have for me?" Barry commented, "Whatever you do, David, do not design another planning group to study whether or not we should go to a two-year MBA program. We have been studying that issue to death and there are pros and cons on both sides." Blake commented, without hesitation, that he had already made the decision to initiate a new and innovative two-year MBA program. He reasoned that all the top MBA programs were two-year programs, and to be considered a top program Cox had to have a two-year full-time MBA program. As the faculty found out, Blake would not even consider keeping the one-year program once the two-year program was designed and ready to be implemented. And while Blake did not discourage discussion of not having a two-year program, it was clear in the minds of a few faculty that the discussion was falling upon "deaf ears." Thus, part of Blake's mission was to move Cox ahead by creating a two-year program and advancing in the rankings.

In addition to implementing a two-year program, much like his predecessor, Roy Herberger, Blake was very interested in internationalizing the curricula of the Cox School. He wanted globalization to extend to all the graduate degrees as well as to the BBA program. As part of his goal to globalize, it was his hope to be able some day to drop all the "international" adjectives from

BusinessWeek

1990 Top 20 Business School Rankings from *Business Week* magazine	
Northwestern	MIT
Pennsylvania	North Carolina
Harvard	Duke
Chicago	Virginia
Stanford	Indiana
Dartmouth	Cornell
Michigan	New York University
Columbia	Texas Austin
Carnegie Mellon	California Berkeley
UCLA	Rochester

courses. It was his feeling that a basic course in marketing, finance, organizational behavior, or any other business discipline should be taught from a world view rather than a domestic view. All courses should be global.

Thus, while Blake admitted to not having a grand mosaic or grand plan, he did have his sights set on a specific mission. That mission was to create a two-year flagship MBA program, internationalize the curricula, and move the Cox School forward in the rankings of major business schools in the United States.

Program Implementation

When Blake joined the Cox School of Business, he inherited a state-of-the-art business school facility. Three years earlier, Herberger had dedicated the new Cox Complex, which included the addition of the Maguire and Crow wings along with a significant renovation of the original Fincher Building. The new wings were connected to the original Fincher structure by internal bridges. Blake credits Herberger for his role in getting the renovation and expansion accomplished. The Fincher Building, which had originally housed all faculty and staff offices, plus all business school classrooms, essentially became administrative and faculty offices. The Maguire Building housed faculty and the undergraduate programs while the Crow Building housed faculty and graduate programs.

Shortly after Blake's arrival, it was no secret to anyone that his focus was and would remain on the graduate programs, particularly the full-time MBA program. Blake was not opposed to undergraduate education. He clearly saw the significance of the BBA program, but he also realized that most of the revenue from undergraduate programs went directly back to the central administration of the university, and he felt that, if he was going to have an impact on the graduate programs, he would have to have the budget to be able to realize that impact.

Blake was at the helm to oversee the development of several new programs, some of which had been discussed or tried by previous administrations without much success. Most of these new developments were MBA-focused. Specifically they included the new two-year, full-time MBA program (FTMBA), the Business Leadership Center (BLC), the MBA Enterprise Corps (MBAEC), globalization of the curricula, and the establishment of strategic partnerships with business schools around the world. He also supported the development of the Business Associates Program (BAP), the counterpart to the MBA Associates mentoring program.

Two-Year FTMBA

As noted above, Blake made it clear to all concerned that he would push hard for a new, two-year full-time MBA program upon his arrival at the Cox School. While he conceded that Cox had developed a very effective marketing niche with the one-calendar-year, three-trimester FTMBA, he strongly believed that Cox could not "get its due" without the traditional two-year MBA format. He did not believe that the program content had to be traditional, and he worked hard to ensure that it was not just "copycat stuff," but he did believe that the classic two-year program was necessary for Cox. He did not have full agreement from all faculty members, and there was much discussion about the downside of leaving the well-established one-year program in place.

Faculty in favor of the one-year program argued, sometimes vehemently, that Cox had gained its recent national press because of the one-year niche program. They further argued that Cox was putting out good students with the "three semester" program, and why should the school go through the trouble of instituting a totally new program that would likely end up a "cookie cutter" program? At least, the one-year supporters reasoned, Cox should keep the one-year program and maintain its market for those students who wanted the degree in just under one calendar year rather than twenty-one months with a summer off between years.

Blake, and the supporters of the two-year program, felt that Cox's one-year students were at a recruiting disadvantage in that many recruiters had suggested that they did not believe the students were getting the same quality

(quantity?) of education as their competitive peers. Further, two-year supporters agreed with Blake's assessment that Cox would never be able to stay consistently high in the business school rankings without having a two-year
program. They offered the fact that none of the business schools ranked in the
top twenty had one-year programs, or maybe more accurately stated, each of
them had a two-year program. It was further argued that the two-year program would allow Cox to develop even stronger business ties than it already
had by providing top-quality MBA candidates as interns for both profit and
not-for-profit organizations.

Blake made the decision, with support from the majority of the faculty, to
design a new two-year program and, upon its implementation, to eliminate
the popular and successful one-year program. Those who supported this position felt that the resources necessary to design, implement, and maintain an
excellent two-year FTMBA program would be considerable and maintaining
the existing one-year program in addition to the new program would create a
serious burden on the budget and support staff. The die was cast.

On September 11, 1990, just nine months after Blake's arrival at SMU and
Cox, a press release contained the following heading: "SMU's Cox School of
Business Announces New Two-Year M.B.A." In the release, Blake was quoted
as saying, "Our goal is to become one of the very best business schools in the
country. . . . But to compete with the top schools in the country, this step up
from a one-year curriculum to a full two years is an important change in our
program."

Blake's sense that his colleagues were ready for this significant change
seemed accurate. He recalled a story that, while he was a young assistant professor at the University of Pittsburgh, he was put on an MBA curriculum-revi-
sion committee. He said the committee never really made any progress for
about seven years until he became the associate dean and moved things forward. "Sometimes," he said, "things just need a little push from the top." Blake
felt, based on all of his discussions with the faculty early in his arrival at Cox,
that the faculty had planned, discussed, and debated the two-year issue long

enough and he was simply in the right place at the right time. By his accounting, Blake thought that several faculty were indifferent to the change and a few were strongly against it, but most were in favor of the refocus and resultant new program.

All new product concepts need product champions, and Blake found his in Blake Ives, an imposing figure at almost seven feet tall. Ives was a forward-thinking professor who held an endowed chair in management science. He was a creative person and had the respect as well as charm to effectively move the implementation of the two-year program. He instituted "implementation committees" rather than planning committees, and intentionally set tight

SMU NEWS RELEASE

Office of News and Information

Southern Methodist University, Box 174

Dallas, Texas 75275-0174

Contact Laura Brumley

Edwin L. Cox School of Business

214-987-7650   214-692-3678

September 11, 1990

SMU'S COX SCHOOL OF BUSINESS
ANNOUNCES NEW TWO-YEAR M.B.A.

DALLAS (SMU) — Southern Methodist University's Edwin L. Cox School of Business will expand its current one-year Master of Business Administration program to a two-year curriculum effective in the fall of 1991, Dean David H. Blake announced today. The new M.B.A. will focus on teaching the fundamentals of management from a global perspective and will feature distinctive new programs for personal development, career counseling and practical internships.

David Blake, faculty, and students at MBA orientation in new two-year program

deadlines so that no one would feel as if there was time to waste before making important decisions.

The new program would have the standard courses in accounting, marketing, organizational behavior, finance, and technology but would offer some new wrinkles. There would be a verbal and written communications requirement that would be handled through the newly developed Business Leadership Center (discussed more fully below). There would also be a social-responsibility requirement that students work in groups at not-for-profit organizations and solve a business problem or set of business problems for those organizations. There was also a social-responsibility requirement that new MBA candidates engage in a day of service for organizations such as the North Texas Food Bank. Blake felt that this social-responsibility requirement was an important one in that it made an outreach to the Dallas Metroplex community that was important for the community and was not the normal fund-raising or business linkage program typically done by schools of business throughout the country. The feedback from students was generally positive, at least until they felt the time-pinch of their credit courses.

Globalization

One of the key changes of the new MBA program, as well as the curricula in general, was globalization. Blake had a background in international affairs and a keen interest in making the Cox School curricula as globally focused as possible. He confided that it was his dream and hope that early into the twenty-first century there would be no special courses in international marketing, international finance, global organizational behavior, international accounting, and so forth. As stated earlier, he believed that all courses, even the introductory ones, should be taught from a global context. Blake had followed the hopes of Herberger with respect to globalization, although Herberger's intent to rid the Cox School of departments (disciplines) and "internationalize the faculty" did not make it very far with the Cox faculty.

Global Courses

As part of the new FTMBA program, there would be a required global course that would be taken by all MBA candidates. This course had been mandated by the AACSB. A variety of faculty, including Blake, taught the course. Some did not necessarily have the global experience that students expected in such a course. Eventually, the global requirement was dropped from the program, mostly due to student complaints about the inconsistent level of teaching brought about by the highly diverse global experiences of the faculty responsible for the course over time.

International Exchange Program

In addition to the global course, Blake created a series of strategic alliances with schools around the world that he called the International Exchange Program. Schools engaged in alliances with Cox would send a small number of their students to Cox; in turn, Cox would send small numbers of its students to alliance campuses for study. The exchange program was designed to be an elective yet integrated component of the new FTMBA program. Blake, through the efforts of Richard Stoller, director of the International Exchange Program, began developing the exchange alliances in 1991 after almost a year of planning. Cox started initially with six programs in three world zones: Pacific Rim, Western Hemisphere, and European Economic Community. Eventually, there were twelve international locations where Cox students could spend part of their MBA training; in exchange, the Cox School hosted students from the alliance schools for part of their training. Typically, the MBA students who chose the exchange option spent one semester out of their four-semester programs studying abroad.

The alliance schools included Escola de Administração de Empresas de São Paulo da Fundação Getulio Vargas, São Paulo, Brazil; Instituto Tecnológico y de Estudios Superiores de Monterrey, Monterrey, Mexico; Instituto de Estudios Superiores de Administración, Caracas, Venezuela; Manchester Business School, University of Manchester, Manchester, England; and the

Center for Business Administration, University of Antwerp, Antwerp, Belgium. Further members of the alliance were École Nationale Supérieure du Petrole et des Moteurs, Paris, France; École Supérieure de Commerce, Dijon, France; Escuela Superior de Administración y Dirección de Empresas, Barcelona, Spain; Instituto de Empresa, Madrid, Spain; International University of Japan in Niigata, Japan; Nanyang Technological University, Singapore; and the Graduate School of Management, University of Melbourne, Melbourne, Australia.

The 1994 goals of the International Exchange Program were to increase the international experiences and foreign-language skills of students, faculty who wanted to teach in the programs, and staff who would have significant interactions with these schools. Further, Blake wanted to increase student participation in the program by at least 25 percent. Because internships were an

Japanese students Naoya Kawamura, Hisashi Kinoshita, and Shinichi Numata

Fall 1994–1995 exchange students with Rich Stoller (standing left)

important component of the new two-year program, Blake wanted to provide at least two internship opportunities at each alliance school. He also wanted to provide an international trip, with tuition abatement, for what was then called the Part-time MBA Program.

The International Exchange Program published a modest newsletter called the "Exchange Network" that included students' articles describing their experiences abroad. The newsletter typically included a letter from Blake, a summary-of-the-world column, career perspectives, and a commentary from Richard Stoller. It was typical for about sixteen international students to come from alliance schools to study for a semester at Cox and anywhere from a dozen to about twenty Cox students to go abroad during the years of the program. When Blake left SMU for the University of California at Irvine, the program, as instituted by Blake, began to fade away. However, a new global program would be instituted by his successor, Al Niemi, a few years later. We will cover that in more depth in chapter 7.

MBA Enterprise Corps

One of the real coups of the Blake administration was garnering an invitation for the Cox School to be a charter member of the MBA Enterprise Corps. Fashioned after the Peace Corps, initially funded by Frank H. Kenan, and started by Jack N. Behrman at the University of North Carolina at Chapel Hill in fall 1990, the Enterprise Corps invited twenty business schools to participate in the endeavor. Sixteen accepted. In addition to Cox at SMU, the founding-member business schools came from the following universities: the University of California, Berkeley, the University of Chicago, Columbia University, Cornell University, Dartmouth University, Duke University, Indiana University, the University of Michigan, the University of North Carolina, Northwestern University, New York University, the University of Pennsylvania, Stanford University, the University of Southern California, and the University of Virginia.

Lisa and Blake Kresl in the Czech Republic for MBA Enterprise Corps

While Cox was the only one of the invitees not ranked in the top twenty-five of *Business Week,* Behrman and Blake were good friends, and Behrman knew of Blake's strong international interests. Both had written independently in the international investments and multinational corporation areas, and they had done some joint research. When Blake accepted the invitation to join the corps, he assigned Barry to manage Cox's participation. Unbeknownst to Behrman, Cox did not yet have a two-year MBA program, one of the criteria for acceptance into the corps!

When Barry attended the initial meeting and Behrman made the comment that all schools there had top-tier two-year MBA programs, Barry experienced several minutes of panic as Behrman went around the room and asked the representatives to talk briefly about the international components of their two-year programs. Just before Barry left SMU for the meeting, one of his finance colleagues commented, "Don't screw this up, Barry!" Barry, thinking the Cox

Pam and John Walter at Vatican on break from work in Poland for MBA Enterprise Corps

School might be expelled from the corps before even getting on board, simply said that Cox was designing a new two-year MBA program and was very proud to be included in the mix of schools represented at the meeting. Behrman simply responded that it was great to have Cox on board as a member but that it could not submit its one-year students as candidates for the corps. That would have to wait until the two-year program was actually implemented. Barry's heart rate slowly returned to normal, but seeing his finance colleague on campus can still generate heart palpitations!

So, the MBA Enterprise Corps was founded and consisted of a consortium of the sixteen schools that accepted the invitation. Each school sent one candidate to the corps. The candidate was a newly minted MBA graduate and would have to commit to working in a foreign country for a small- to medium-sized foreign firm for one year.

In late 1990, the corps launched a pilot program from four schools with eight MBAs. They went to Czechoslovakia, Hungary, and Poland and worked in a recording studio, venture capital fund, and organizations promoting privatization, democracy, and free enterprise. Over the first five years of the corps' existence, MBAs served in organizations in Bulgaria, China, the Czech Republic, Estonia, Ghana, Hungary, Indonesia, Lithuania, Poland, Russia, Slovakia, Tanzania, and Uganda. The major funding came from the U.S. Agency for International Development with additional contributions from foundations and corporations. Paul Fulton, president of corporate sponsor Sara Lee, commented:

> I don't know of a better training ground for future global managers than what is delivered through the MBA Enterprise Corps. The skills that Corps participants gain are immeasurable in the business environment—maturity, resourcefulness, understanding a different culture. It's these skills that place Corps members in front of their peers in post-Corps employment.

Corps members were having great times and making significant contributions. Barry finally convinced the corps administration, including Behrman, that SMU's one-year graduates were up to the task of representing the corps just as well as students from the other fifteen schools. Barry's research assistant, John Walter, had expressed a strong interest in going to Poland as a corps member and interviewed in Chapel Hill for a position. Walter was approved, and he and his wife, Pam, moved to Poland to serve in the corps. The next year, Barry's research assistant, Blake Kresl, and his wife, Lisa, ventured to the Czech Republic for service in the MBA Enterprise Corps. For several years, Cox MBAs, including Jared Houser, another of Barry's research assistants and the first African American to go to Poland, represented the Cox School in excellent fashion in developing countries around the world. The Cox School MBAs were rubbing shoulders with MBAs from the most elite business schools in the world, and those Cox ambassadors had no problems holding their own.

The corps has since moved its headquarters from Chapel Hill, North Carolina, to Washington, D.C., and has merged with the Citizens Development Corps. The Enterprise Corps now has fifty-two member schools, and since its inception it has sent more than 560 volunteers to four continents. Cox continues to participate, albeit in a much smaller way.

The Business Leadership Center

Another component of the two-year MBA was the requirement that all students go through the Business Leadership Center and pass both verbal and written communications assignments. While this was a requirement, there was no credit granted for the work. Nevertheless, students could not graduate without having passed the communications hurdles. In the September 11, 1990, press release mentioned above, Blake commented about the "integral role" of the BLC in the new MBA program. He stated, "Beginning in the first

Paula Hill, Ed Cox, and David Blake at the BLC offices

semester of the educational experience, each student will be assessed and coached on a variety of personal attributes including effective communications skills, motivational skills, planning and follow-through capabilities and sensitivity to ethical situations. . . . The center will help students graduate as business people ready to have an impact on organizations and assume leadership roles." A pilot of the leadership program was conducted on the last one-year MBA class in January 1991. As a result of its perceived success and student feedback, the BLC was to become a permanent fixture in the two-year FTMBA.

The BLC was conceived by Blake, funded by Ed Cox, and headed by Paula Hill, who remains the leader and motivator of the center today. In the first brochure printed about the center, it was stated that "The Business Leadership Center at the Edwin L. Cox School of Business was developed *by* leaders to *develop* leaders." As part of the center's activities, MBA students were required to be proficient in presentation techniques and business writing. The center provided a variety of workshops and tutorials to aid the students in meeting this proficiency requirement. Students designed their own training programs, and the center provided seminars to the students over their two-year experience. The initial program included:

FIRST SEMESTER	Academic and Career Success
SECOND SEMESTER	Communication and Interpersonal Skills
THIRD SEMESTER	Teamwork and Team Building
FOURTH SEMESTER	Coaching, Developing, Motivating, Influencing

Specific workshops and tutorials covered effective presentation techniques, leadership assessment, goal setting, advanced business writing, listening skills, communication skills, visionary leadership, teamwork fundamentals, consulting skills, managing conflict, and coaching skills. Blake believed that the BLC would provide a distinct competitive advantage for the new MBA program.

One of Cox's graduates, Joann Ferguson, managing director for Mservice in Poland commented, "Every business school tries to find a competitive advantage. The Cox School has found that in the Business Leadership Center." Many of the MBA graduates felt that the BLC provided practical, real-world training and that that training was one of the most important tools they received from their Cox MBA.

The Business Associates Program

As previously noted, the Associates Program was conceived and developed by Bobby Lyle in the early 1970s. This is a mentoring program for MBA students that consists primarily of businessmen and businesswomen providing career advice for the MBAs. In late 1988, a BBA student named Eric Ferris was sent to Tom Barry's office. Barry was then associate dean for Herberger, and Betsy Bayer (director of the undergraduate program) wanted Barry's assessment of a mentoring program for the BBA students. Barry and Ferris discussed criteria that would have to be met, and Barry voiced his concern that BBA students might not be as responsible as they should be in meeting their mentors on a regular basis. Ferris convinced him otherwise. While the Business Associates Program (BAP) was started under Herberger and supported by Acting Dean John Slocum, it gained full momentum under Blake.

Activities of the BAP included luncheon meetings, company meetings observed by the BAP students, golf outings, attendance at business seminars, and visits and executive shadowing at mentors' companies. In the first edition of the BAP white paper, the objectives were to motivate students, facilitate the process of acquainting the business community with SMU's BBA students, enhance career opportunities and career decision making, aid in the transition from the university to the business world, develop business character, and advise and educate students on business and economic trends.

The Business Associates Program has enjoyed success and continues in the Cox School of Business today. Some eighty junior and senior BBA students and another eighty businessmen and businesswomen participate in the program.

Strategic Assessment of Academic Programs

As already stated, while Blake did not have a grand planning strategy for the Cox School, based on his own admission, he did assign Barry to design a strategic assessment for all four of the academic degree programs and the Business Information Center (BIC). Herberger had started the BIC, and Blake felt that it was an important distinctive competency of the Cox degree programs. In that light, he gave full support to the BIC and its staff. The strategic assessment was, in part, driven by the call of Interim President Kirby to create and implement a strategic plan for the university as a whole. The strategic assessment of Cox's academic programs consisted of a vision statement, a credo, and value statements for teaching, research, and service.

Vision Statement

The Cox vision statement read,

> The Edwin L. Cox School of Business is dedicated to improving continuously its quality and reputation as a top-tier school noted for intellectual rigor, creative approaches to research and teaching, commitment to fostering leadership, and the development of each member of our community.

Credo

The credo for the Cox School was much longer but, in essence, it promised dedication to the following key points: the pursuit of scholarship, the discovery of and sharing of knowledge, a focus on high-quality work and professional conduct, increased ethical awareness, expansion of the vision to include peoples and activities of the world, assistance to graduates in achieving success in their initial careers, encouragement of graduates to engage in lifelong learning, assistance to graduates in becoming leaders of their communities, creation and advancement of the body of knowledge in business and management, the fostering of personal and professional development in an environment of respect, and responsibility to and for the community in which we live and work.

Teaching Value Statement

The Teaching Value Statement for the Cox School stated the faculty's and administration's commitment to the enhancement of student learning, including a commitment to provide Cox students with the most up-to-date knowledge, understanding, and insight into management and business issues. Effective curricula for the students would include those that would strike an appropriate balance between theory and practice; integrate across traditional functional boundaries; develop student competencies in problem solving, critical analysis, professionalism, teamwork, and communication; challenge students through the creation of high standards and high aspirations; and provide appropriate feedback on student performance and academic programs.

The Teaching Value Statement encouraged the development of inclusive, innovative learning and open dialogue between and among faculty, students, and administrators.

The Research Value Statement

The Research Value Statement called for the faculty to conduct research that adds to and/or improves the extant stock of knowledge in their respective and allied disciplines. It was felt that research contributed to a better understanding of business and society, especially when it was high quality and provided high visibility to the various communities in which the faculty operated. The by-product of high-quality, high-visibility research was the enhancement of the image and reputation of the individual faculty producing that research as well as the Cox School and SMU as a whole.

Research was defined as creating or empirically validating ideas and theories whether those ideas and theories were normative or descriptive. Research included the synthesis of theory as well as the creation of theory. The evidence of research might include unpublished papers as well as those published in the highest-quality journals, although it was clear that Cox was moving in a direction where the highest-quality journals in one's discipline mattered the most when research contributions were evaluated.

Research quality was to be judged by Cox School peers and colleagues, journal editors and reviewers, colleagues outside of the Cox School, and SMU administrators involved in the evaluation process. Research is a key ingredient of the Cox faculty member's portfolio, "although the nature and evidence of that research may change over the course of one's career."

Service Value Statement

Blake wanted the faculty to understand and believe that the Cox School valued the service of all faculty members at all levels. Further, Blake expected service from all faculty although, as the research criteria for tenure and promotion grew more stringent, junior faculty were required to do less service such as committee work for the school and university. As the Service Value Statement read,

> All faculty are expected to demonstrate commitment to Southern Methodist University and to the Cox School through active committee and task force participation. However, the extent of faculty participation may change with faculty rank, position in the career life cycle, and teaching and research productivity. For example, newly hired junior faculty are not normally expected to assume major committee responsibilities upon their arrival.

Most important to Blake regarding service was the message that being a good citizen of Cox and SMU was an essential component of the Cox faculty's portfolios but adjustments would be made depending upon the career life cycle and productivity of each faculty member. However, those who did engage in excellent service activities would know that they would be recognized for that service by the dean's office.

Key Accomplishments and Key People in Blake's Administration

Blake feels that many people in the Cox School, throughout the university, and in the communities outside of the university contributed to the accomplishments that occurred during his watch. He feels that the faculty's willingness to accept change, even when some of them did not believe in the direction of the change, was a key reason for his successes. Blake succeeded in hiring high-quality junior faculty from top schools and encouraging quality senior faculty to make contributions to the overall efforts of the Cox School and its programs.

Blake considers the establishment of the two-year MBA degree to be one of his most significant accomplishments during his tenure. As a whole, the faculty and administrative staff supported that venture, as noted previously. There were, however, "ankle biters" in Ives's terminology—those who would stand hard against every proposed change. Eventually, most of them came around to Blake's way of thinking with respect to the two-year program and all of the changes that were inherent in that program.

As a result of the two-year MBA and increased standards of admission to this flagship program, the image and reputation of the Cox School were enhanced within the school, around the university, and in important external communities. The Cox School was not where Blake wanted it when he left, but he left it with a better reputation than it had when he arrived. MBA student profiles and GMAT scores were increased over his tenure as dean. Job placement of graduates was improved, particularly for the FTMBAs. This happened, in part, because of Blake's commitment to make the placement office more than a "part-time affair."

Blake believed that he helped create a shift in culture in the school and in the university. He elevated the status of key administrative (non-faculty) people and convinced new junior faculty and many senior faculty that change was in their best interest as well as in the best interest of the Cox School and SMU. Improved quality of students and faculty could lead to the attraction of even more high-quality faculty and students. Blake estimates that the faculty grew from around fifty upon his arrival to sixty-five at his departure. This was important because he believed that Cox was losing good students in the admissions process because the curriculum of the FTMBA program did not offer the number of electives MBA candidates could get at competitor schools, including the University of Texas at Austin. In order to offer the electives, there had to be an ample number of faculty to do so. One final argument that Blake continually made for increasing faculty size was that it would improve Cox's reputation as these faculty met more stringent standards of teaching and research for tenure. Further, it is easier, in Blake's terms, to hide five dead-wood faculty members among a hundred colleagues rather than among just fifty colleagues. Regarding "deadwood," Blake was very willing to challenge faculty who he believed were not pulling their weight in the classroom, re-search, and/or service, even to the point of minimizing their raises.

Blake had engaged in a series of rather pointed debates with the central administration of the university regarding Cox's budget and the school's con-tributions to the university at large. He argued constantly that the business school must have more control of the revenues it produced in order to make headway against the top national elite schools of business in the United States. He was always concerned about the "excess contributions" made to the uni-versity by both the Cox School and the School of Law. Blake was not as suc-cessful in this budgeting arena as he hoped he would be, and he felt that the university was slow to make a serious budget commitment to the school.

Part of the explanation of the budget issue lies in the financial realities that were confronted by Ken Pye early on in his arrival at SMU. Shortly after Blake arrived at Cox, and as noted earlier, President Pye mandated a 9 percent budget cut across the university. No area was exempt from that drastic, but necessary measure. Blake, along with Barry and other key administrators, had to let several employees go. A few were relocated to other parts of the university, but most had to leave SMU. It was a gut-wrenching and sad time to have to let almost a dozen good people go from Cox, but the financial exigencies of the university demanded that it be done.

Another budget issue that Blake dealt with was the limitation on extra compensation that SMU faculty members could make in addition to their contractual salary. As a result of this compensation limitation, executive education in Cox was not at the level that Blake thought it should be for a school with the growing reputation of the Cox School. Blake fought to change this limitation as well as to get the university to think more entrepreneurially about the revenues generated by the EMBA and PTMBA programs. Blake felt that the SMU administration was an "undergraduate focused" administration and that it was difficult for him to convince the administration that it should be more entrepreneurial with regard to its budget.

When Blake approached the university with the recommendation that the Cox School offer its own placement service and that the investment in these funds would be a good one, the university at first balked, suggesting that placement could be done centrally. The university also suggested that Cox was spending an awful lot of money on admissions, another function that could be done centrally. In the end, Blake was successful in persuading university administrators to let go of some of the purse strings with the promise from

Blake that revenues and revenue sharing would improve both for Cox and SMU as a result of these new investments.

Because of the efforts of Gerald Turner and other SMU officials, EDS (originally Electronic Data Systems) opened one of the buildings on its educational campus to SMU. One program offered toward the end of Blake's time as dean was the MBA degree. Eventually, EDS gave four buildings to SMU, the first of which was given shortly after Blake left the Cox deanship. This location later came to be known as SMU-in-Legacy. The campus was located in Plano, Texas, where a number of high-tech professionals worked. It would be easier, Blake reasoned, for those professionals to attend an MBA program that was physically near their workplace rather than have to travel to the main campus of SMU.

Blake admits that he was not the most successful fund raiser in the history of business schools or the Cox School, but he believes that one of his important successes was getting initial funding from Ed Cox to support the Business Leadership Center. The BLC came to be known as the Edwin L. Cox Business Leadership Center as a result of Blake's deliberations with Ed Cox and the latter's generosity toward and support of the BLC. Blake states that Paula Hill, director of the Cox BLC, was the key to the tremendous success of the BLC during his administration (and today as well).

The Cox School was to go through the re-accreditation process under Blake's tenure. This is always an arduous task filled with much self-auditing and paperwork to be provided to the AACSB. The process usually takes a good two years, and the task of spearheading that re-accreditation was handed to Associate Dean Dan Costello. Costello did a good job of dealing with the bureaucracy of the process, and the Cox School sailed through the re-accreditation with flying colors.

As stated earlier, David Blake gave credit for his accomplishments to a host of people in and outside of the Cox School. Blake Ives, Paula Hill, and Dan Costello have already been mentioned. Blake felt that his two academic associate deans, while very different in backgrounds and styles, both helped him immensely. With respect to Barry, he commented, "[He] had an enormous capability of not being ruffled and keeping a broader perspective, and an absolute fierce determination that somebody's self-interest shouldn't get in the way of the educational process." Rex Thompson was "thoughtful and analytical . . . and has a sharper mind than anybody I've ever met. . . . He was instrumental in some of the budgetary issues."

Blake credits Richard O. Mason and Andrew H. Chen, endowed chairs in management science and finance, respectively, as being "the kind of senior faculty members that senior faculty members ought to be." Blake contends that he was lucky to have joined the Cox School when he did and to have quite a few endowed chairs who were willing to help, through a lot of time and talent, make possible the changes he wanted instituted.

In addition to Costello, Blake mentioned other key staff/administrators who helped him immensely in his quest for moving the Cox School to a new plateau. Among them he included Mary Sarver, who was responsible for budget operations. Sarver was a very pleasant and competent person, soft-spoken even in the heat of battle. Blake tells the story that one day a department chairman walked into her office shortly after he had been "raising hell." This chairman had just lost his temper with one of his assistants. He then went to the financial office, and by that time Sarver already had heard the story. She simply said, "Mr. Chairman, I understand that you have been misbehaving again." She completely and diplomatically disarmed the chairman, and he calmed down, admitted his guilt, and moved on with his business.

Another passionately committed staff member was Monica Powell, director of MBA programs. She initially began her career in Cox as director of the EMBA program but eventually oversaw all of the MBA programs. Powell was a bundle of energy in a small package and had extremely youthful looks. Putting her in charge of executive MBA students seemed, at first glance, a foolish thing to do. Nevertheless, Powell was up to the task and more. She understood that EMBA students had to be handled carefully. They had to be fed and pampered, and Powell was effective at that. At the same time, she had no problem mentoring EMBA students who were in academic trouble and convincing them that they had to meet the standards or leave the program.

As mentioned earlier, Betsy Bayer, a long-time Cox School employee, was the director of the BBA program. Undergraduate students loved the BBA office because everyone there provided the students with the utmost attention and care. At times, the BBA program had 1,200 students, and Bayer managed the program just as efficiently as when it had only 700 students. She would convince the faculty—many of whom were partial to MBA programs—that the BBA students were special too, and she expected the department chairs to assign their best teaching faculty to the undergraduate students as well as the graduate students.

Blake felt that he was at odds most of the time with central administration, but he gives a lot of credit to Jim Kirby for his willingness to jump into the interim president position and not just try to "keep the ship afloat." Kirby instituted, as noted earlier, the strategic plan for the university and tried to make the university more entrepreneurial in nature. During his tenure as dean of the school of theology, Kirby had experienced central administration's tendency to take from the schools to support the general programs of the university. While this is necessary, Kirby and Blake agreed that things could change to aid the individual schools but not at the expense of the university as a whole. Blake contends

Betsy Bayer, BBA director

that Kirby worked very hard to give the individual schools more voice in the process of effectively managing themselves. Blake also felt that his peer deans were all collegial and willing to help each other except maybe "when we began to talk about budgets."

Blake was perceived by his colleagues as being more of an "inside" versus "outside" dean. These are difficult pigeonholes in which to place deans, but that is what faculty do. Although Blake did not spend large portions of his time outside the school raising money, he did mention that he received significant help from several key business and social leaders in Dallas. These included Ed Cox, Cary Maguire, John Massey, several members of the Collins family, Bob Folsom, and Dorothy Cullum. All these people spent a lot of time with Blake, gave him advice and support, and helped him on his part of the journey toward the enhanced recognition and reputation of the Cox School.

Reflections on David Blake's Administration

When asked to reflect on his time as dean at the Cox School, Blake talked mostly about the positive elements of Dallas, SMU, and the school. While he felt a lot of frustration with the "fights" he endured with central administration, he felt that the Cox School got more and more support as he moved through his tenure there. He knew that Herberger had left a very good foundation, especially with facilities and the BIC. Blake felt that he himself improved upon that foundation for Al Niemi, who was to succeed him as the dean of the Cox School.

Blake remembered that when he arrived he found a school, in his terms, that was comfortable with itself and a university that was maybe a bit "country clubish." He found great comfort in turning faculty and staff who felt alienated from the system into supporters for change. That, he said, was a lot of fun. The school "allowed us to dream" and to try to realize those dreams; Blake enjoyed the opportunity to innovate and try to be different from the cookie-cutter business schools that existed. He enjoyed the challenge of improving the quality of the student body and the faculty, especially the young faculty that were hired during his tenure.

It is not unusual at any school for faculty and administrative staff to chafe at changes, but the Cox School was different according to Blake. People were generally motivated to improve the school. There were disagreements, and not everyone liked Blake or approved of the changes he wanted to make, but he was well-respected and considers himself to have been a success at Cox and SMU. Blake has fond memories of Dallas and the key people who helped him accomplish his goals. The Cox School of Business had wonderful facilities and a good technology base to support the faculty and students in their scholarship endeavors. In short, Cox was a fun culture, and it made Blake's job easier than what he experienced in his other appointments as dean.

Blake left the dean's position at the Cox School in December 1996 for personal reasons. He spent some time researching in a rather secluded office in the Fincher Building of the Cox Complex while trying to help run his wife's business. But his desire for decanal work was overpowering, and in October 1997 he left Dallas to accept the position of dean of the Graduate School of Management at the University of California in Irvine. He served in the dean's role until June 2002, and then left administration altogether to work on research as a professor of strategic management at UC Irvine.

Blake continues to research and write in the areas of multinational corporations and political economy, strategic leadership of organizations, business in technology-driven economies, and the management of universities. He continues to serve on accreditation visitation committees and is on several corporate boards. He also stays active as a management consultant for major corporations. He lives with his wife, Mary Sarver Blake, in San Luis Obispo, California.

Blake-Niemi Transition

When David Blake announced that he was leaving the deanship of the Cox School of Business, central administration named Michael E. (Mick) McGill as interim dean of the school. McGill served the Cox School in this acting capacity from December 1996 to May 1997. McGill was an extremely popular choice

David Blake relaxing in California, 2005

to serve in the interim dean position, and, like some of his predecessors, he did yeoman's work in keeping the school moving forward for Niemi's arrival.

McGill was born in northern California and trained in political science and public administration at the University of California, Santa Barbara; California State University, Fullerton; and the University of Southern California, where he earned his PhD. Prior to his arrival as an assistant professor of organizational behavior at SMU in 1971, McGill was a city planner for Garden Grove, California; a lecturer at Cal State Fullerton; and a consultant to the Center for Training and Development at USC.

McGill was a very energetic, creative, and popular professor and administrator during his tenure at SMU. He was one of the key figures in the Cox School's early venture into executive education and the executive MBA program. He was involved in much of the creative curriculum structure previously mentioned in the Grayson chapter, and he was (and is) a close colleague of Bobby Lyle and the authors. McGill's California roots afforded him the desire and willingness to be "a little different." He would throw monthly Friday afternoon parties in his office, which included a pinball machine and a variety of his own paintings and other "works of art."

When asked why he took the acting dean's position, knowing that he was often at odds with administrators, he said that he thought he had an opportunity to do some things that needed to be done before the new dean arrived at Cox. He further said that he had no illusions about being the full-time dean and that there had been, in his opinion, a disconnect with the dean's office and the faculty and he wanted to reconnect them.

While McGill agrees that interim deans cannot do a lot, especially when their terms run for only about five to six months, he felt that he made an impact on the salaries of the Cox faculty during his brief tenure as dean. One of Blake's concerns had been the relatively low faculty salaries for a business school that was trying to become an elite business school. McGill worked well with central administration to solve some of the faculty salary inequities that continued to exist in the Cox School. Also, because of his passion for teaching and his realization that teaching is the purpose of universities, McGill got the faculty to accept a more significant role for teaching at Cox and SMU. McGill was a persuasive speaker and could get an audience to "eat out of his hand." He had "hard-core" research faculty agreeing with him that teaching had to be considered significant in the Cox School. He reasoned that students paid high tuition costs and expected top-quality faculty in the classroom. They also expected to be mentored outside of the classroom. McGill had credibility with the faculty because he was perceived to be one of the premier classroom teachers both in Cox and in the university as a whole.

While McGill was dean, he instituted the Friday afternoon "fireside chat" in the very elegant room known then as the Dean's Parlor. This is the same area that was originally called the Fincher Parlor and housed many furnishings from Mrs. Fincher's home. Some consid-

Interim Dean Michael E. McGill

ered the parlor to be a somewhat extravagant room with tasteful, but lavish décor and furniture. It was here that McGill instituted the first fireside chat. He thought, "What better way to have a fireside chat than to have a real fire in the fireplace in the parlor?" Along with the fire in the fireplace, there were wine and cheese trays to soothe diverse palates. This was circa January 1997. It was a chilly afternoon, an afternoon ideal for a cozy fire. Some of the faculty in the room had been using the parlor since the early 1970s and had never seen a fire in the fireplace, and apparently for good reason! Shortly after the ceremonial lighting of the fire by McGill, the fire alarm went off and the building was cleared. Over the years, the chimney had become so clogged that there was no place for the smoke to go except back down the chimney and into the lavish parlor. The fire was quickly extinguished without injury or destruction. The fire department did not seem too upset at being called on an "almost false alarm," and the undaunted McGill continued his chat *sans* fire. Future fireside chats continued, but this was the first and last one with a "real fire." The story, however, will enjoy a very long life.

During his career, McGill was a consultant for several major firms, including Mobil Oil, Southwestern Bell, Hoechst Celanese, Brunswick, State Farm, and Associates First Capital Corporation. It was the latter organization that would offer him a significant management position, prompting him to leave SMU in May 1997. He became executive vice president of human resources and administration at the Associates. McGill made most of his mark on the Cox School not as interim dean but as a professor of organizational behavior who constantly called on himself and his colleagues to make significant changes in the way they thought, taught, and administered business education. He would always play a key leadership role in change processes. When McGill left Cox and SMU, he was missed by many. But he readied the school for the next dean, Al Niemi.

CHAPTER SEVEN

NIEMI'S DRIVE TOWARD
NATIONAL STATURE, 1997–PRESENT

I really thought I could be an agent of change and accomplish a lot
[at Cox]. Going to a small private [school] and an economic epicenter
like Dallas, Texas, was a whole new challenge.

AL NIEMI

ALBERT WILLIAM NIEMI JR. officially joined the Cox School of
Business in July 1997. He appeared at the school ready to go in June,
about a month and a half before he was officially to start. Prior to serving as
the Cox School dean, Niemi was dean at the School of Business, University of
Alabama, Birmingham, from July 1996 until June 1997. Though he spent only a
year at Birmingham, he spent fourteen years as dean at the University of
Georgia in Athens. Prior to being dean at Georgia, he held various positions as
professor and administrator, beginning with his appointment as an assistant
professor of economics at Georgia in 1968. Niemi is an economist through
and through. He earned three degrees in economics. His AB is from Stonehill
College, and his MA and PhD are from the University of Connecticut.

Niemi had early thoughts of becoming a lawyer, but his passion for the
study of economics led him to pursue that discipline. He decided early in his
career that he would become an academic, and calculates that more than fifteen thousand students have been in his courses. Niemi earned his PhD at the
age of twenty-five, was tenured at twenty-eight, became a full professor
when he was thirty-two, and was named to an endowed chair at the youthful

Dean Albert W. Niemi Jr.

age of thirty-five. He began his deanship at Georgia when he was thirty-nine years old.

When asked why he came to SMU, Niemi said that one of Cox's previous deans, Roy Herberger (chapter 5), and he had been on the accreditation team for the University of Colorado in October 1996. Herberger told Niemi that Cox was going to be looking for a new dean shortly and that Niemi should investigate the position. Niemi was a good student of economics. Though he was a native of the Northeast, it was clear to him that the liveliest financial development of the latter part of the twentieth century and the early part of the twenty-first century was going to occur in the Sunbelt. He thought that Dallas was a particularly attractive location for business and that SMU and the Cox School enjoyed a growing reputation in the academy. He thought that Cox was a "great opportunity," and if he were going to leave his current position at the time, it would be for a private university in an urban setting that was poised for economic growth. Herberger told Niemi that the Cox School offered one of the five best deanships in the country and held tremendous opportunity for advancement. So Niemi was ready for Dallas, but would Dallas be ready for Niemi and his incredible level of enthusiasm?

The Dallas Environment

When Niemi arrived in Dallas, the city's growth rate had slowed from the prior decades. In 1990, Dallas had a population of 1,006,877. Two and a half years after Niemi's arrival, the population of Dallas had grown to only 1,083,500 by the start of the new century. This growth only represented approximately 8,000 persons annually over the decade. Nevertheless, the Dallas Metroplex area continued to attract new residents from all regions of the United States and the world, with cities such as Richardson, Plano, Irving, Garland, Mesquite, and Duncanville emerging as important entities in the area. Dallas's vibrant economic environment continued to attract regional and national corporate headquarters, and its entrepreneurial spirit continued to attract small- and medium-sized businesses along with the corporate giants.

Changing downtown Dallas skyline

So from the time of the founding of Dallas in 1841 to the arrival of Niemi, Dallas had grown from a log cabin along the banks of the Trinity River and an estimated population of twenty-five families to a Metroplex of over one million persons, one of the ten largest cities in the United States. SMU had always relied on the resources of Dallas and its generous citizens to help support the mission and goals of the university and of the school of business since its inception in 1921. As we will see, Niemi would take advantage of Dallas's interest in and support of SMU and the Cox School.

The SMU Environment

Niemi began his Cox deanship just a little over two years after Gerald Turner's arrival as SMU's tenth president. As stated in the previous chapter on David

Blake, Turner had inherited a strategic plan from Interim President Kirby and continued to move forward with the strategic plan, placing his own imprimatur on the strategic direction of SMU. Turner also initiated two other major planning tools shortly after his arrival at SMU in June 1995. The first was the development of a master plan for the future renovation of old buildings and the construction of new buildings for the SMU campus. The second was the most ambitious capital campaign ever developed by an SMU president.

The SMU Centennial Master Plan was developed because of Turner's interest in assuring students, faculty, staff, alumni, friends, and supporters of SMU that there was a plan for the effective and efficient use of the limited space on SMU's campus. The campus is landlocked, and donors were beginning to show interest in providing significant funding for new, expanded, and renovated buildings. There had to be a plan in place that could guide, in some orderly fashion, the efficient and effective location of these future buildings. A local architect, Good Fulton & Farrell, was hired to work with key administrators to design and implement the plan. The SMU Centennial Master Plan was designed and approved by the Board of Trustees in May 1997.

Under the master plan, Niemi and his colleagues in the Cox School witnessed the continuing change of the physical landscape of the SMU campus. More than twenty-five major new construction, renovation, and infrastructure projects have been completed during Turner's administration at this writing. Among these projects are the Fondren Library Center, with the Laura Bush Promenade; the Perkins Chapel renovation; Gerald J. Ford Stadium and Paul B. Loyd Jr. All-Sports Center; Meadows Museum and parking garage; two additional parking garages; Junkins Electrical Engineering Building; Doak Walker Plaza; the Calatrava *Wave* sculpture; Fondren Science Building renovation; Laura Lee Blanton Student Services Building; the James M. Collins Executive Education Center (part of the Cox School of Business); and the expansion and renovation of the Dedman Center for Lifetime Sports. The funding necessary for all of these projects was approximately $300 million.

In order to help fund these and other building projects as well as new academic programs, endowed chairs for faculty, and financial aid for students,

Turner put together the most successful capital campaign—Campaign for SMU: A Time to Lead—in the history of SMU. At the completion of the campaign, it was labeled the most successful fund-raising venture in the history of the North Texas area. Turner and his colleagues raised the impressive sum of $542 million. In seven short years, Turner had changed the financial and physical landscape of Southern Methodist University.

Not one to rest on his laurels, President Turner led the charge for the second strategic plan for SMU—Strategic Plan 2001–2005: Education for Leadership in a Global Society. This continuation of the strategic planning process reaffirmed the initial six goals in the first plan but incorporated a new goal, the enhancement of the academic quality and competitiveness of SMU. Turner and his key development colleagues are in the preliminary stages of the next capital campaign and are planning the festivities for 2011 to celebrate the one hundredth anniversary of the founding of SMU.

In a recent speech to the South Central Jurisdiction of the United Methodist Church, Turner reaffirmed his commitment to his values and mission for SMU. In part, he said:

Laura Lee Blanton Student Services Building

My model for this University was "SMU in Dallas," responsive to its partnerships and influenced in its formation by the historic forces of the United Methodist Church and the citizenry and culture of Dallas, but with a national and even international mission to be listed among the premier private universities. This means that we won't just be a liberal arts college for the Church, nor will we just be a confederation of professional schools for the city. We have to maintain a strong core of liberal arts requirements for all graduates, as well as provide nationally ranked professional and graduate schools. . . . There has to be a model that provides enough flexibility to allow universities going forward to attract and empower the enormous support from diverse corners that is required to attain national distinction and still be meaningfully related to the Church. Our model for SMU requires it, and we are committed to helping develop it.

So what Robert Stewart Hyer began in 1911, Turner continues ninety-five years later. SMU is an institution that is proud of its Methodist heritage as well

Capital Campaign kickoff, April 18, 1997

as its original partnership with the small city of Dallas and its continued partnership with the large city of Dallas and the surrounding Metroplex. This heritage and partnership, along with the continuing stream of faculty, students, and staff who come and go from this institution, consistently keep its presidents focused on enhancing the substance and quality of the educational experiences at SMU. It is, then, with this more recent backdrop of Dallas, the city, and SMU, the university, that Al Niemi began his tenure as the eighth dean of the Edwin L. Cox School of Business.

Al Niemi's Philosophy and Managerial Style

As noted in the discussion of Dean Blake's tenure, deans do not like to be characterized as "inside deans" or "outside deans." But, in reality, each dean has his or her own strengths that lead to such characterizations. As we will see, Niemi has made, and continues to make, extensive changes inside the organization of the Cox School of Business. Few would refute this. But compared to the majority of his predecessors, his most significant influence can be seen and felt among the external constituencies of the Cox School.

When one first meets Niemi, she or he finds a man nattily dressed, with a large smile, firm handshake, a pat on the back, and words of enthusiasm about the futures of Dallas, SMU, and the Cox School of Business. And because he is well trained as an economist, he always has a "list" of numbers supporting his optimistic predictions for the three partners. Niemi also has a keen sense of marketing. He understands selling, public relations, and the broader discipline of marketing. His presence exudes enthusiasm, and it is evident that he has both a passion and a love for being the dean of the Cox School.

When Niemi asks business executives to interact with the Cox School, he does not just ask them to be guest lecturers, donors, or advisors. He asks them for a "passionate commitment" to the school—its students and faculty—for the long haul. He expects all the guest lecturers to become part-time instructors and all the advisors to become involved in the mentoring programs of Cox or its Executive Board. He tells the business community that he needs their passion, their involvement, and their true engagement with the Cox School and SMU.

Part of Niemi's style is to do his homework—to get engaged in the business at hand. When he first arrived at SMU, he spent the better part of his first one hundred days "working the Dallas community" so that he knew all the major players and they knew him, his faculty, his students, and his ambitions. During those first one hundred days, Niemi says he met more than one thousand constituents or constituents-to-be at breakfasts, lunches, and dinners. He also spent time "walking the halls of the Cox complex" getting to know the faculty on a first-name basis. Niemi was hired because of his significant experience as a dean and his engaging, enthusiastic personality. SMU's administration as well as the faculty of the Cox School knew that more had to be done in the future than had been done in the past in the fund-raising arena for Cox. In this regard, Niemi fit in perfectly with Turner's capital campaign plans and goals.

Niemi rightly believes he had the support of the Cox faculty to be "out and about," inspiring past and prospective donors about the futures of Cox and SMU. Niemi's philosophy is about attaining the very highest quality faculty and students and encouraging their interactions with each other. Fund raising is only a means to achieve the quality necessary to advance into the group of elite schools of business. In his words, "fundraising is all about creating the support of the faculty, creating the scholarships to entice the students to come here, providing them a terrific experience while they are here, and then helping them get started in their careers." This is what an external dean must do. But Niemi goes on to say, "I've always told prospective deans, or young deans, that you really can't go outside and be an ambassador for your school until you have the support of your faculty. You can't be an external dean if things aren't right inside."

Since his arrival at SMU, Niemi has been focused on business school rankings. When Cox is ranked high in one of the top five polling magazines, Niemi raises and waves the banners of achievement through the halls of the Cox School. He is not bashful about bragging about the placement of Cox near the

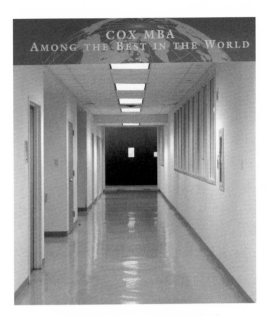

A rankings banner at the Cox School

elite schools of business in the country and the world. He is constantly doing public relations work to get the Cox School of Business name among those who can help the reputation and image of the school. But Niemi is a realist. He understands the fragile nature of "newcomers" to the top of the rankings heap; he also knows that Cox must have the products—the successful graduates—who rise quickly through the ranks of their respective organizations and provide both positive publicity for Cox and human and financial resources for its students, faculty, and programs.

In short, Niemi hires the very best faculty and staff that he can. He insists that his program directors continue to raise the bar for admission standards in all the Cox School programs, particularly the FTMBA program. He "wheels and deals" with important players in the local, regional, and national SMU communities. He is a passionate ambassador for Cox and SMU. The remainder of this chapter looks at the impact that he has made at the Cox School since his arrival in mid-1997.

Vision and Goals

In our interviews with the deans, we always asked if they received any specific directives from the president of the university. Most said they had not, but Niemi indicated that he was assigned one specific goal by Gerald Turner. As part of his formal interview for the job at Cox, Niemi had breakfast at the Doubletree with Turner. Niemi said, "Gerald made it very clear what the marching orders were." Those orders were to increase the visibility of the dean and the Cox School in the Dallas business community. Turner knew that previous deans had made inroads, but he felt that a significantly larger presence in Dallas for the Cox School was essential to his lofty aspirations for the university and the Cox School.

Niemi had no objection to this goal because he fully understood that if the business community would get "engaged with the school" that engagement would work to the benefit of SMU and Cox students, especially through the creation of jobs for students. Turner's directive was also congruent with Niemi's perceptions that there was much development work to be done at the Cox School, and Niemi made development one of his key goals. Niemi considered this goal a "no brainer" and one that was crucial to him and the university if the Cox School and SMU were to be successful in engaging Dallas business constituents. He knew how to relate to the business community, and he knew how to raise money. He had the ability to get external constituents excited about the Cox School, and his goal of significantly enhancing the development operations of Cox was in tune with his overall vision to improve the quality of the faculty, student body, and alumni relations.

Niemi believes that "an academic institution can never be better than the accomplishments of [its] alumni." He says that universities and business schools are in the people business, and the quality of the students and faculty makes the reputations of those universities and business schools. Where students go for their careers when they leave universities and business schools is an important barometer of reputation. According to Niemi, Harvard and Stanford are what they are because they have outstanding students and faculty, and the graduates of these business schools tend to "go very far when they hit the workplace." In short, then, the importance of development is to get funding to provide adequate support for the highest-quality students and faculty, who will, in turn, enhance the Cox School's reputation.

Cox alumni giving had been at about 8 percent when Niemi arrived, and he felt he could increase participation to 40 percent—at least that was (and remains) his goal. Niemi was amazed that there was no history of class giving in the Cox School. That would change early in his tenure. Niemi's goals also included focusing on the FTMBA program, the program most deans of business schools consider their flagship program. In spite of what people might think about rankings (we will have more to say about them later), they are considered important to students in choosing what business school to attend.

When Niemi first arrived at SMU and the Cox School, business school rankings focused mostly on full-time MBA programs. Once he ramped up the MBA programs at Cox, Niemi also had a goal to improve the quality of students seeking the BBA degree. He would develop new emphases in the BBA program, including the very successful BBA Scholars program, to which we will return shortly.

We stated earlier that, while Niemi is a trained economist, he has a good flair for "all things marketing." One of his strongest suits is public relations, and as part of his overall development and quality-improvement goals, Niemi had the goal of providing a significant infusion of life and energy into Cox marketing and communications activities, including national public relations programs. It was important to Niemi that both SMU and Cox became "players" in the national media. Niemi felt that the enhancement of the reputation of the Cox School of Business was in large part a function of the continuing enhancement of the name of Southern Methodist University as well. Rankings became an important part of Niemi's overall development vision for the Cox School.

Another important "no-brainer goal," according to Niemi, was the expansion and upgrading of the Cox School's executive education activities. This

Kevin Knox (left) and alumni in Newport, California

was one of the ideas that he and Interim Dean McGill had discussed. Both correctly believed that Dallas was a great market for executive education, and there was no reason why the Cox School could not provide a significant portion of the executive development needs of the local and regional business communities. After all, Cox and Dallas had partnered in executive education for decades. One program that had excellent regional and local reach was the Southwest Graduate School of Banking (SWGSB) mentioned in chapter 3. SWGSB is housed in the Cox School's Collins Executive Education Center.

Like deans who preceded him, particularly Herberger and Blake, Niemi also sought to make a mark for the Cox School through more extensive globalization efforts. Further, he was also interested in providing better career

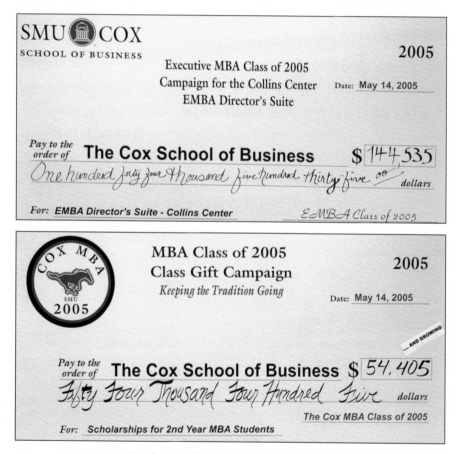

Graduation gifts from EMBAs and FTMBAs

services to both graduate and undergraduate students. Finally, Niemi still holds the aspiration, if not a specific goal, to have a PhD program associated with the Cox School. Only three top-fifty business schools—Tuck at Dartmouth, Georgetown, and SMU—do not have doctoral programs. Niemi realizes that PhD programs are very demanding on human and financial resources, but he believes that Cox should have some kind of a program at the PhD level, even if it is in cooperation with another school within the university.

So Al Niemi hit SMU running with the goals of enhancing development, alumni relations, and Dallas business community relations and, at the same time, significantly improving upon the quality of the faculty and students and their experiences in the Edwin L. Cox School of Business.

Goal Implementation

Niemi's contention is that development and fund raising are activities that provide means to an end. Development is crucial to establish commitments, and fund raising is crucial to attain financial resources. This is especially true in private universities and schools, and is becoming even more critical in public universities and schools. But these resources, Niemi would argue (and correctly in our opinion), simply provide the means for enhancing the reputation of the Cox School. And in order to enhance its reputation, the Cox School must have outstanding faculty, outstanding students, outstanding staff and administrators, and outstanding programs.

Development under Niemi

As noted earlier, Niemi spent his first one hundred days meeting one thousand key constituents. He quickly implemented Turner's directive to become significantly more visible in the Dallas business community. Through scores of breakfast, lunch, and dinner meetings, Niemi became highly visible among key Dallas business people. He did not, however, stay glued to the city of Dallas. Niemi quickly learned that in the previous seventeen years prior to his

Al Niemi (left) at alumni reception, Washington, D.C.

arrival there had been only two key Cox School events outside the state of Texas. One occurred in New York and the other in Los Angeles. During his first year, he and Assistant Dean Kevin Knox conducted fourteen events outside of Texas. Knox had been Niemi's director of development for seven years before they both arrived at SMU. He is now executive director of the Cox Alumni Association as well as Niemi's assistant dean.

As part of his outreach to the Dallas and broader communities, Niemi made significant changes in the composition of the Executive Board. Upon his arrival, about 90 percent of the Executive Board members were from Texas and 85 percent were from Dallas. Today the Cox School Executive Board is much more geographically diverse with the number of members from Houston going from four to nine and the number from other states rising from six to thirteen. Additionally, Niemi has increased the gender and ethnic diversity of the board, increasing the number of women from seven to twelve and the number of minorities from zero to seven. There are also two members from Mexico on the board. Niemi has stated on many occasions and in front of many different audiences that he believes he has one of the most supportive boards of any business school dean in the country.

Holding firm to his belief that a business school can go only as far as its alumni, Niemi made it a point to find out where his alumni had gone. Prior to Niemi's arrival, there was not what he refers to as a "formal alumni relations program for Cox alumni"; the school had not developed a strong alumni association. And the alumni giving rate for the Cox School was, in his terms, "a pathetic 8 percent," a rate he believed to be one of the lowest for business schools in the country. At the time of our interview with Niemi, he said that 25 percent of Cox alumni were now giving annually to the school, and he hoped to someday achieve a 40-percent rate—high but achievable according to Niemi. A 25-percent giving rate is about average for good business schools, but the very best achieve the 40-percent figure, and some have even higher rates.

As part of his alumni outreach program, Niemi launched *Cox Today* and the *Cox Review.* These are both professional publications filled with intriguing glossy photos and stories about the Cox School and its faculty, students, and alumni. *Cox Today* is published and distributed twice annually while the *Cox*

Cox Executive Board in action

Review is published and distributed once a year. Both are targeted to the more than thirty thousand Cox alumni and approximately five thousand friends of the Cox School. Alumni and friends also receive a weekly electronic newsletter.

Under Niemi, the Cox School established a formal alumni reception program in major cities throughout the country. At last count, twenty-five cities were visited for alumni receptions, including such cities as Atlanta, Boston, Chicago, Dallas, Houston, London, Mexico City, New York, San Francisco, and Washington, D.C. Further, Dallas–Fort Worth area alumni now gather monthly to hear about the activities of the Cox School. Niemi also developed a thick directory of alumni and established an International Alumni Board. The board meets twice annually with one meeting at SMU and the other off campus. Members of the board come from more than a dozen states stretching from New England to California, as well as other countries, including Mexico, Brazil, and India.

Under Niemi's leadership of the Cox School, endowment has increased from $78 million to $142 million. Prior to Niemi's arrival, only forty-six gifts totaling $100,000 or more had been given to Cox, but during his first eight years, ninety-five gifts of $100,000 or more were received.

The Collins Center is the fourth building serving the Cox School of Business. It is the home for working professionals enrolled in Cox's executive MBA program as well as for working professionals who want to continue their education through executive development offerings. In addition, the Collins Center, a four-story, 67,000-square-foot building, houses the Southwest Graduate School of Banking (as noted earlier), the KPMG Institute for Corporate Governance, and the Norman E. Brinker Institute for Restaurant and Hospitality Management. The $19-million facility has five classrooms, the Crum Auditorium with seating for three hundred people, a large ballroom, an atrium, a dining room, a boardroom, conference rooms, fifteen breakout rooms, an executive lounge, a business center, and staff offices for executive programs. Almost fifty corporate foundations and sponsors contributed to the Collins Center, joined by individuals on the Cox Executive Board and other significant friends of the Cox School.

Cox Today

Cox Review

Most would agree that Niemi played one of the most significant roles as dean of the Cox School in creating friends in the Dallas and broader communities, and harnessing major financial and human support for achieving excellence at the Cox School of Business.

Niemi's Pursuit of Faculty Excellence

When Niemi started as dean of the Cox School in the fall of 1997, the school had sixty-two faculty. Under his leadership the number has increased to seventy-four. Over half (thirty-nine out of seventy-four) of Cox's full-time faculty have been hired during Niemi's first eight years. Further, the Cox School, at this writing, has twenty endowed chairs. Four remain open, but when these are filled, about 25 percent of the Cox faculty will hold a chair. Niemi states that teaching is very important in his hires, but there is little question that a faculty member's potential to add to the research skills of the existing faculty is very critical to Niemi and his colleagues. He hires faculty from "brand-name schools"; these scholars have illustrated the potential, even in their doctoral programs, to be top-quality researchers. He, like many deans and department chairs, looks for "research star" potential.

In fact, as Niemi told us in his interview, he seeks faculty who are both excellent researchers and excellent teachers. Niemi, his senior associate dean, William R. Dillon—a member of the Marketing Department and a nationally known researcher—and the faculty members' respective department chairs evaluate faculty annually, a process instituted and followed by several previous deans. Niemi states that 50 percent of a faculty member's evaluation is based on teaching (and 50 percent on research), and he believes that it is very important, especially in a private university, to focus on high-quality teaching and reward it when it is attained. Only certain faculty can excel at both teaching and research. And they are in high demand from universities and business schools all over the country.

Americans love rankings. The world loves rankings. And rankings are important—in almost all walks of life. Research productivity rankings are published on a regular basis across disciplines in business schools as well as other major academic units in universities. Who are the most productive scholars? What are the best journals? What schools and universities employ the most productive scholars? What schools and universities produce the most productive scholars? On October 1, 2004, Niemi sent Provost Ross Murfin a memo highlighting the research productivity of the faculty in the Cox School. Based on a paper in the *Academy of Management Journal,* co-authored by Niemi and published in 2000, Niemi told Murfin that the Cox School ranked thirty-seventh in publications in the top two or three journals in each business school field between 1986 and 1998, and thirty-fifth for the more recent period 1994 to 1998. Niemi said to Murfin, "This performance is quite remarkable when you consider that the research rankings are not adjusted for the size of faculty and we are competing with large public universities with two to three times more faculty."

Niemi went on to provide Murfin further evidence of the scholarly efforts of the Cox School faculty. He told Murfin that in a more recent research paper, published in 2003, authors from Rice and Pepperdine examined the research productivity of business school faculty across eight business disciplines by measuring the number of citations in scholarly journals. The researchers ranked the top thirty universities. SMU ranked among the top thirty in five disciplines: economics, finance, information systems, marketing, and strategy. Only Harvard, MIT, Stanford, Michigan, Chicago, NYU, and UCLA were ranked across all disciplines. Niemi closed his memo to Murfin by stating that SMU's Cox School had compared very well to several of its benchmark business schools at universities such as Vanderbilt, Emory, Washington (Saint Louis), Georgetown, and Notre Dame.

We will talk more about what makes a business school outstanding and the role of teaching and research in that ranking process in our final chapter. Suffice it to say for now that since the middle 1970s, SMU's business school has sought to increase the number of research stars on its faculty as well as add excellent classroom teachers. This effort was begun by Alan Coleman and continued through the tenures of Herberger, Blake, and now Niemi. Quality faculty beget quality faculty. Quality faculty are well known nationally. National

Collins Executive Education Center

reputations, as a general rule, are built upon excellent research records and not excellent teaching records.

During his interview, Niemi said that until two years ago he had never lost a faculty member that he wanted to keep. While at Cox, and in contrast to some of his predecessors, Niemi made some very high salary adjustments to keep certain key people. But he also lost several key faculty. He noted, however, that those faculty were lost because of personal decisions that he could not overcome, and it was unlikely, according to Niemi, that even significant salary increments could have kept them. In the last analysis, Niemi understands the importance of quality faculty, and he works hard to hire the very best faculty available.

The Pursuit of Excellent MBA Students

In the early 1970s, the average Graduate Management Aptitude Test (GMAT) score for the full-time MBA (FTMBA) program candidates at the school of business was in the low 500s. When Niemi joined the Cox School, that average had risen to 600 and, as a quality indicator, was not among the top fifty programs in the United States. In 1998, the GMAT average rose to 612, and Cox MBAs in the full-time program were tied for fiftieth place with their peers at the universities of Florida and Tennessee. However, by 2003, only five years later, the average FTMBA GMAT score was 665, placing Cox twenty-sixth among top-fifty business school FTMBA programs. For various reasons, not the least of which was the dwindling number of applications of students to FTMBA programs nationwide, the Cox average dropped slightly (661) in 2004, but Cox moved up two spots in the top-fifty rankings to twenty-fourth.

At this point it is important to note that there has been a sharp decline in the national enrollment of students in FTMBA programs over the last five or so years, but a sharp increase in the enrollment in part-time MBA programs. By early 2004, 80 percent of graduate business students were enrolled in weekend or evening programs, and full-time enrollment had declined by 20 percent. These national enrollment trends have been similar at the Cox School.

From 1997 to 2004, FTMBA enrollment fell from 272 to 212 students, a significant decrease. However, the professional or part-time MBA (PMBA) program increased during that time from 404 to 621, a very significant increase. Further, over the same period of time, executive MBA (EMBA) enrollment increased from 116 to 164 candidates. In short, during that time span, Cox's graduate enrollment increased overall by 26 percent.

While rankings of business school programs originally focused on FTMBA programs, the pollsters soon began ranking EMBA programs, and then finally part-time or professional MBA (PMBA) programs. Throughout the 1990s and into this decade, the Cox EMBA program has enjoyed a strong reputation. Cox EMBAs now rank second in the nation based on number of years of work experience and second in the nation based on starting median salaries. EMBA students are typically local students since they work full time for area businesses. Students recently admitted to the program come from over fifty companies, including firms such as 7-Eleven, Accenture, Blockbuster, EDS, GE, Motorola, Nokia, State Farm, Texas Instruments, Dow Chemical, Verizon, and Wells Fargo.

Cox School PMBA students also have strong credentials, and Cox ranks among the nation's twenty most selective programs for working professionals. Again, like EMBA students, PMBA students are local residents working for a variety of firms. Recent classes hail from more than eighty local businesses,

Cox EMBA/PMBA Rankings	1997	1998	1999	2000	2001	2002	2003	2004	2005
EMBA									
Business Week	NR		Top 20		19		18		16
U.S. News & World Report					12	19	15	14	15
Financial Times					24	19	24	15	30
PMBA									
U.S. News & World Report			NR	NR	NR	NR	22	14	12
Forbes									10

Associate Board mentor Bobby B. Lyle and students

including companies like American Airlines, Bell Helicopter, Citigroup, Deloitte & Touche, Hewlett-Packard, IBM, JC Penney, Lockheed Martin, and Trammell Crow. The PMBA program has been enhanced by participation in the Business Leadership Center, Career Services, and the Global Leadership Program.

The BBA Scholars Program

As noted above, Niemi's early focus upon his arrival to SMU's Cox School was graduate programs. However, in 2002, Niemi felt that the quality of the BBA student body could be significantly enhanced, and he launched the BBA Scholars Program. This program allowed first-year students to be admitted directly into the Cox School for purposes of interacting with Cox counselors and receiving invitations to select Cox School speaker series. The new BBA Scholars Program injected a high dose of quality to the undergraduate business school program, a program historically considered among the strongest in the country by pollsters. Program administrators, principally Stephanie

Dupaul and her staff, visited 215 high schools in 2003–2004 and planned to visit 250 in 2004–2005.

The Cox School Executive Board supports the BBA Scholars Program to a large extent. Board members currently account for twenty-six of the forty-three scholarships in the BBA Scholars Program, each representing a commitment of $20,000—funded in four $5,000 annual payments. The remaining seventeen scholarships came from the Cox School endowment. Early results are promising. The class of 2007 has 119 students enrolled in the program with an average Scholastic Aptitude Test (SAT) score of 1309 compared to SMU's average for all undergraduates of about 1200. The class of 2008 has 114 students enrolled with a 1329 SAT average, and the class of 2009 has a 1336 average. Niemi admits that the litmus test of the success of this program will be to see how the BBA Scholars do in the job market in 2007 and beyond. He has a lot of confidence in the quality of these particular BBA students and expects them to do very well in their careers.

The BBA Scholars Program caps twenty-five years of increasing quality at the undergraduate level. The minimum grade point average for admission has risen from 2.5 to 3.2. It should be noted that the Cox School has always been attractive to good students because it has consistently staffed undergraduate courses with some of the school's best faculty.

Of course, the improvement in the quality of the BBA program has fostered a change in the profile of undergraduates, much as the character of the MBA students has changed. In the Grayson era, the undergraduate student primarily came from Texas and the Southwest, with the Midwest the next most significant recruiting pool. While these areas are still popular, both SMU's and Cox's reputations and national recruiting efforts have created a broader national base for students.

Student Services Enhancements

As we noted in earlier chapters, the Cox School Associate Board, a mentoring program for MBA students, was established in the early 1970s and has provided invaluable career counseling and internship services. Niemi has strengthened the Associate Board by (1) adding about fifty executives to the board, (2) diversifying the board to include a substantial increase in the number of female and minority members, (3) improving the access of the board members to the MBA students through electronic means as well as with a number of structured social interactions between students and mentors, and (4) hiring an Associate Board Coordinator. All mentors are now on the Cox Web site, and matching of students and mentors is more efficiently and effectively facilitated through a host of on-line processes. The coordinator can provide both mentors and students with a consistent contact who is always available when there are questions, challenges, comments, or issues to be discussed.

Prior to Niemi's tenure as dean of the Cox School, the MBA Career Management Center (CMC) was open only to FTMBA students. Previous deans had worried about the reaction of corporate partners who were sponsoring students in the part-time and executive MBA programs to the school providing career advice to those sponsored students who might move to other companies upon completion of their MBA degree requirements. Niemi did not have this concern, especially after canvassing about twenty major employers of Cox's PMBA students. The companies felt that if they were not attractive enough to keep their employees without the SMU degree, they would not be able to keep them with it either. So Niemi and his colleagues opened up the CMC to both PMBA and EMBA students, and the students in these two degree programs now account for about 50 percent of the career counseling appointments in the center.

Historically, BBA students in Cox relied upon the University Career Counseling Center, now known as the Hegi Career Center. In an effort to improve career counseling and advising to undergraduate students in Cox, Niemi launched Cox BBA Career Services Group, which works closely with the university's Hegi Center. Through its interaction with the Hegi Center, Cox Career Services enhances the career-search process for BBA students and undergraduate corporate business recruiters. As an example, during the 2003–2004 academic year, Cox career service professionals held over 850 meetings with Cox

BBA students to advise them on their futures. The feedback Niemi receives from students and recruiters suggests that the new program in career counseling for undergraduates has had a very positive impact on the undergraduate experience in the Cox School.

MBA Globalization

Niemi feels that the globalization of the MBA curriculum is essential in order to effectively educate Cox's MBA students and compete with other MBA programs for the same top-quality students. In 1999, Niemi launched the American Airlines Global Leadership Program, which required all FTMBA students to participate in a global experience, and for which they receive four credit hours.

Cox Global Leadership Program in Shanghai, China

The program involves study in Europe, China, India, and Latin America. At the start of their first year of study, the students begin an intensive study of the business and culture of the country that they will visit. They spend six months preparing a document that can reach two hundred pages in length to help prepare them for their trip. Following this comprehensive research program, Cox FTMBA students travel abroad for two agenda-filled weeks of interactions with business leaders, public officials, and others to reinforce their understanding of major global economic and business issues.

The students are then required to present what they learned in a seminar format upon their return. International students are not allowed to return to their home countries for international study but must travel to another foreign country. Thus, students from Japan cannot go to any Asian country but must go to Europe or Latin America. Over the five years of the program to date, students have visited Taipei, Shanghai, Beijing, Hong Kong, Tokyo, Kyoto, Nara, Osaka, Seoul, or India. In Latin America, they have learned about global business in Monterrey, Santiago, Buenos Aires, São Paulo, and Rio de Janeiro. In Europe, London, Paris, Zurich, Munich, Frankfurt, Stockholm, and Budapest have been host cities for the MBA students.

Niemi's initial globalization thrust was directed toward the FTMBA program. Since its launching, however, he has moved the global experience to both the PMBA and EMBA programs, although EMBA students have had a global experience requirement for more than fifteen years. Cox PMBA students can study abroad in several different countries, including Mexico, France, China, Germany, Denmark, and India. Cox EMBA candidates are required to have two global experiences. At the end of their first year of study, they travel to Latin America. In the spring semester of their second year of study, they travel to China.

BBA Leadership Institute

As noted in the last chapter, on Blake, the FTMBA program has had a Business Leadership Center (BLC) since early in the 1990s. As he did with the BBA

Scholars Program, Niemi sought to further enrich the BBA experience by launching a counterpart program to the BLC that he called the BBA Leadership Institute (BBALI). It is a BLC for BBA students. It provides a voluntary, non-credit course, and in its first offering over one hundred BBA Scholars enrolled. The undergraduates experienced a crash course in presentation skills. They were taped giving presentations during the first week of class, then during the last week of class. Niemi says that the results were nothing short of "miraculous." These first-year scholars turned from often-terrified speakers to very confident speakers during the course.

Modular MBA Courses

Always keeping one eye on the competition, Niemi became disenchanted that the Cox School's MBA curriculum continued to maintain the traditional fifteen-week semester format for all of its courses. He observed that many of the benchmark competitors were about to implement or had already implemented integrated modular course systems. In effect, semesters are divided into smaller time blocks so that a semester might contain as many as nine courses rather than a more traditional number, say five, courses. Modules also encourage greater integration of content from different disciplines.

European schools of business moved to the modular program in the 1980s. According to Niemi, the Cox faculty "went kicking and screaming," but after two to two and a half years of persuasion by Associate Dean Dillon, the modular system was instituted in the FTMBA program. Niemi believes the modular system offers MBA students more course alternatives, and the courses themselves provide more "meat" for the students. There tends to be less redundancy in elective courses across areas, and students frequently have two concentrations of study (e.g., marketing and finance) instead of just one as they had under the traditional three-credit-course system. For faculty, modules often allow them to carry their full teaching loads in one semester and devote the next semester to research. As with any curricular program, the modular system is not perfect. Some faculty and students still have not totally accepted it. Nonetheless, it is the program of choice for many top-ranked FTMBA programs. The PMBA program also offers an integrated modular system and requires forty-eight credit hours to complete. The EMBA program employs the integrated modular style; however, under the cohort or team approach, elective courses are chosen to suit the cohorts as a whole.

Key Accomplishments and Key People in Niemi's Administration

While Niemi feels that he has made some excellent headway in moving the Cox School of Business toward greater national prominence, he knows that much work is to be done in spite of the accomplishments that have been achieved.

Cox School Rankings

Niemi is a master promoter, and one of the key signs of prominence for business schools is business school rankings. In spite of concern about the reliability of rankings, students, faculty, and the business world use them to "sanction" a business school's place in the status hierarchy. One measure of a business school dean's success is the upward movement of his or her school in the rankings (or maintenance if it sits at the top). Niemi admits that rankings have their problems, but he also knows, based on feedback from Cox students, that the students use rankings in the decision-making process, especially regarding graduate school selection. Says Niemi, "So my focus on the rankings is that I think we have to take them seriously because students look at them. . . . Every student [I interviewed] over the last two years has looked at *Business Week* and the *Wall Street Journal*. . . . And about half of them are looking at *U.S. News & World Report*. . . . I pay attention to them [the rankings] because I know especially *Business Week* and the *Wall Street Journal* have the capacity to drive a lot of business our way. . . . I'd love to be in everybody's top twenty-five."

Niemi rightly contends that reputation lags behind the reality of quality in business school programs, both on the way up as well as on the way down the status ladder. Much of the rankings has to do with the public's perception of a

A BRIEF HISTORY OF COX SCHOOL RANKINGS	1997	1998	1999	2000	2001	2002	2003	2004	2005
BBA									
U.S. News & World Report				32	34	31	36	34	35
Fiske								Top 16	
Gourman Report	22								
MBA									
Business Week	23	Top 50*		Top 50*		Top 50**		Top 50**	Top 50
Wall Street Journal					9	26	30	14	20
U.S. News & World Report	NR	NR	36	42	35	34	51	52	54
Financial Times			24	34	31	31	37	39	37
Forbes				23	17		36		31
Entrepreneur					NR	NR	NR	7	5
EMBA									
Business Week	NR		Top 20		19		18		16
U.S. News & World Report					12	19	15	14	15
Financial Times					24	19	24	15	30
PMBA									
U.S. News & World Report					NR	NR	22	14	12
Forbes									10

* Below Top 25   ** Below Top 30

given school. Niemi suggests that it might take another twenty-five years for the Cox School's FTMBA program to reach the top twenty-five schools in all the polls. A business school is what people *think* a business school is. People believe that Harvard and Stanford are outstanding universities; therefore their business schools are perceived to be outstanding. The key for the Cox School, again, remains with its success in placing its graduates and the paths those graduates take in their respective organizations. Niemi is also quick to remind people that the two-year FTMBA program at Cox is only a little more than a decade old, and it has a long future ahead. Further, he contends that the future of MBA programs lies squarely with working professionals programs such as the EMBA and PMBA. These programs now often account for 80 percent of the number of students in MBA programs. Here, among the five top pollsters, only seven universities have business schools listed in the top twenty of all five polls: Northwestern, Chicago, UCLA, NYU, USC, Emory, and SMU.

The Collins Executive Education Center

Niemi offers the Collins Center as one of his success stories. As noted earlier, all data on MBA programs show that there is growth in evening and weekend programs. The additional space now available in the Collins Center will allow expansion of these professional programs such as the EMBA program. Further, Niemi believes that the building sends a strong signal that continuing executive education in business is vitally important to Cox and SMU. Niemi sees a trend in some corporations to relinquish inhouse training and return it to universities, where he says it belongs. The pendulum is going to swing back; corporations will return their focus to their core businesses; and universities, especially business schools, will regain primary responsibility for training business executives. As mentioned earlier, the center houses the Southwest Graduate School of Banking, KPMG Corporate Governance, and the Brinker Institute. Other new professionally oriented programs will be housed in the Collins Center.

Global Leadership Program

Niemi is particularly proud of the Global Leadership Program (GLP). He believes Cox MBAs are better trained in international business than is the case in most other business schools. This is, in part, because of the program's immersion requirements. Feedback from the students suggests that the GLP significantly changes the way they think about the world, and Niemi says this shows up in their second year of study. Niemi even goes so far as to contend that the Cox GLP might be more "global" than the global programs in European schools. For example, he suggests that when a French student goes from France to Germany the culture shock may be less than that of an American student going from Atlanta to New York! When Niemi first talked to students in the MBA program, they told him that the largest single void in the program was global business. Niemi is convinced that he has successfully begun to fill that void, not only for the FTMBA program but for the PMBA and EMBA programs as well.

Faculty and Student Quality

Niemi is most proud of the quality of faculty and students who have come to the Cox School during his tenure. He believes he is hiring potential research and teaching stars, and that the students in all the degree programs attest to an increase in quality. These results can only enhance the rankings and improve the reputation and status of Cox in the future.

Niemi has made some significant adjustments to awards given to faculty (and staff) in the Cox School. Upon his arrival, faculty received a variety of awards for teaching and research as well as research grants. Niemi enhanced the awards system considerably. For example, whereas the outstanding teacher in the BBA program and the MBA program historically received $1,000, under Niemi those recipients now receive $5,000. In addition, four runners-up in each of those categories received $1,000 a piece.

With respect to the outstanding research award, before Niemi's arrival the recipient received $1,000, but he or she now gets $5,000. To further enhance and reward research productivity in the Cox School, Niemi increased the $12,500 Corrigan grants to $16,500 and Corrigan professorships from $16,500 to two-ninths of a recipient's academic-year salary. Further he increased the Cullum research grants from $12,500 to $16,500 and instituted $16,500 Dunlevy grants.

In addition to these adjustments in teaching and research, Niemi instituted, with the help of Carl Sewell, an Outstanding Service Award. The recipient receives $5,000. These changes have stimulated faculty research and teaching productivity and effectiveness. Consistently improving faculty along with in-creasingly high-quality students, as evidenced by rising GMAT and SAT scores, work experience, salaries, and other metrics, support Niemi's assertions that things are moving in the right direction in the Cox School and that they will continue to get better.

Key People to Niemi

All the deans that we interviewed were reluctant to list names of key people for fear of leaving out very important people. Nevertheless, we asked Niemi, as we did his four predecessors whom we interviewed, who some of the really key people on SMU's campus were (and are) in his administration as well as those key people outside of the SMU campus. We started with internal people, and the first person Niemi mentioned was Gerald Turner. He commented that Turner is an unusual president in that he wants to give his people the ball and let them run with it. Some presidents are very intrusive, but Turner lets you do your job. Niemi appreciates that, and stated, "He is a terrific guy to work for."

Carl Sewell, Cary Maguire, and John Tolleson

Continuing at the top, Niemi then mentioned Provost Ross Murfin. "[He] is just the best provost I've worked for. Again, Ross doesn't get in the way." Niemi went on to say that he likes having a central administration at SMU that lets him be entrepreneurial and do what he thinks should be done in order to enhance the reputation of the Cox School of Business. Both Turner and Murfin have provided Niemi that freedom.

Niemi then moved to the Cox Executive Board and commented that he was particularly hesitant in naming people because the full board (past and present members) has always been so cooperative and supportive. He mentioned first and foremost, Ed Cox. He continued with Cary Maguire, Carl Sewell, and John Tolleson, the first, second, and current chairs,

Dee Powell

respectively, of the Cox Executive Board. All have served or currently serve as SMU trustees as well. He also mentioned numerous other key friends of Cox and SMU, an impressive corporate roll call too long to list here. Niemi felt that there were simply too many key faculty and staff to begin naming any of them. He did mention that Associate Dean Bill Dillon has outstanding credibility with the faculty because of his academic reputation and productivity, and that allows Niemi to do the things he needs to do to accomplish his goals and objectives. Niemi also mentioned that his assistant to the dean, Dee Powell, who also worked for Herberger, Slocum, Blake, and McGill, was (and is) very efficient in running the affairs of the dean's office. We let him off of the hook at that point.

Disappointments

When asked if he had any disappointments while at the Cox School, Niemi immediately commented on an early concern about the budget system at SMU. He did not believe that the budget, as set up, was in the Cox School's best interest or that Cox was particularly healthy from a budget perspective. The budget system inherited by Niemi was one that had been created by Blake in concert with Turner, Murfin, and Blake's fellow deans, and Niemi agreed that while programs (especially MBA programs) were growing in Cox, the budget arrangement was fine. Under that arrangement, revenue from new growth was given to the schools that generated that revenue; nothing had to go back to central administration. What concerned Niemi, and other deans, is that the base of the budget kept growing each year, making it more and more difficult to realize growth revenues that amounted to much. Niemi spent a good part of four years trying to convince central administration that a new budgeting system was necessary before finally realizing his goal.

Beyond the budget situation, Niemi did not mention any other disappointments. He indicated that because he is a positive person, when he asks for support and is rejected he simply says that he did not ask the "right way." He endeavors to rethink and return for another, more successful day. In short, like all effective sales people, Niemi does not personalize rejection.

Niemi's Reflections on the Dean's Job

When asked for the most significant changes he has made in the Cox School to date, Niemi mentions the budget changes first. He also notes that his administration raised $50 million over his first six years as dean. He believes he has positively increased the quality of the faculty as well as of the students in all three MBA programs and the BBA program. He admits that Cox's FTMBA program is not yet a top-twenty-five school across all polls, and it may take longer than he will have as dean to get it there. However, under his administration great strides in quality and reputation have been made. This is evidenced in the ranking data for the BBA program and all three MBA programs in the table on page 255.

The BBA Career Center and BBA Scholars Program are two more significant changes that Niemi points to in his self-assessment of his tenure to date. He also adds, in reaction to our notion to label him an "outside dean," that while he has raised a lot of money, built up Cox's endowment, and built the Collins Center, he also has fostered significant support for faculty fellowships and student scholarships. He has fostered new programs such as the GLP and

Maria and Al Niemi and family on Hilton Head outing, 2005

new internal processes (integrated modular courses in the FTMBA program) to continually raise the performance levels in the Cox School and ultimately enhance the reputation and respect for the Edwin L. Cox School of Business.

When asked about his fondest memories of his deanship at Cox to date, Niemi instantly mentions Dallas and what a wonderful place it is to live and work. It is a large city, but its neighborhoods provide a small-town feeling and atmosphere. It has one of the most supportive business communities in the country. Working in a private university such as SMU is a joy after the bureaucracy and "paranoia" of large, public institutions. SMU and Cox are collegial places, and that is very important to Niemi.

Niemi is proud of his record to date as dean of the Cox School. He warns, however, that because Dallas is such a vibrant city, and has so much interaction from all over the country, SMU and Cox "must stay on their toes." Competition has been rigorous and will continue to be felt from universities and corporations that want to do their own executive education. "So we can never take anything for granted, but we are in a strategically very good position." And in response to our question of whether he is an "inside" or "outside" dean, Niemi smiles and says, "I really would rather be thought of as someone who raised money only to make things better."

CHAPTER EIGHT

THE CHALLENGE OF A
NEVER-ENDING JOURNEY

*The all-encompassing challenge facing the business school of the future
is how to select among all the demands that will be made on it.**

LYMAN W. PORTER AND LAWRENCE E. MCKIBBIN

I T HAS BEEN OUR INTENT, in the brief history conveyed in the previous
chapters, to provide the reader with a snapshot of eighty-five years of
growth of the Edwin L. Cox School of Business. We have done this through its
partners—Dallas and SMU—by highlighting the accomplishments of the Cox
School's eight deans to date—William Hauhart, Laurence Fleck, Aaron Sartain, Jack Grayson, Alan Coleman, Roy Herberger, David Blake, and Al Niemi.
They, along with their colleagues on the faculty and staff, in the student body,
and in the broader SMU and Dallas communities, have, as the commercial
used to say, "come a long way, baby."

In this final chapter, we wish to make a few summary comments about
the deans, in part as individuals, but mostly as a group with similar goals and
aspirations for the school of business at Southern Methodist University. Our
colleagues who worked with the various deans may not always agree on the
respective strengths and weaknesses of the deans, but they would all agree

---

*Lyman W. Porter and Lawrence E. McKibbin, *Management Education and Development:
Drift or Thrust into the 21st Century?* (New York: McGraw-Hill, 1988), 340–41.

that each dean had the business school as a primary focus in his life during his tenure.

We also wish to present the challenge facing deans in the future. We believe that leadership of all organizations, including those in higher education, necessitates a good dose of strategic thinking across a broad range of complex issues. Decision making "by the seat of one's pants" is, and must remain, a relic of the past. Further, we think that there have been and will continue to be common threads among these deans and their eventual successors. As an example, the race for rankings, if one believes that rankings are an effective metric of excellence, is never ending. So, too, is the journey for excellence and prominence for the Cox School. While few would question that the school has made substantial progress, there would be near consensus that there is more to be done. The journey is never ending, even when goals are met, because new goals are established constantly, especially when new deans come on board, and the performance standards are continually raised.

How Did They Do?

It is our undivided opinion that each of the eight deans of the business school at SMU made contributions that aided the present-day Cox School in achieving the reputation that it now enjoys. This is true even though some programs in which deans invested significant resources were ultimately phased out or failed. Each dean invested considerable energy and time during his career for the good of the Cox School.

William Hauhart correctly read the business climate in Dallas and throughout the country, and realized that Dallas and the Southwest region of the United States needed a strong private-school business curriculum. His vision inspired the founding of the business school, and he led it for twenty-five years, an amazing feat in itself. He was responsible for the school receiving its first nod of accreditation from the AACSB. Under his direction, the school grew from a small department of two students and several faculty to five hundred students and thirty faculty.

Hauhart passed the baton to Laurence Fleck, who headed the school during the time when massive numbers of World War II veterans entered the university and the school. Under Fleck, the business school grew in both numbers of students and numbers of courses. New departments sprang up. Fleck's close association with the business community, and their mutual respect for each other, led to the development of a variety of institutes in the school as well as internships and cooperative work programs with business organizations. Several new majors came into existence under Fleck, and a beautiful new facility—the Fincher Building—was built.

During Fleck's administration, Aaron Sartain started a Department of Personnel Administration, which was to become the Organization Behavior Area years later. It was Sartain, the former chairman of the Psychology Department in the Humanities and Sciences Division at SMU, who took the reigns from Fleck. Sartain helped his colleagues at SMU who were outside the business school gain an appreciation of the school as something more than a place for vocational education. During Sartain's tenure the strong relationship between the school and the business community continued. The SMU Foundation for Business Administration was formed, and Sartain engaged influential businessmen, including Ed Cox and Bill Clements, to interact with the school. Further, an influential group of academics and business leaders reviewed the school's operations and advised the school on its path to becoming an elite business school. Increased faculty pay and curriculum change were paramount conditions.

Whether the School of Business Administration was ready for change or not, it got a full dose with Jack Grayson. Grayson turned the rather tradition-bound, business-community-oriented school on its head. Grayson likely made more enemies in his first year at SMU than his three predecessors did in their cumulative forty-eight years. A superb visionary with a penchant for innovation, Grayson got the school to think in dramatically different ways, such as installing a one-year MBA program and introducing students directly into the main decision-making processes of the school. While he wanted to interact with the business community as much or more so than his predecessors, he also alienated some members of that community. He worked hard to put the SMU business school on the national map, and he succeeded. But Grayson underestimated the power of the faculty to resist change in general and many of his changes in particular. Grayson worked tirelessly for change and gathered around him a group of colleagues who were committed to his values and vision. Under Grayson, the school, the university, and Dallas learned the benefits of change along with the pains of that change.

Alan Coleman was much more traditional than Grayson in his thinking about how the business school could be improved. Coleman engaged in a determined and successful effort to retain the accreditation of the undergraduate program and to achieve accreditation for the MBA program. Under his tenure, additional endowed chairs were secured for the school. Faculty were convinced to move from "brand name" schools to SMU before the Cox School had established itself as a fairly well-known brand at the national level. Coleman was a diplomat and, like Sartain, worked well with his fellow deans around the campus. A devotee of the arts, Coleman had a good relationship with the Meadows School and supported the innovative and rather unique arts-management joint master's degree program. Coleman focused on hiring faculty who were above-average teachers and researchers. His "steeples of excellence" speeches continually referred to the Stanford business school and how it was similar to the SMU Cox School of Business "not too many years ago." Coleman's tenure would focus on improved quality of both faculty and students.

Roy Herberger's attempt to eliminate individual subject areas and make all faculty internationally focused was hauntingly reminiscent of some of the dramatic changes that Grayson called for a little over a decade earlier. Herberger was not successful in meeting this goal; however, he continued to add to the quality of the faculty by filling more endowed chairs and setting higher standards for tenure and promotion. He also would build a contemporary business school complex, including the electronic business library and information center (BIC). He would refurbish the outdated Fincher Building and add two new wings that resulted in a truly first-class, state-of-the-art business school complex. Herberger motivated a good number of faculty to think about international business and its importance for Cox students.

David Blake would make one of the most radical changes in the Cox School since the Grayson years. He eliminated the very successful one-year MBA niche program in favor of a more traditional two-year curriculum. He instituted a global business course requirement for all MBAs as well as a business leadership portfolio of requirements and social responsibility activities. In support of these ideas, Blake conceived the Business Leadership Center, which continues as one of the school's hallmarks. Blake argued strongly with central administration that the budgeting process was ineffective and continued that message until he finally was able to convince the president and provost that a new budget model was in order. Blake was almost singlehandedly responsible for the Cox School joining the MBA Enterprise Corps, where Cox kept company with the top twenty business schools in the country. While Blake worked with several key members of the business community, he would be known more as an inside dean concerned about curricula, faculty evaluation processes, and strengthening the role of key staff positions.

Al Niemi created a level of enthusiasm in the business community that was probably not seen during the tenure of any other SMU business school dean. He greatly expanded the Cox Executive Board and created alumni events in cities such as New York City, San Francisco, and Chicago. He also recognized the growing number of international alumni and took his alumni events overseas as well. Along the way, he created a Global Leadership Program that has added a significant international dimension to all these graduate programs. He put significant resources into both graduate and undergraduate placement services. The recent dedication of the Collins Center on September 9, 2005, was attended by a glittering array of Dallas's most prominent business people. Niemi's long-time effort regarding the Collins Center is expected to pay dividends for the school's EMBA program and its various professional-development programs.

Under Niemi, Cox has flourished, by previous standards, in the national rankings. And Niemi has promoted those rankings without hesitation. The

standard input ranking criteria—GMAT scores, GPAs, and work experience—
have continued to improve under Niemi's leadership. The output criteria—
salary enhancements, jobs at graduation, and others—have improved as well.
He created a BBA Scholars program and added high-quality faculty and graduate students. He continues to pursue excellence passionately.

This brief historical review has summarized the contributions of each of
the eight deans to the growing status of the Cox School. The path to national
recognition has been replete with twists and turns, yet there are some key features to the direction provided by the school's leaders. There appear to be four
consistent aspirations among all eight of the deans. The most obvious one is
the relationship the Cox School has established with the Dallas business community since the school's founding in 1920. Second is the attempt of each dean
to get more and better students to the school. Third is the goal of each dean to
hire and retain the very best faculty that were available to SMU. And finally,
each in his own style, embraced change along the way.

Collins Center looking southeast

If one believes—as we do—that the Cox School has made significant strides under every dean in at least a few significant ways, then one has to ask the question of how the Cox School continues to improve its quality and prominence in the future. What will it take to become truly elite? While we do not know the answers, we provide some conjectures below. We break these conjectures into two parts: necessary but insufficient conditions and crucial conditions. We begin with the necessary but insufficient conditions.

Necessary but Insufficient Conditions

If one were to spend a week, a month, or a year at each of the top thirty schools of business in the United States, one would find several commonalities among those thirty major players. First, those top thirty business schools—in almost 80 percent of the cases—are housed in the top thirty universities. Further, all the schools have the basic conditions of excellence under control. These conditions include the ability to do the following:

- Matriculate and retain the very best students in the world.
- Hire and retain outstanding faculty from all over the world.
- Attract significant discretionary resources for key people and programs.
- Design and maintain excellent faculty and student support systems.
- Increase or maintain their rankings.

The Best Students in the World

The best business schools typically have outstanding students who are highly diverse on several fronts: ethnicity, race, gender, geography, religiosity, career aspirations, and interests. In the finest schools, students learn from students as well as from professors and assignments. The standard metrics of student excellence include the quality of their prior school(s), work experience, leadership skills, undergraduate and graduate standardized test scores, grade point averages, and earning power. These attributes will differ among BBA, MBA, and PhD programs. The very finest students—the best and the brightest—at the very finest schools of business are provocative in the classroom. They encourage each other and their professors to excel almost as much as the professors encourage them to excel. Great students beget great students. Only the best and the brightest get into the very best business schools—at least in good economic times.

The very best students matriculate to the very best business schools because of brand equity, certain professors (in the case of PhD programs), rankings, and a host of other attributes, not the least of which is career potential upon graduation. This might mean graduate school at another brand-name institution or placement in the corporate world. Students at the elite schools, again in good economic times, tend to get the most offers from the most institutions for the most benefits, typically measured by high compensation packages. Competition for the very best students is keen, and the applicant pools for these students are "owned" by the elite schools for the most part. It is a difficult group to break into, but without elite students it is difficult to be an elite business school.

Outstanding Faculty

There are a lot of really good faculty at all ranks of the professorial ladder. However, the number of schools chasing the relatively few number of faculty stars makes the competition for those stars grueling, even at the entry level for future stars. Compensation packages to attract faculty exceed current faculty compensation packages, inequities appear, and compression problems abound. But business school deans live in a free-market world, and, for the most part, star business professors can write their own tickets. These stars are in short supply and high demand—Economics 101 dictates price. Deans live with this reality, and so do their faculty.

The very finest faculty bring to the table portfolios of outstanding research and publications and reputations that usually precede them. They may or may not be the very best classroom performers, but they typically are adequate in this regard. It is the rare faculty member that sets the standards in his or her research discipline and in the classroom as well. Among deans and faculty, national business school reputations are, for the most part, built on research productivity—quantity and quality. Quantity by itself will not do. Quality is the name of the game. The academy at large knows who the top researchers are—at least in one's own discipline—but the academy is not sure who the top teachers are. Students are quick to recognize the best teachers as they experience those professors in the classroom setting.

Most quality faculty are also good citizens of the business school, university, and community at large. They care not only about their research productivity but about their students, their colleagues in and out of the business school, and the efficient and effective operations of the school, university, and academy.

Significant Discretionary Resources

In order to meet the first two necessary but insufficient conditions, deans of business schools must have a lot of discretionary money. Their coffers must be full. How else will they get the best and the brightest students and faculty stars? Top business schools buy top business school students and star faculty. There are some exceptions, but not many.

The elite universities and business schools have significant development (fund-raising) programs. Development officers and deans that have a penchant for fund raising can attain endowments and gifts from alumni and other friends of the university and the school. Endowments to business schools are often restricted for certain purposes: endowed chairs, buildings, scholarships, or special programs. Unrestricted monies are the most attractive for deans and development officers. Deans can use these discretionary funds in the most productive way for people, programs, and capital projects.

Deans of business schools also make deals with central administration regarding tuition revenue and income from special programs. These are lucrative and very important sources of funds. Business schools usually generate strong positive cash flows, and, as entities within a university, the rich have to support the poor. There is always disagreement about the "tax rate" of business schools and law schools. Deans, like most of us, would like to keep it all "at home," but the central administration demands financial support for the university as a whole. Negotiations take place, and agreements are created. However, in some instances these agreements cause some deans to leave. These deans perceive that over time financial limitations thwart their attempts to take the school to the next level.

Deans can also rely on auxiliary revenue, for example, alumni contributions, sales of business school memorabilia, and so forth. In short, business school deans and central administrators of universities must maintain some flexibility in the budgeting process. They must be held accountable for the proper expenditure of funds by establishing the correct priorities and distributing funds to those priorities accordingly.

Strong Support Systems

Business school deans must have excellent support systems for their faculty and students. The most critical ingredient is the hiring of outstanding staff to design and implement those support systems. For students, strong support systems include generous scholarship programs and excellent career services. For faculty, support systems include effective reward and evaluation systems. Ancillary support for faculty in the form of course and research assistance is essential. The school must have top-notch administrative and educational support staffs that free faculty to concentrate on their professional endeavors. And, of course, the staff members themselves must be evaluated and rewarded according to their contributions to the overall mission and goals of the business school.

Business School Rankings

Some consider business school rankings a necessary evil; others consider them just plain necessary. Business school deans are very adept at using rankings to their advantage when the rankings are good, and minimizing the rankings when their school falls in a poll. In the latter case, the dean might go so far as to question the statistical significance of the fall. But when his or her school ranks high, rankings are important, valid, and reliable. This is human nature, and deans are human.

There are several major ranking polls for business schools in the United States and throughout the world (mostly Europe). They include *Business Week, U.S. News & World Report, Wall Street Journal, The Economist, Forbes,* and *Financial Times,* to name a few. Deans will use not only overall place ranks but individual attribute ranks, such as GPAs, GMAT scores, work experience, salaries, number of offers, and others. A good example is illustrated in the SMU COX advertisement that ran in March 2005 (see the figure on page 275). The ad was part of a special advertising supplement in the *Dallas Morning News* for MBA programs in the Dallas–Fort Worth area. In addition to overall ranks ("Recognition"), notice how various aspects of different ranking organizations are used in the ad. Business school deans always put their best foot forward, and Al Niemi is second to none in this regard

There have been many arguments that rankings lack both validity and reliability. The only true measure of a school's worth is the quality of the education it provides, and this is difficult to measure. Most ranking measures are input measures rather than output measures, such as how much students have learned and how that learning has helped them in their future personal and professional career paths. Nevertheless, rankings are with us, and they are here to stay. Deans and their admissions staff are quick to point out that students carry the most recent rankings around with them as they go to consortia to determine what universities and schools of business they will attend. The Cox School has improved its rankings significantly over the last decade for its three MBA programs and its BBA program. No dean in Cox's history emphasized rankings more than Niemi, and when Cox improves in a ranking he unabashedly publicizes that fact. That's part of the brand equity game.

Through the eight and a half decades since its inception, the Cox School has continued to improve—with slight dips now and then—in all the "necessary but insufficient conditions" required to make it one of the elite business schools. By the metrics generally used in the academy, Cox has improved on all counts. It has improved its undergraduate and graduate student body, the quality of its faculty, its financial resources, its support services to students and faculty, and its rankings. The Cox School must continue to improve in all these arenas. But is that enough? Maybe not.

Moving Forward

Most people would say that the Cox School of Business is not yet one of the elite business schools. It has come a long way and is going in the right direction. However, it cannot rest on its laurels. The authors would assert the necessity for a more focused future path by distinguishing itself in some unique way.

When one thinks of the Harvard Business School, often ranked as the top business school in the world, one thinks of outstanding general management education and the case method of teaching. Chicago's business school is known for its very strong analytical and quantitative orientation. Yale is known for its nonprofit, public-sector focus. Dartmouth's Tuck School is typically known for its general management program and team building. It is the only top-twenty business school without a PhD program. The University of Michigan's business school is respected for its practical training and manufacturing orientation. The Wharton School is a standout in finance, while Northwestern University's marketing program is highly respected. Generally, the elite schools have clear distinctive competencies. With this in mind, we turn, now, to the crucial conditions.

Crucial Conditions

We believe that there are four crucial conditions that deans of the Cox School should pay attention to now and in the future. They include (1) the development of a strong and distinctive niche for which the Cox School can become well known and respected, (2) strategic planning involving a focus on priorities and funding, (3) increasing affiliation with the larger SMU community and the Dallas business communities, and (4) the fostering of an enduring organizational culture.

We Think
Highly Of Our Programs.
So Do Many Others.

NETWORK OPPORTUNITIES
The geographic breadth of Cox's alumni network is ranked #9 in the world, 5th among U.S. Business schools, and #1 in Texas by *The Economist*. Cox has active alumni chapters in every major city in the U.S. and many leading international cities.

RECOGNITION
Cox's full-time MBA is ranked among the leading programs in the world by *BusinessWeek, U.S. News & World Report, Forbes, The Wall Street Journal, Financial Times,* and *The Economist*. Cox's Executive MBA is ranked among the top 20 in the U.S. by *BusinessWeek, U.S. News & World Report,* and *The Financial Times*. In the only ranking of Professional MBA programs, Cox ranks #14 in the U.S. according to *U.S. News & World Report*.

DIVERSITY
Researching the most prestigious schools in the country, *Hispanic Trends* ranks Cox one of the top 25 business schools in the U.S. For Hispanics.

SUCCESS
According to *The Financial Times* Cox's Executive MBA graduates rank 7th in the world in terms of compensation five years after graduation.

STUDENT QUALITY
In all three MBA programs, full-time, Professional MBA, and Executive MBA, Cox's student quality ranks among the top 25 business schools in the U.S.

FACULTY QUALITY
Princeton Review ranks Cox faculty #7 in the nation based on their accessibility. *Academic Assessments* ranks Cox's faculty among the top 30 in the nation based on scholarly citations in leading academic journals in economics, finance, information systems, marketing and strategy.

INTERNATIONAL STUDY
Global opportunities abound with study abroad programs as well as international business experience with the American Airlines Global Leadership Program in Latin America, Asia and Europe.

For more information, visit www.smuexecedu.com or call 214.768.9022

SMU COX
SCHOOL OF BUSINESS

SOUTHERN METHODIST UNIVERSITY

Dallas Morning News, *March 29, 2005*

Discovering a Strong Niche

In reality, business education is a commodity. While inputs to business schools vary, a detailed analysis of curricula across BBA and MBA programs results in the conclusion that most curricula are the same. Hoping to gain recognition, a school may create venues for every market opportunity. Programs and activities come and go, some seemingly successful while others are short-lived. In spite of the attempt by some deans, business schools cannot be all things to all people. Not every program and activity within a business school can be the best or even outstanding compared to competitive schools. It is critical that business schools find their niches—their strengths—and set priorities in those areas. These priorities should include matriculating the right kinds of students and faculty, as well as garnering the right resources and resource support for specific niche programs.

Al Niemi and his successors must find the Cox School's niche or niches. They may be different by program. And they may change over time. The very best business schools not only adapt to changing times; they are on the leading edge of those changes. Equally important, the school's vision and values must be clear and accepted by all the major players. The Cox School has tried a variety of unique thrusts in its history. Among others, they include the following:

- Experiential learning (Grayson)
- A single required course in the BBA program (Grayson)
- Leadership, e.g., the Business Leadership Center (Blake)
- A one-year MBA Program (Grayson)
- Dual degrees with arts administration and law (Coleman, Niemi)
- Graduate and undergraduate business mentoring (Grayson, Herberger)
- Social-responsibility requirements, including team projects for local organizations (Blake)
- Entrepreneurship vis-à-vis the Caruth Institute (Grayson)
- Globalization (Herberger, Blake, Niemi)
- Specialized masters' degrees (Niemi)

One or more of these could be a focal niche for Cox. We will not try to make a choice. But Cox should have a niche—something in which the Cox School excels. This identity needs to become common knowledge among business school deans. It should be something that attracts students to Cox, something that Cox's constituents find indispensable. For example, the school's niche might be leadership, at least for its FTMBA program. Perhaps Cox could develop a program of joint degrees with engineering, economics, and other departments and schools around campus and become known as a school that produces graduates who are experts in multiple fields. Cox could enhance its focus on global business. Two prior deans attempted global programs, though they did not succeed. We will address the reasons for the downfall of these programs in the next section. While we cannot identify specific niches for Cox's future leaders, we can suggest a process for discovering them.

Strategic Thinking, Planning, and Executing

Strategic thinking is mostly about systematic thinking—the antithesis of simply reacting to changing circumstances. We do not accuse any Cox School dean of doing the latter or of avoiding the former. We simply recommend that thinking strategically, rather than thinking programmatically or in terms of activities, is smart business. Strategic thinking leads to effective planning and the efficient allocation of resources so that programs and actions can be effectively executed. Strategic thinking is the beginning of the creation of sustainable competitive advantages, as important to business schools as it is to corporate organizations.

Strategic planning requires organizations to understand their strengths and weaknesses, trends in the education industry, domestic and world socio-economic affairs, and the interests of the school's major stakeholders. While the business community and students are immediately identified as significant stakeholders, the school's faculty and staff may be the most important.

In this way, strategic thinking and planning provide the basis for the school's leaders to set direction for their school—their vision, mission, goals, and values. Warren Bennis, the renowned leadership author, has studied hundreds, even thousands, of successful leaders. He notes that, as our Cox deans have proven, leaders have many different styles and characteristics. Bennis concludes that the best leaders all share one talent—they have the capacity to create a compelling vision, one that takes people to a new place. They then translate that vision into reality. We underscore this tenet while adding that a dean's job is to engage everyone in providing leadership. Gone are the days when the role of leadership was vested in one or only a few individuals in an organization. Once the direction of the school has been established, the leaders can create and implement strategies and programs guiding them toward the vision. The old saying that "if you don't know where you're going, any road will get you there" is accurate. Business school deans who focus on programs without giving thought to how those programs fit the culture and resources of the school may find themselves on "any road" rather than on the road to their vision.

What is the vision of the Cox School? What is its mission? What are its values? Where does it want to go? For what does it want to be known? Where are its strengths and weaknesses regarding its students, faculty, administrators, staff, and financial resources? What should it emphasize—graduate education, undergraduate education, executive education, research, teaching, community service? Because the options are almost innumerable and the resources are limited, it is necessary to focus on reasonable priorities derived from the strategic thinking process. Priorities drive efficient funding. They also drive conflict because those not included in the priorities may feel left out. But it does not have to be that way. There are some aspects of Cox that are already strong and may not need to be strengthened. People in these areas could feel slighted unless they become part of the vision, mission, and priorities. There are other areas—maybe in higher demand or more nearly unique—that should receive priority attention. As the tenure document states for its faculty, the Cox School of Business must be superior in at least one "thing" and good in "everything" else.

Enhancement of SMU and Business Community Interaction

We have highlighted the three-way partnership throughout this book. Unique strategies and programs can be developed with enhanced interaction between and among other schools and departments on the SMU campus, and with the increasingly diverse Dallas business community. We believe that there is potential in this partnership for the creation of an exciting vision and mission for the Cox School.

There are not many organizations in society that are more compartmentalized than institutions of higher education. Business schools have historically been islands unto themselves. While the Cox School experiences healthy collegiality and there is some interdepartmental research, typically at Cox and elsewhere finance faculty collaborate with finance colleagues, marketing with marketing, strategy with strategy, and so on. Research is not as interdisciplinary as it could be. Young tenure-track faculty are mandated to publish in their mainstream journals and not to stray too far from their main fields. Some senior faculty will collaborate from time to time with colleagues from other disciplines, but this is the exception rather than the rule. More interdisciplinary work involving both the business community and other areas on the SMU campus could be highly advantageous for the Cox School, its faculty, its students, and its constituents.

This is not to suggest that everyone must stop their current work and become engaged with strangers. We only suggest that there are tremendous untapped talents and resources in the business community and throughout SMU. Maybe this is part of the future niche(s) of the Edwin L. Cox School of Business.

Building an Enduring Organizational Culture

Organizational culture is an overused and misunderstood concept, yet we see it as one of the four crucial conditions for the Cox School to engender as the search for prominence continues. We use the phrase "enduring organizational culture" to refer to the manner in which the Cox School conducts its affairs. An organization must be flexible so that it recognizes and adapts to changing conditions. Changes in academia may seem to occur at a snail's pace that often frustrates or even infuriates. This frequently occurs when organizations fear change. Often the fear is grounded in the history of an organization whose members recall innovations that were unsuccessful. Often the failed effort had significant negative consequences for faculty and staff. Nonetheless, the failure of any academic organization to anticipate, recognize, and adapt to significant change can prevent it from achieving its potential.

On the other hand, an organization that views change as an ally rather than a foe will have in place processes that foster progressive change. A mechanism to encourage and reward ideas emanating from every level in the organization is an example of a mechanism that embraces change as an ally. This stance toward change will enable the organization to effectively utilize the strategic planning systems outlined in a previous section. If the organization has not embraced change, the strategic planning systems will produce the time-consuming and unproductive efforts that most of us have experienced. The "grand plan" has little or no value and any future effort to develop a plan receives little support.

"That's the way we do it around here." Individuals may not use these words, but the effect is often found in organizations that are overwhelmed by change. Policies and procedures may be the mechanism whereby useful ideas are smothered. The more an organization departs from performance-based reward systems, the better it can ignore change and continue to wallow in mediocrity—in our case, wallow in the middle of the rankings. The reward system is so important to creating a culture responsive to change that one of the most respected managers of our time, Jack Welch, former CEO of GE, said that even the individual who delivers outstanding results but violates positive cultural norms, such as sharing information with colleagues, must be expunged because that person will contaminate the culture.

An enduring culture, then, is one where its members embrace a shared mission and relentlessly pursue the organization's goals. They passionately preserve and protect performance processes and norms and welcome change as the driver for sustainable growth. It is our experience that the Cox School, through much of its history, has not devoted sufficient time to the development of an enduring culture. To be sure, it may be one of the most daunting tasks a dean can face, but it can have enormous benefits in the pursuit of excellence.

Some Parting Thoughts

As noted earlier in this chapter, it is typical that the elite business schools are housed at elite universities, that is, if one is to accept the rankings of *Business Week* and *U.S. News & World Report,* for example. There are some exceptions to this generalization, but they are in the clear minority. Given the evidence, it appears rather certain that academic units of a university are enhanced or constrained by the elite status of their respective universities. By all accounts, SMU is an excellent university. The Cox School of Business is an excellent business school. Neither has yet attained the ranks of the elite. In order for the Cox School to make that class, it is likely that SMU will have to help get it there by achieving the same status. As business schools go, Cox's FTMBA is typically ranked in the second twenty-five top business schools in most polls, and SMU is typically ranked in the second fifty of top universities. Both will need to continue to achieve the necessary but insufficient conditions of excellence and the critical conditions as well.

Deans have incredibly difficult jobs. They are expected to effectively manage a variety of diverse constituencies including faculty, staff, students, central administrators, board members, and citizens at large. They are expected to raise significant amounts of money, make the right curricular decisions, hire the right faculty, admit the right students, and much more. No wonder that the average tenure of the dean of a business school is about 4.5 years (recent data suggest only a two-year life span, but we doubt that). Deans must continually renew themselves and continually excite the motivational spirit of all of their constituents. There are deans that can do these things. They are passionate and committed; they are focused. And we hope they continue to come to the Cox School at SMU for the next eighty-five years and eighty-five more after that.

We hope that you have enjoyed reading this journey of the Cox School's quest for prominence as it aspires to join the exclusive club of elite business schools as much as we have enjoyed compiling it for you. Recall at the beginning of the book that we proposed that people such as John Neely Bryan, Robert Stewart Hyer, and William Hauhart were builders. So too are their successors, including all the leaders of Dallas, SMU, and the Cox School of Business. We illustrated the building spirit of these leaders through the words of William Wadsworth Longfellow in one stanza of his poem "The Builders."

We believe—now that we have arrived at the end of this book's chronicle of the Cox School's journey—that a stanza from one of Longfellow's more popular poems—"A Psalm of Life"—encapsulates the spirit of all of these people—leaders and followers alike.

Lives of great men all remind us
We can make our lives sublime,
And, departing, leave behind us
Footprints on the sands of time.

We congratulate and thank all the men and women who have, even in the smallest ways, contributed to the progress of the Edwin L. Cox School of Business. Most of their accomplishments cannot be measured in ways that do them justice. It is our hope that the passion and productivity of all those who preceded and follow you, the reader, infuse the Cox School with a level of quality and potential that will make us and our predecessors extremely proud. Here's to Dallas, SMU, and the Cox School—partners in a challenging and never-ending journey toward prominence.

SOURCES

Acheson, Sam. "Selecman as a Methodist Leader." *Dallas Yesterday,* March 22, 1971.

Adams, Lorraine. "At SMU, Faculty's Sun Rises: Crisis Heightens Role in Picking President." *The Dallas Morning News,* March 15, 1987.

Adams, Lorraine, and Connie Pryzant. "A Game Plan forGreatness." *The Dallas Morning News,* April 14, 1987.

Alsop, Ronald J., ed. *The Wall Street Journal: Guide to the Top Ten Business Schools 2003.* New York: Simon & Schuster, 2002.

Bayer, Betsy. Personal interview by Thomas E. Barry and Eugene T. Byrne. April 22, 2003.

Bennis, Warren. *On Becoming a Leader.* 2nd ed. New York: Addison-Wesley, 1994.

Bernhard, Annette. "Proposals Called Helpful in Search for New President." *The Dallas Morning News,* May 2, 1987.

———. "SMU Sees Drop in Donations for Fiscal Year, Report Says." *The Dallas Morning News,* June 20, 1987.

Bilton, Nora Katherine. Personal interview by Thomas E. Barry. January 8, 2003.

Blackistone, Kevin B. "Economists Move Base to N. Texas: Weinstein, Gross Have Left SMU." *The Dallas Morning News,* June 2, 1989.

Blake, David H. "Comments from the Dean." *Exchange Network,* Spring 1995.

———. Personal interview by Thomas E. Barry. February 5, 2003.

Boles, Walter E., Jr., Theodore R. Eck, and Sydney C. Reagan. Cover letter and excerpts from *Report of the Task Force on the School of Business Administration.* Southern Methodist University, Dallas. December 15, 1962.

Bradshaw, Bob. "Business School Schedules Student-Faculty Caucus." *The Daily Campus,* October 6, 1970.

———. "Participants Express Reactions to Business Caucus." *The Daily Campus,* October 9, 1970.

Brown, Don. "Popular Business Prof to Resign." *The Daily Campus,* September 30, 1970.

Byrne, Eugene T. Personal interview by Thomas E. Barry. January 23, 2003.

———. Personal papers. 1968–1983.

Byrne, Eugene T., and Douglas E. Wolfe, eds. *Developing Experiential Learning Programs for Professional Education: New Directions for Experiential Learning.* San Francisco: Jossey-Bass, 1980.

Canavan, Patrick. Letter to Dean C. Jackson Grayson Jr. September 29, 1970.

Coleman, Alan B. Contributed papers. DeGolyer Library. Southern Methodist University.

———. Personal interview by Thomas E. Barry and Eugene T. Byrne. March 29–30, 2003.

Collins, James C., and Jerry I. Porras. *Built to Last.* New York: Harper Collins, 1997.

Collins, Jim. *Good to Great.* New York: Harper Business, 2001.

Consortium for the MBA Enterprise Corps, Inc. *A Decade of Assistance to Private Enterprises in Transitioning Economies.* Tenth Anniversary Report, 1990–2000.

Dallas Historical Society. "Dallas History: Overview." http://www.dallashistory.org/history/dallas/dallas_history.htm.

Domeier, Doug. "Professor Resigns Amid Controversy." *The Dallas Morning News,* October 1, 1970.

Early, James. *Robert Stewart Hyer and the History and Architecture of Dallas Hall on the Campus of Southern Methodist University.* Dallas: Southern Methodist University, n.d.

Edwin L. Cox Business Leadership Center, Southern Methodist University. *The Measure of a Leader.* Undated.

Edwin L. Cox School of Business, Southern Methodist University. *Assets.* Fall 1988.

———. *Report of the Finance Department of the Edwin L. Cox School of Business.* 1987.

———. *Report of the Strategic Planning Committee.* July, 1981.

———. *A Strategic Assessment of Academic Programs.* December 1994.

———. *1985 Progress Report.* Fall 1985.

Elliott, Karen. "Grayson: 'Academic Gypsy' in Storm's Eye." *The Dallas Morning News,* December 12, 1971.

———. "Resigning Prof Believes He's Made Contribution." *The Dallas Morning News,* October 2, 1970.

———. "SMU's Business Dean Tries to Erase Carbon Copy Image." *The Dallas Morning News,* October 5, 1970.

Erwin, Dorothie. "'Pvt. Dallas' A Go-Getter." *The Dallas Morning News,* December 12, 1971.

Fleck, Laurence H. Letter to the business, professional, and industrial leaders of Dallas. January 9, 1961.

Grayson, C. Jackson, Jr. "The B-School World of Pvt. Douglas Dallas, circa 1980." *Innovation,* 1971.

———. Letter to President Willis Tate. September 7, 1970.

———. Letter to President Willis Tate. October 1, 1970.

———. Personal interview by Eugene T. Byrne. September 2002.

———. Personal papers. American Quality and Productivity Center, Houston, Texas. 1968–1975.

———. "Toward a New Philosophy in Business Education." *Mustang,* August 1969, p. 3.

Greater Dallas Chamber of Commerce. *Dallas: Reflections & Visions.* Dallas: MARCOA, 2000.

Grimes, Johnnie Marie, ed. *Willis M. Tate: Views and Interviews.* Introduction by Marshall Terry. Dallas: SMU Press, 1978.

Guinto, Joseph. "Rutgers Dean Named to Cox Post." *The Daily Campus,* August 28, 1989.

The Handbook of Texas Online. http://www.tsha.utexas.edu/handbook/online.

Hansen, Richard. Personal interview by Thomas E. Barry and Eugene T. Byrne. December 19, 2002.

Hazel, Michael V. "Pioneer Memoirs: An Individual Perspective on the Past." *Legacies* 13, no. 1 (Spring 2001): 4–13.

Herberger, Roy A. *Dean's Letter.* Edwin L. Cox School of Business, Southern Methodist University. Summer 1985, spring 1986, spring 1987, summer 1987.

———. "Message from the Dean." *1985 Progress Report.* Edwin L. Cox School of Business, 1985.

———. Personal interview by Thomas E. Barry. February 4, 2003.

Kenan Center, University of North Carolina, at Chapel Hill. *Building Bridges for Cross-Cultural Management, Five Years of the MBA Enterprise Corps.* Undated.

Kotter, John P. *Leading Change.* Boston: Harvard Business School Press, 1996.

Lyle, Bobby B. Personal interview by Thomas E. Barry and Eugene T. Byrne. January 17, 2003.

———. Personal papers. Lyco Energy Corporation, 1971–1975.

Maguire, Cary. Personal interview by Thomas E. Barry and Eugene T. Byrne. May 12, 2003.

Mason, Don. "B-School Group Requests 'Suspension of Business.'" *The Daily Campus,* October 2, 1970.

———. "McFarland Explains Incidents Leading to Canavan Resignation." *The Daily Campus,* October 13, 1970.

MBA International Exchange Program, Edwin L. Cox School of Business, Southern Methodist University. *International Exchange Programs Strategic Planning.* December 6, 1994.

McDonald, William L. *Dallas Rediscovered: A Photographic Chronicle of Urban Expansion 1870–1925.* Dallas: Dallas Historical Society, 1978.

McGill, Michael E. Personal interview by Thomas E. Barry and Eugene T. Byrne. January 23, 2003.

Miller, Bob. "Corporate Donations Underscore Significance of SMU." *The Dallas Morning News,* November 18, 1986.

Mitchell, Jim, and Gary Jacobson. "Touchstone for a City: Ray Hunt Bridges Gap for Old Guard and New as Leadership Evolves." *The Dallas Morning News,* January 9, 1989.

Murphy, J. Carter. *Recollections: SMU's Department of Economics 1960–1971.* Dallas: Southern Methodist University, 2002.

Niemi, Al. Personal correspondence materials provided to Thomas E. Barry on October 20, 2004.

———. Personal interview by Thomas E. Barry and Eugene T. Byrne. May 14, 2003.

Olivera, Mercedes. "Ground-Breaking Ceremonies Held for SMU Business School Expansion." *The Dallas Morning News,* December 6, 1985.

Orms, Tom. "SMU Aims for Top Ten in Business Schools." *The Houston Post*, December 5, 1971.

O'Toole, James. "When Leadership Is an Organizational Trait." In *The Future of Leadership,* edited by Warren Bennis, Gretchen M. Spreitzer, and Thomas G. Cummings. San Francisco: Jossey-Bass, 2001.

Payne, Darwin. *Dallas: An Illustrated History.* Dallas Historic Preservation League. Woodland Hills, CA: Windsor Publications, 1982.

Porter, Lyman W., and Lawrence E. McKibbin. *Management Education and Development: Drift or Thrust into the 21st Century?* New York: McGraw-Hill, 1988.

Potts, Helen Jo, and Patricia Macsisak. *The Edwin L. Cox School of Business: A Historical Perspective.* Dallas: Southern Methodist University, 1978.

Powell, Dee. Personal interview by Thomas E. Barry and Eugene T. Byrne. May 14, 2003.

Powell, Monica. Personal interview by Thomas E. Barry. May 12, 2003.

Sartain, Aaron Quinn. Autobiographical sketch, undated. Southern Methodist University Archives.

School of Business Administration, Southern Methodist University. *72 Report 73,* p. 7.

———. *Annual Report.* 1975–1976, 1976–1977, 1977–1978, 1978–1979, 1979–1980, 1980–1981.

———. *The Plan.* September 1971, p. 4.

———. *Report.* [1971–1972.]

———. *SMU MBA Handbook.* August 1974.

———. *Student Handbook of the SMU Business School.* January 1974, November 1974, September 1975.

Sewell, Carl. Personal interview by Thomas E. Barry and Eugene T. Byrne. May 15, 2003.

Sherman, Straford. "How Tomorrow's Leaders Are Learning Their Stuff." *Fortune,* November 27, 1995.

Slater, Robert. *Jack Welch and the GE Way.* New York: McGraw-Hill, 1999.

Sloan, L. C. "Business and Educators Develop Mutual Respect." *The Dallas Morning News,* May 5, 1963.

Slocum, John A. Personal interview by Thomas E. Barry and Eugene T. Byrne. January 30, 2003.

Slone, Ronald R. Letter to Dean C. Jackson Grayson Jr. May 16, 1975.

Southern Methodist University. *Bulletin of Southern Methodist University.* 1921–1922, 1922–1923, 1946–1947, 1947–1948, 1948–1949, 1949–1950, 1950–1951, 1951–1952, 1955–1956, 1956–1957, 1959–1960, 1962–1963, 1963–1964, 1964–1965, 1965–1966.

———. *Bulletin of the Edwin L. Cox School of Business.* 1982–1983, 1983–1984, 1984–1985, 1986–1987, 1987–1988, 1988–1989, 1990–1991.

———. *Careers in Business Administration.* Circa 1952.

———. *The Courses in Business: Report on Initial Curriculum Established in the Dept of Commerce, Finance and Accounts.* Circa 1922.

———. Minutes of the Board of Trustees. Books 2, 10, 23.

———. *The SMU Undergraduate Business Associates Program.* 1st ed., 1987–1988.

Southern Methodist University Office of News and Information. "Extraordinary Entrepreneurial Success Lands COMPAQ CEO SMU Award." News release, May 10, 1988.

———. "SMU's Cox School of Business Announces New Two-Year M.B.A." News release, September 11, 1990.

Stoller, Richard. Personal correspondence addressed to Thomas E. Barry. April 27, 2004.

Terry, Marshall. *"From High on the Hilltop . . .": A Brief History of SMU.* Dallas: Southern Methodist University, 1993.

———. *"From High on the Hilltop . . .": A Brief History of SMU.* 2nd ed. Dallas: Southern Methodist University, 2001.

Thomas, Mary Martha Hosford. *Southern Methodist University: Founding and Early Years.* Dallas: SMU Press, 1974.

Thomas, Robert Hyer. Personal correspondence addressed to Thomas E. Barry. May 14 and July 16, 2003.

Van Breda, Michael. Personal interview by Thomas E. Barry and Eugene T. Byrne. May 16, 2003.

Walker, Ronald D. Personal interview by Thomas E. Barry and Eugene T. Byrne. January 15, 2003.

Welch, John F., Jr., Jeffrey R. Immelt, Dennis D. Dammerman, and Robert C. Wright. "Letter to Shareowners." *GE 2000 Annual Report.* February 9, 2001.

White, Jerry. Personal interview by Thomas E. Barry and Eugene T. Byrne. July 14, 2003.

SMU ADMINISTRATION

R. Gerald Turner
President

Thomas W. Tunks
Provost and Vice President for Academic Affairs,
ad interim

Thomas E. Barry
Vice President for Executive Affairs

S. Leon Bennett
General Counsel, Vice President for Legal and
Government Affairs, and Secretary

James E. Caswell
Vice President for Student Affairs

Brad Cheves
Vice President for Development and External Affairs

Dana Gibson
Vice President for Business and Finance

Steve Orsini
Athletic Director

Elizabeth C. Williams
Treasurer

COX SCHOOL ADMINISTRATION

Albert W. Niemi Jr.
Dean

Mary D. Powell
Assistant to the Dean

William R. Dillon
Senior Associate Dean for Academic Affairs

Marcia K. Armstrong
Associate Dean for Masters Programs

Elbert B. Greynolds Jr.
Associate Dean for Undergraduate Programs

Frank R. Lloyd
Associate Dean of Executive and Management Development

Catherine Collins
Assistant Dean for Administration and Finance

George C. Johnson
Assistant Dean for Career Management Center

Kevin Knox
Assistant Dean for External Relations

David E. Perryman
Assistant Dean for Marketing and Communication

Michael S. Caplan
Director of Graduate Student Services

Vicki Cartwright
Director of PMBA and MSM Admissions

Patti Cudney
Director for Full-Time MBA Admissions

Steven Denson
Director of Diversity

Dennis Grindle
Director of MBA Career Services

Linda Kao
Director of MBA Global Programs

Tom Perkowski
Director of Executive MBA Program

Paula Hill Strasser
Director of the Edwin L. Cox Business Leadership Center

COX SCHOOL OF BUSINESS FACULTY

Evrim Akdogu
Assistant Professor of Finance

Ellen Allen
Lecturer in Information Technology and Operations
Management

Jeffrey W. Allen
Associate Professor of Finance

Jeffrey R. Austin
Lecturer in Accounting

Thomas E. Barry
Professor of Marketing

Amit Basu
Charles Wyly Professor of Information Systems

Charles A. Besio
Lecturer in Marketing

Anita D. Bhappu
Assistant Professor of Management and Organizations

Sreekumar R. Bhaskaran
Assistant Professor of Information Technology and
Operations Management

Nilabhra Bhattacharya
Assistant Professor of Accounting

Richard A. Briesch
Assistant Professor of Marketing

Brian R. Bruce
Senior Lecturer and Director of the Finance Institute
and Portfolio Practicum

William B. Brueggeman
Clara R. and Leo F. Corrigan Sr. Professor
of Real Estate

Jay Carson
Assistant Professor of Management and Organizations

Chester G. Chambers
Assistant Professor of Information Technology and
Operations Management

Andrew H. Chen
Distinguished Professor of Finance

James C. Collins Jr.
Lecturer in Information Technology and Operations
Management

David C. Croson
Associate Professor of Strategy and Entrepreneurship

Michael L. Davis
Senior Lecturer in Finance

Hemang A. Desai
Associate Professor of Accounting

William R. Dillon
Herman W. Lay Professor of Marketing and
Professor of Statistics

Edward J. Fox
Assistant Professor of Marketing

Judith H. Foxman
Lecturer in Marketing

Mel Fugate
Assistant Professor of Management and Organizations

Amar Gande
Assistant Professor of Finance

Bezalel Gavish
Eugene J. and Ruth F. Constantin Distinguished Professor
of Business

Elbert B. Greynolds Jr.
Associate Professor of Accounting

J. Douglas Hanna
Associate Professor of Accounting

Jeffrey R. Hart
Lecturer in Finance

Peter A. Heslin
Assistant Professor of Management and Organizations

Daniel J. Howard
Professor of Marketing

Ellen F. Jackofsky
Associate Professor of Management and Organizations

Joakim Kalvenes
Assistant Professor of Information Technology and
Operations Management

Neil J. Keon
Assistant Professor of Information Technology and
Operations Management

Roger Anthony Kerin
Harold C. Simmons Distinguished Professor
of Marketing

Barbara W. Kincaid
Senior Lecturer in Law

James T. Kindley
Senior Lecturer in Marketing

Chun H. Lam
Associate Professor of Finance

David T. Lei
Associate Professor of Strategy and Entrepreneurship

Qin Lei
Assistant Professor of Finance

Joseph Magliolo III
Professor of Accounting

Richard O. Mason
Carr P. Collins Jr. Distinguished Professor of
Management Sciences

David C. Mauer
Phyllis Gough Huffington Professor of Finance

Darius P. Miller
Associate Professor of Finance

Gary T. Moskowitz
Senior Lecturer in Strategy and Entrepreneurship

Albert W. Niemi Jr.
John and Debbie Tolleson Distinguished Professor of
Business Leadership and Economics

Robin L. Pinkley
Associate Professor of Strategy and Entrepreneurship

Mina J. Pizzini
Assistant Professor of Accounting

Steven R. Postrel
Assistant Professor of Strategy and Entrepreneurship

Amy V. Puelz
Senior Lecturer of Information Technology and
Operations Management

Robert Puelz
Associate Professor of Insurance and Financial
Services on the Dexter Endowment

Miguel A. Quinones
Professor of Management and Organizations

Priyali Rajagopol
Assistant Professor of Marketing

Robert W. Rasberry
Assistant Professor of Management and Organizations

Susan M. Riffe
Senior Lecturer in Accounting

Ulrike Schultze
Associate Professor of Information Technology and
Operations Management

John H. Semple
Associate Professor of Information Technology and
Operations Management

Raj Sethuraman
Associate Professor of Marketing

Wayne H. Shaw
Helmut Sohmen Distinguished Professor of Corporate
Governance

Tasadduq Shervani
Associate Professor of Marketing

Suzanne B. Shu
Assistant Professor of Marketing

John W. Slocum Jr.
O. Paul Corley Distinguished Professor of Management
and Organizations

James L. Smith
Cary M. Maguire Professor of Oil and Gas
Management

Eli M. Snir
Assistant Professor of Information Technology
and Operations

Marion G. Sobol
Professor of Information Technology and Operations
Management

Gregory A. Sommers
Assistant Professor of Accounting

Rex W. Thompson
James M. Collins Professor of Finance

Michael F. van Breda
Associate Professor of Accounting

Donald M. VandeWalle
Associate Professor of Management and Organizations

Kumar Venkataraman
Assistant Professor of Finance

Michel R. Vetsuypens
Professor of Finance

Gordon Walker
Professor of Strategy and Entrepreneurship

Catherine Weber
Senior Lecturer in Law

Wendy M. Wilson
Assistant Professor of Accounting

Executive-In-Residence

Edward Ahnert
Executive-in-Residence

Emeritus Professors

Marvin L. Carlson
Professor Emeritus of Accounting

Alan B. Coleman
Professor Emeritus of Finance

Dudley Walz Curry
Professor Emeritus of Accounting

Robert J. Frame
Professor Emeritus of Finance

Richard W. Hansen
Professor Emeritus of Marketing

Thomas V. Hedges
Associate Professor Emeritus of Accounting

Elaine Janosky Hudson
Assistant Professor Emerita of Accounting

Sydney Chandler Reagan
Professor Emeritus of Real Estate and
Regional Science

John A. Stieber
Assistant Professor Emeritus of Finance

Rhonald D. Walker
Associate Professor Emeritus of Accounting/
Business Law and Taxation

Helen W. Watkins
Associate Professor Emeritus of Business Law and
Taxation

Leland Michael Wooton
Associate Professor Emeritus of Management and
Organizations

Frank A. Young
Associate Professor Emeritus of Insurance

INDEX

Page numbers in **bold** indicate photographs or illustrations.

ABOUT THE TYPE

The text of this book was set in Monotype Dante, a digital version of the hot-metal typeface designed by master printer Giovanni Mardersteig (1892–1977). Characterized by its even color and classic proportions, Dante was first used by Mardersteig in 1955 at his Officina Bodoni press for an edition of Giovanni Boccaccio's classic, *Trattatello in laude di Dante* (trans. Little Tractate in Praise of Dante).

This book was printed on a Heidelberg Speedmaster 102 press by Padgett Printing Corporation, Dallas, Texas. The text and duotone photographs were printed on 70 lb. Finch Opaque Smooth; the dustjacket was printed in 6 colors and finished with a gold foil emboss. Smyth sewn case binding in Cialux Nordic blue cloth, and foil stamping in gold by Big D Bindery, Dallas, Texas.

Book design and composition by Mark McGarry,
Texas Type & Book Works, Dallas, Texas.